Cambridge English

Grammar for IELTS

with answers

剑桥雅思
语法精讲精练

（英）DIANA HOPKINS
（英）PAULINE CULLEN 编著

耿耿 译

CAMBRIDGE
UNIVERSITY PRESS

西安交通大学出版社
XI'AN JIAOTONG UNIVERSITY PRESS

图书在版编目(CIP)数据

剑桥雅思语法精讲精练＝Grammar for IELTS with answers／(英)霍普金斯(Hopkins，D.)，(英)库林(Cullen，P.)编著. —西安：西安交通大学出版社，2013 (2016.8 重印)

ISBN 978-7-5605-5715-1

Ⅰ. ①剑… Ⅱ. ①霍… ②库… Ⅲ. ①IELTS—语法—自学参考资料 Ⅳ. ①H314

中国版本图书馆 CIP 数据核字 (2013) 第 219316 号

陕版出图字：25－2007－068 号

Cambridge Grammar for IELTS with answers，first edition by Diana Hopkins and Pauline Cullen first published by Cambridge University Press 2007

This edition for the People's Republic of China is published by arrangement with the Press Syndicate of the University of Cambridge，Cambridge，United Kingdom.

书　　名　剑桥雅思语法精讲精练
编　　著　(英) Diana Hopkins，(英) Pauline Cullen
译　　者　耿　耿
责任编辑　黄科丰
封面设计　大愚设计
出版发行　西安交通大学出版社
地　　址　西安市兴庆南路 10 号(邮编：710049)
电　　话　(010)62605588　62605019(发行部)　(029)82668315(总编室)
读者信箱　dywh@xdf.cn
印　　刷　北京精乐翔印刷有限公司
字　　数　120 千
开　　本　787mm×1092mm　1/16
印　　张　17
版　　次　2016 年 8 月第 1 版第 8 次印刷
书　　号　ISBN 978-7-5605-5715-1/H・1584
定　　价　45.00 元

Acknowledgements

My thanks go firstly to my editor, Jessica Roberts, who has worked tirelessly and patiently with me and kept me going through her endless words of encouragement. Thanks also to my commissioning editor, Alison Sharpe, whose encouragement and gentle persuasion have led the project to completion, and to Anna Teevan, who saw me through the initial stages. Many thanks also to all at Cambridge University Press who have contributed along the way, and to the teachers and readers involved in commenting on the material. And of course I would like to thank Pauline Cullen, without whom this book may never have quite reached the final stages and whose contribution has been much appreciated.

Finally, a thank you to my children Laura and Alexander, my partner, Ned Garnett and my mother, for their support, encouragement and help at every stage.

Diana Hopkins

The authors and publishers would like to thank the following teachers and readers who commented on the material in its draft form:

Guy Brook-Hart, Valencia, Spain; Mike Gutteridge, Cambridge, England; Vanessa Jakeman, Hove, England; Barbara Thomas, Cambridge, England.

The authors and publishers are grateful to the following for permission to reproduce copyright material. It has not always been possible to identify the sources of all the material used and in such cases the publishers would welcome information from the copyright owners.

p.14: *New Scientist* for the adapted article 'Good vibrations help jumping spiders to hunt' by Peter Aldous, 24 February 1996 from www.newscientist.com; p.60: *The Economist* for the text adapted from the article 'Dressed to dazzle' by Barney Southin, and for p.71: listening text adapted from 'Back on the treadmill' by Konstantin Kakaes, *Economist Intelligent Life*, Summer 2004, © The Economist Newspaper Limited; p.64: ESA for adapted listening text 'World's Largest Switchboard for Climate Monitoring' from www.innovations-report.com; p.87: Wcities for the adapted text from www.wcities.com, Wcities © 2006; p.88: adapted from an article 'Great Guide – Buying a Backpack' in the *Rambler*, former members' magazine of the Ramblers' Association, www.ramblers.org.uk; p.103: Professor Rajendra Persaud for the text 'Practical Intelligence Lends a Hand' taken from www.caribvoice.org; p.113: Roger Hedge for the adapted text 'Discovery and Prehistory of Soap' from www.butser.org.uk; p.140: Professor John Maule for the adapted article 'How Consumers Decide' from www.faradaypackaging.com; p.160: Bristol Magazines Ltd for the adapted article 'We are family' by Philip Dalton from *BBC Wildlife Magazine*, November 2004; p.180: Auspac Media for the adapted text from 'Robotic Approach to Crop Breeding' by Jennifer Manyweathers, *Australasian Science Magazine*, March 2006; p.206: Scientific American Inc., for article adapted from 'Experience Versus Speed' by Marion Sonnenmoser, *Scientific American Mind*, Volume 16, Number 2, 2005, Copyright © 2005 by Scientific American Inc, All rights reserved.

Photographs: Alamy Images/©Stockdisc for p8 (crt), /©Mark Sykes for p8 (crb), /©D Hurst for p11 (r), /©Lebrecht Music & Arts PL for p27, /©Rena Pearl for p80 (l), /©B.Mete Uz for p80 (m), /©Sciencephotos for p140, /©Motoring Picture Library for p144 (l), /©Epictura for p144 (ml), /©Image Broker for p169; Corbis Images/©Bettmann for p11 (l), /©David Ball for p38 (c), /©Gideon Mendel for p41, /©Charles Jean Marc/Sygma for p42, /©Viviane Moos for p80 (r), /©Richard Klune for p98 (l), /©Stephen Frink for p 98 (r), /©Royalty Free for p144 (cr), /©Chris Collins for p144 (br), /©Keith Dannemiller for p150, /©Guenter Rossenbach/Zefa for p188, /©Photocuisine for p198; Dell for p8 (cl); Empics/©AP/Vincent Thian for p69; FLPA/©Mark Moffett/Minden Pictures for p14; Getty Images for pp8 (r), 38 (r), 90; Photolibrary.com/©Thom DeSanto for p8 (c), /©Royalty Free for p38 (l); Punchstock/©Image Source for p144 (tr), /©Digital Vision for p160, /©Image Source for p154, /©Bananastock for p210 (l); Rex Features for pp8 (l), 32, 64, 210 (r); Royal Ontario Museum ©ROM for p112 (reproduced with permission); Topfoto/©UPP for p158.

Key: l = left, c = centre, r = right, t = top, b = bottom

Picture Research by Hilary Luckcock

Contents

To the student

Who is this book for?

本书适用于任何一位准备参加雅思考试的考生。虽然雅思考试中没有专门的语法测试项，但是正确使用语法对于在雅思考试中取得好成绩至关重要。

本书包含了雅思考试中可能出现的所有语法点，既可用作雅思备考教程，也可作为英语语言课程的额外语法练习。本书可供语言培训课程使用，也可作为考生自学的辅导教材。

How do I use this book?

本书有两种使用方法。方法一：从第一单元开始循序渐进直至最后一单元。方法二：使用前先做一下第vii页的学前测试，找到自己最需要提高的部分并从该单元开始学习。

What is in this book?

本书共包含25个单元，每单元由4部分组成：

A: Context listening

本部分介绍了与雅思考试相关的语法内容，使考生学习Grammar部分时更容易理解语法知识，另外还为考生提供了必要的听力练习。考生可以听录音并解答问题，然后在学习Grammar部分之前对照答案进行检查。

B: Grammar

考生在进行语法练习之前应先学习本部分内容。书中的每个语法点均附有解释和范例。在做Grammar exercises部分时也可回顾本部分内容。

C: Grammar exercises

考生可在此部分进行语法练习并对照书后答案进行检查。

D: Test practice

每单元均有测试题目，有助于考生练习雅思考试中的不同部分。测试题目之后附有针对某个特定语法点的额外练习。

The Key

答案包括：

■ 所有练习的答案。做完练习后可与答案进行核对，如果有问题，可通过答案了解哪些语法点需要再次学习、巩固。

■ Test practice部分各种题型的解题技巧。

■ Test practice部分所有写作试题的样本答案。考生可在完成答题后参考该部分，仔细揣摩样本答案的语言使用和思路组织。

Recording scripts

书中附有每单元Context listening部分的录音文本。考生应在解答完问题之后再阅读此部分。阅读录音文本时再次结合听录音材料对雅思考生而言是富有成效的练习方式。

The Entry test

使用本书前先做Entry test中的习题，然后对照答案进行检查，从而认识到自己语法学习中的不足，根据个人情况选择需要重点学习哪个单元。

To the teacher

本书精确而全面地讲解了顺利通过雅思考试需要掌握的必备语法知识，既可作为雅思考生的自学材料，也可供课堂教学使用。

The Entry test

此部分可以帮助考生诊断语法错误并了解亟待提高的语法点，既适合个人练习也可作为课堂练习使用。

A: Context listening

本部分适合课堂使用。许多内容可用于小组或学生的两两练习。

B: Grammar

本部分适合个人学习。如果有特别需要强调的语法点，可与学生展开讨论。

C: Grammar exercises

本部分既可在课上使用也可作为课后作业。教师可鼓励学生独立练习或一起讨论练习中的难点。

D: Test practice

本部分包含了基于每单元语法点的测试题目，通过练习这些题目，可使学生熟悉雅思考试的题型。每道题目后面都紧跟一个Grammar focus task，旨在提高学生对该单元所包含的特定语言点的认识。本书在听力、学术类阅读、普通培训类阅读、学术类写作、普通培训类写作的每一部分都至少包含一个练习题目。

在课堂上，对于未通过雅思考试的学生而言，教师可重点使用Test practice部分对学生进行额外训练。本书为所有学生提供了宝贵的语法练习机会，同时也为学术英语（EAP）课程提供了有效的教学资源。

You can do this test before using the book to help you choose what to study. Choose the correct answer, A, B or C, for each question. When you have finished, check your answers on page 223. The key tells you which units are most important for you.

1 Most university students .... on campus in their first year.
A lives
B live
C are living

2 From this graph we can see that the economy .... at the moment.
A improves
B improve
C is improving

3 They .... personal computers when my father was a student.
A hadn't
B didn't have
C weren't having

4 I .... want to be a practising doctor but now I'm more interested in research.
A was used to
B used to
C would

5 The teacher .... us how to do the experiment when the fire bell rang.
A showed
B shown
C was showing

6 I finished my essay yesterday but .... it in to the tutor yet.
A I've given
B I haven't given
C I didn't give

7 .... the experiment three times now with different results each time!
A We've done
B We did
C We've been doing

8 When I arrived the lecture .... so I didn't find it easy to follow.
A started
B had started
C had been starting

9 She .... well at school but that changed when she became friends with a different group of girls.
A did
B had done
C had been doing

10 .... the doctor at 2.00 this afternoon so I can't go to the lecture.
A I'm seeing
B I see
C I will see

11 My sister .... economics and politics when she goes to university.
A is going to study
B studies
C will study

12 While we're working on the project our boss .... on a beach in Greece!
A will sit
B will have sat
C will be sitting

13 If the trend continues, the average income .... by 107% by 2020.
   A will increase
   B will have increased
   C will be increasing

14 You can base your geography assignment on .... country – it doesn't matter which.
   A a
   B some
   C any

15 There aren't .... places left on the course so you'd better apply soon.
   A much
   B many
   C lots of

16 I don't know whether to accept the job offer. It's ....
   A a difficult decision
   B the difficult decision
   C difficult decision

17 For those of you new to the company, this leaflet is full of ....
   A a valuable information
   B the valuable information
   C valuable information

18 The manager interviewed .... candidates in turn.
   A each of the
   B each
   C every

19 I know it's not much of a present but I made it ....
   A me
   B myself
   C by myself

20 You should visit Bath. It's .... city.
   A a historical and interesting
   B a historical interesting
   C an interesting historical

21 The government has released some .... data showing how schools are not providing an adequate education to our children.
   A shocking
   B shock
   C shocked

22 You really should go to Namibia. The scenery is .... stunning and the people are very friendly.
   A very
   B fairly
   C absolutely

23 This factory produces some of .... cameras in the world.
   A best
   B the best
   C the most best

24 .... people live in the countryside than 100 years ago.
   A Less
   B Few
   C Fewer

25 The bookshop .... the end of the road is excellent.
   A at
   B on
   C in

26 There were millions of people around the world .... the football match live on television.
A watched
B watching
C were watching

27 Scientists finally .... find a cure for the disease after years of research.
A managed to
B can
C could

28 She got a terrible mark in the exam so she .... very hard at all.
A mustn't have worked
B can't have worked
C didn't work

29 What .... in order to get a permit to work in your country?
A do I need to do
B must I do
C ought I do

30 When you write your essays you .... copy ideas from books without referencing them properly.
A mustn't
B don't have to
C have to

31 Doctors have .... us to cut down on salt in our diets if we want to reduce the risk of getting heart disease.
A insisted
B suggested
C advised

32 .... this newspaper report, more women smoke than men nowadays.
A Apparently
B According to
C Supposedly

33 My parents encouraged .... this course.
A me to do
B me doing
C me do

34 What will you do if ....
A you don't get a good IELTS score?
B you didn't get a good IELTS score?
C you won't get a good IELTS score?

35 A recent government report has warned that .... we act immediately to reduce pollution, there will be serious consequences for the planet.
A provided that
B in case
C unless

36 If I didn't have to work tonight, ...
A I'd be able to relax now.
B I'm able to relax now.
C I'll be able to relax now.

37 I wish that man .... tapping his fingers on the table. It's really annoying me.
A stopped
B had stopped
C would stop

38 I'm aiming .... a band 7 in IELTS.
A on
B for
C to

39 Do you have any knowledge .... how our education system works?
A of
B on
C for

40 The minister .... is responsible for education has just resigned.
A which
B who
C what

41 The University of St Andrews .... is the oldest university in Scotland.
A which was founded in 1413
B , which was founded in 1413,
C , that was founded in 1413,

42 Many children these days do not have a healthy diet. .... is possible that this is because less healthy foods are cheaper than healthy ones.
A What
B That
C It

43 The charity is trying to find ways to save and .... the world's endangered animal species.
A the charity is trying to find ways to protect
B to find ways to protect
C protect

44 In the past we threw a lot of our kitchen waste away, but today many items such as plastic bottles and newspapers ....
A are recycled
B recycle
C need recycling

45 I can't pick you up from the station on Wednesday because .... on that day.
A I'm fixing my car
B I'm having my car fixed
C I need my car fixed

46 These drugs are the best medicine available as a treatment at the moment, ... they are expensive, unfortunately.
A although
B because
C so

47 Learning a foreign language is important because it helps you to understand other cultures better. .... it can be a useful skill in many areas of work.
A However,
B Despite this,
C In addition,

48 .... I can't go to the conference as I've got to go to Sydney on business.
A Frankly
B Unfortunately
C Personally

49 .... I think it's useful to write an outline of your essay before you start to write the first draft.
A Interestingly,
B Definitely,
C Personally,

50 The .... of dark red spots is one of the first signs of the disease.
A appearance
B appearing
C appear

(答案请见P223)

A Context listening

1 You are going to hear a woman interviewing a student for a survey about what people do in their free time. Before you listen, look at the pictures. Which activities do you think the student does in his free time?

2 🎧 **1** Listen and check if you were right.

3 **1 ◄◄** Listen again and decide if the following statements are true or false. If a statement is false, write the correction.

1 Peter is waiting for his friends. ....

2 He isn't studying much this month. ....

3 His parents own a shop. ....

4 He practises the guitar most mornings. ....

5 He frequently uses the Internet. ....

6 His cousin is living in America at the moment. ....

7 Peter doesn't support any football teams. ....

4 Look at your answers to Exercise 3 and answer these questions.

1 Which sentences are about a situation that is permanent or a fact? ....

2 Which sentences are about everyday habits? ....

3 Which sentence is about an action happening at the moment of speaking? ....

4 Which sentences are about a temporary situation? ....

B Grammar

1 Present simple （一般现在时）

+	verb/verb + (*e*)*s*	*He **plays** tennis.*
−	*do/does not* + verb	*She **doesn't play** tennis.*
?	*do/does* ... + verb?	***Do** you **play** tennis?*

一般现在时用于：
- 经常性的习惯或反复发生的动作：
  *I **get up** really early and **practise** for an hour or so **most days**.*
  *I **use** the Internet **just about every day**.*
  描述频率的词汇包括：（如 *always, generally, normally, usually, often, sometimes, rarely, never, every day, every evening*）。

- 永久性的情况或状态：
  *My parents **own** a restaurant.*
  ⚠ 要表达某件事持续了多久时，应使用现在完成时，而非一般现在时。
  *I **have worked** there since I was 15.* (**not** ~~I work there since I was 15~~ : see Unit 3)

- 陈述事实或广为接受的真理：
  *Students **don't generally have** much money.*
  *If you **heat** water to 100°C, it **boils**.* (see Unit 17)
  在表示这个意义的时候，常使用下列词汇：*generally, mainly, normally, usually, traditionally*。

- 提供指导或指示：
  *You **go** down to the traffic lights, then you **turn** left.*
  *To start the programme, first you **click** on the icon on the desktop.*

- 讲述故事、电影、书籍和戏剧：
  *In the film, the tea lady **falls** in love with the Prime Minister.*

2 Present continuous （现在进行时）

+	*am/is/are* + verb + *-ing*	*He's **living** in Thailand.*
−	*am/is/are not* + verb + *-ing*	*I'm **not living** in Thailand.*
?	*am/is/are* ... + verb + *-ing*?	*Are they **living** in Thailand?*

现在进行时用于：
- 现在的情况或状态：
  *I'm **studying** really hard for my exams.*
  *My cousin **is living** in Thailand **at the moment**.* (= he doesn't normally live there)
  此类经常使用的单词或短语包括：*at the moment, currently, now, this week/month/year*。

- 说话间正在发生的动作：
  *I'm **waiting** for my friends.*

◆ 趋势或正在变化的情况：
*The Internet **is making** it easier for people to stay in touch with each other.*
*The price of petrol **is rising** dramatically.*

◆ 经常发生的动作，常与*always*、*constantly*、*continually, forever*这类副词连用，表示羡慕、批评等情绪：*always, constantly, continually, forever*。
*My mum's **always saying** I don't help enough!* (complaint)
*He's **always visiting** exciting places!* (envy)

3 State verbs （状态动词）

因为状态动词本身的意思是想表述一种事实而不是暂时的事情，所以状态动词通常并不出现在现在进行时的句子里。状态动词表达想法、感情、感知、占有和描述等状态。
以下是一些状态动词的例子：

◆ 想法：*agree, assume, believe, disagree, forget, hope, know, regret, remember, suppose, think, understand* 。
*I **assume** you're too busy to play computer games.*

◆ 感情：*adore, despise, dislike, enjoy, feel, hate, like, love, mind, prefer, want*。
*Do you **mind** if I ask you a few questions?*
*I **love** music.*

◆ 感知：*feel, hear, see, smell, taste*。
*This pudding **smells** delicious.*

⚠ 当谈论事情正在发生时，可以使用 *can*:
*I **can smell** something burning.*

◆ 占有：*have, own, belong*。
*My parents **own** a restaurant.*

◆ 描述：*appear, contain, look, look like, mean, resemble, seem, smell, sound, taste, weigh*。
*You **look like** your mother.* (= a permanent situation, not a temporary one)

⚠ 当意思本身表暂时性时，一些状态动词可以使用进行时。比较以下几组句子：
*What **are** you **thinking** about?* (now)
*I **think** you should tell her exactly what happened.* (my opinion, so not temporary)

*I'm **tasting** the sauce to see if it needs any more salt.*
*The sauce **tastes** delicious.*

*She's **having** a great time.* (*is having* = is experiencing, not possession)
*Students **don't** generally **have** much money.* (*have* = possession)

C Grammar exercises

1 Choose the best endings for sentences 1–8.

1 Fiona is watching television   **(a)** because her favourite film star is on.
         b when she has time.

2 I'm having my lunch   **(a)** at one o'clock every day.
         b early today as I have an appointment.

3 I do the shopping   **(a)** at the same time every week.
         b today for a friend who's ill.

4 What are you doing   **(a)** to your sister when she behaves badly?
         b to your sister? Leave her alone!

5 I wear casual clothes   a at the weekend.
         (b) because we're having a party at lunchtime.

6 Teachers work hard   **(a)** to get the concert ready for next week.
         b but they get long holidays.

7 The company's financial situation is improving   a now that it has a new Chief Executive.
         (b) when there is greater demand for its products.

8 Serge is thinking of retiring early   a every time something bad happens at work.
         (b) because he isn't happy at work any more.

2 Fill in the gaps with the correct form of the verbs in brackets.

1 I'm busy right now. I _'m filling in_ (*fill in*) an application form for a new job.

2 My tutor _sees_ (*see*) me for a tutorial every Monday at two o'clock.

3 John _doesn't studying_ (*not/study*) very hard at the moment. I _don't think_ (*not/think*) he'll pass his exams.

4 'What _he does_ (*he/do*)?' 'He _tries_ (*try*) to fix the television aerial.'

5 Animals _breathe in_ (*breathe in*) oxygen and _give out_ (*give out*) carbon dioxide.

6 Be quiet! I _want_ (*want*) to hear the news.

7 In my country we _drive_ (*drive*) on the right-hand side of the road.

8 My friend Joe's parents _travelling_ (*travel*) round the world this summer, and probably won't be back for a couple of months.

9 The college _runs_ (*run*) the same course every year.

10 Numbers of wild butterflies _fall_ _are falling_ (*fall*) as a result of changes in farming methods.

3 Fill in the gaps with the verbs in the box in the correct present tense.

agree · catch up   cause   have   go up   know   think   ~~use~~

We 1 ...... use ...... energy for three main things: electricity production, heating and transport. For the first two, we 2 ...... have ...... options such as solar and wind power, or natural gas. But oil is still the world's number one source of energy, and for transport at least, there is currently no alternative. In China, domestic energy consumption 3 catch up ...... year by year and demand in similar regions 4 ... go up ...... fast. We are 5 ... knowing ... how to use energy more efficiently now than in the past but the worldwide rise in demand 6 went up cause ...... concern amongst experts. Some experts 7 ... think ...... that oil supplies will start to fall within the next twenty years. Most experts 8 ... agree ...... that we need to find a new source of energy soon.

4 Look at the following extracts. There are six incorrect verbs. Find and correct them.

Extract A

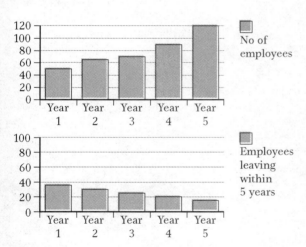

From the graphs, we are seeing that the number of employees employed by this firm increases each year and the number of employees leaving after less than five years decreases.

1 can see
2 increase
3 decreased

Extract B

The sun heats the ground. This is warming the air nearby and the warm air rises into the sky. As the air is rising, it becomes cooler and the water vapour inside it change into droplets of water. These join together to form a cloud.

4 ....
5 rise into
6 changes

D Test practice

Listening Section 1

Questions 1–3

Choose the correct letter, A, B or C.

> *Example*
> Which sport is the woman interested in?
>   A gymnastics
>   (B) swimming
>   C tennis

1 How long is the heated pool?

    A 15 metres
    B 25 metres
    C 50 metres

2 Which of these is free for all members?

    A the beginners swimming class
    B the training session
    C the keep-fit class

3 Which of these does the woman need to book?

    A swimming lanes
    B gym equipment
    C sauna

Questions 4–10

Complete the notes below.

Write **NO MORE THAN THREE WORDS AND/OR A NUMBER** *for each answer.*

Yoga classes

- held on Monday, **4** .... and .... mornings
- weekend evenings from **5** .... to ....
- attend **6** .... per week
- see instructor to change **7** ....
- cost £1.50

Meet John **8** ....

Office located on first floor

Meet at **9** .... tomorrow

Tel: **10** ....

Look at the following extracts from the conversation and <u>underline</u> the tenses that the speakers used.

1 I'm *wanting* / *want* to do some sports activities.
2 Our tennis team *are always looking* / *always look* for new people.
3 *Are members having to* / *Do members have to* pay to use the pools?
4 We're *not actually allowing* / *don't actually allow* anyone to book the swimming lanes or the gym equipment.
5 What time *is suiting* / *suits* you?
6 Great, well, I'm *thinking* / *think* that's everything.

2 Past tenses 1

past simple; past continuous; *used to*; *would*

A Context listening

1 You will hear a man giving a talk on the radio about protecting your home from burglaries. Before you listen look at the pictures below. Make a list of all of the items.

2 🎧 **2** Listen and answer the following questions.

1 Which three items from your list were stolen?

2 Why did the man tell this story?

   A to show that crime has increased

   B to show that crime can happen at any time

   C to show that burglars can open any lock

3 **2◄** Listen again and complete these sentences.

1 A few weeks ago a woman .... to report a burglary.

2 It .... at five in the afternoon when she .... the news on TV.

3 This woman .... the front door locked.

4 When her son got older she .... the door unlocked whenever she was at home.

5 The burglar simply .... in through the front door.

6 The son .... anything because he .... to music.

7 Then the burglar .... into the front room, ... all the cupboards and .... a valuable collection of CDs.

4 Look at sentences 1–7 above and answer the following questions.

1 Which two sentences provide a background scene and an action? ....

2 Which two sentences talk about a single completed action in the past? ....

3 Which sentence describes a series of completed actions in the past? ....

4 Which two sentences talk about a repeated action in the past? ....

5 Which four tenses or structures are used in sentences 1–7? ....

B Grammar

1 Past simple (一般过去时)

+	verb + -ed (or -d)	He **worked** for the police.
−	did not + verb	She **didn't work** for the police.
?	did ... + verb?	**Did** they **work** for the police?

⚠ 不规则动词
许多动词都是不规则的：**went** (*go*), **came** (*come*), **wrote** (*write*) (see Appendix 1)
注意：*be* 动词也是不规则的：*I/he/she/it* **was**; *you/we/they* **were**

一般过去时用于：

◆ 过去已经完成的动作。通常情况下，句中会提及时间：
*A few weeks ago a woman **called** to report a robbery at her house.*
如果时间已知，句中则不需要提及时间：
*How **did** the burglar **break** in without anybody hearing him?* (in the story I just told you about)

◆ 按照发生顺序描述的一系列动作：
*The burglar **came in** through the front door, **picked up** the woman's handbag, **emptied** it out and **stole** her purse.*

在表明事件的顺序时，通常会使用诸如 *next*、*then* 之类的词语。
***Then**, the burglar **went** into the front room, **opened** all the cupboards and **took** a valuable collection of CDs.*

◆ 过去的习惯性动作：
*When her son got older he often **went out** to visit his friends after school.*
注意：*used to* 和 *would* 也可以用于表示过去的习惯性动作（见 *used to* 和 *would* 的语法讲解）。（见 B3）.

◆ 过去长时间保持的、现在已经发生改变的状态：
*Bill Murphy **worked** for the police force for over 17 years.*

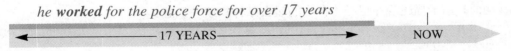

*Explorers at that time **believed** that the world was flat.*
注意：*used to* 也可以用于表示此类状态。（见 B3）.

2 Past continuous （过去进行时）

+	was/were + verb + -ing	She **was watching** the news.
−	was/were not + verb + -ing	They **weren't watching** the news.
?	was/were ... + verb + -ing?	**Were** you **watching** the news?

过去进行时用于：

◆ 为某一动作或事件（通常用一般过去时）提供场景。通常会用到 *when*、*while* 和 *as* 这样的词汇：
*It happened at five in the afternoon **while** she **was watching** the news on TV.*
*He **was doing** his homework in his bedroom **when** the burglar came into the house.*

he **was doing** his homework

THE PAST   NOW

the burglar **came** into the house

在同一时间可能进行多个动作：
*He **was listening** to music and **working** on his computer.*

◆ 强调某个动作而不关注动作的完成情况。比较以下两个句子：
*For a while last year I **was working** at the cinema, **studying** for my degree and **writing** a column for the local newspaper.* (we don't know if the actions were completed or not, or whether they happened at the same time)
*Last year I **worked** at the cinema, **studied** for my degree and **wrote** a column for the local newspaper.* (suggests all of the jobs are now complete, and probably happened in that order)

⚠ 状态动词（见Unit 1）一般没有进行时态。

3 *Used to and would* （Used to 和 would）

+	used to / would + infinitive	She **used to / would lock** the door.
−	did not + use to + infinitive	I **didn't use to lock** the door.
?	did ... use to + infinitive?	**Did** they **use to lock** the door?

used to +原形（动词）或者*would* +原形（动词）用于描述过去的习惯性动作：
*She **used to keep** the front door locked.* (but she stopped doing this)
*She **would leave** the door unlocked whenever she was at home.*

⚠ 注意：*Would* 一般不出现在被动语态和*Yes / No*题目中。

used to +原形（动词）用于描述现在已经不存在的过去某种持续性状态：
*Bill Murphy **used to work** for the police force.* (but he doesn't now: **not** ~~Bill Murphy would work for the police force.~~)

当描述某种状态持续了多久的时候，不用*used to*：
*Bill Murphy **worked** for the police force for over 17 years.* (**not** ~~Bill Murphy used to work for the police force for over 17 years.~~)

⚠ 注意：*would*不能与状态动词同用。

C Grammar exercises

1 Fill in the gaps in this model answer with verbs from the box in the past simple.

> *Thanks to modern technology, there have been enormous changes in the workplace over the past 100 years.*
>
> *What are the most significant changes that have occurred and what changes do you foresee in the next 100 years?*

allow	~~be~~	be	be	invent	increase	lay
mean	own	receive	replace	ride	take	walk

The pace of change in the world of technology is amazing. It **1** ....*wasn't*.... (not) long ago that the postal service **2** .... our only way to communicate over any distance. It **3** .... days and sometimes weeks to receive letters from within the same country. As a result, the news in the letters **4** .... already out of date when people **5** .... them. In the workplace, this **6** .... that business was mostly conducted locally, over relatively short distances.

When Alexander Graham Bell **7** .... the telephone in 1876 it **8** .... the foundation for the communication systems we have today. The telephone **9** .... two people to communicate instantly across a great distance. Eventually computers **10** .... typewriters and dramatically **11** .... the speed of our daily work life. Nowadays the Internet is an essential part of every business.

However, it is not just communications that have changed. Only 50 years ago most people **12** .... (not) a car. People **13** .... to work or **14** .... bicycles. Changes in travel as well as the increased speed of communications have led to the global business world that we have today.

2 Fill in the gaps with the past simple or past continuous form of the verbs in brackets. In which gaps could you use *used to*?

I 1 ....had........... (*have*) a wonderful biology teacher, Mrs Hughes. She 2 .... (*make*) us excited about the subject because she was so interested herself. I remember one lesson in particular; we 3 .... (*study*) different types of plants, and Mrs Hughes 4 .... (*describe*) the different parts of the flower. She 5 .... (*pick up*) a purple flower, I can't remember exactly what it was, and then suddenly we 6 .... (*notice*) that she 7 .... (*cry*)! She 8 .... (*apologise*) and 9 .... (*say*) that sometimes nature was so beautiful it just made her cry! We 10 .... (*not/know*) what to do at first, but it certainly 11 .... (*make*) us think. Something similar 12 .... (*happen*) while she 13 .... (*show*) us how to work the microscope. She 14 .... (*examine*) a slide of some plant tissue and she 15 .... (*smile*) all over her face. She suddenly 16 .... (*get*) all excited and 17 .... (*say*), 'Isn't it wonderful?' Some students 18 .... (*laugh*) at her when she 19 .... (*not/look*) but I didn't. Somehow her enthusiasm 20 .... (*inspire*) me, and I 21 .... (*start*) to like biology.

3 A teacher and student are talking about local customs. Fill in the gaps with the verbs in brackets in the correct form. Use *would* or *used to* where possible.

Teacher: What sort of things 1 ...did you use to do.. (*you/do*) as a child?

Yoko: Oh, when I was a child growing up in Japan there were many customs that we 2 .... (*follow*). For example, I remember we 3 .... (*move*) house when I was seven and we 4 .... (*visit*) our new neighbours with gifts. At that time the tradition was that people 5 .... (*give*) gifts of Japanese noodles, but it is different now and people tend to give things like soap or towels or nothing at all.

Teacher: 6 .... (*have*) one tradition that you particularly remember?

Yoko: Yes, one tradition that I 7 .... (*really/like*) was in the spring when the cherry blossoms were out. As a family we 8 .... (*go*) into the countryside and we 9 .... (*spend*) the day eating, drinking and singing. One year my father 10 .... (*take*) a lovely photo of me and my sisters and I still keep that picture on my wall today.

Teacher: And 11 .... (*you/have to*) do anything you didn't like?

Yoko: Yes. I remember how we 12 .... (*have to*) clean the house thoroughly. This ceremony is called Osoji and my sisters and I 13 .... (*not/look forward to*) it very much!

4 Read the test task and a student's response. Tick (✓) the <u>underlined</u> verbs if they are right, and correct them if they are wrong.

> **Describe an unforgettable trip you once made.**
> **You should say:**
> > **where you went**
> > **why you went there**
> > **what happened**
> **and explain why you remember it so well.**

I remember a trip I once **1** <u>made</u> to my grandmother's house. She **2** <u>would live</u> about 30 kilometres away from us and we **3** <u>used to going</u> there quite often with our mother. On this occasion we **4** <u>set off</u> to my grandmother's after school on a cold winter's day. When we were about to leave we **5** <u>were noticing</u> that some snow was beginning to fall, and as we **6** <u>were driving</u> along we **7** <u>were realising</u> that it **8** <u>snowed</u> more and more heavily. Suddenly we had to brake hard as the car in front stopped suddenly. We **9** <u>were skidding</u> and **10** <u>went off</u> the road into a ditch! It was pretty scary, but we were lucky and none of us were hurt. We got out of the car, and my mother **11** <u>was phoning</u> for help on her mobile phone. While we **12** <u>were waiting</u> for help it **13** <u>was stopping</u> snowing and we **14** <u>sang</u> lots of songs to keep ourselves cheerful. Eventually the truck **15** <u>was coming</u> and pulled our car out of the ditch. The car wasn't badly damaged, but we **16** <u>decided</u> to turn round and go home. We didn't manage to see our grandmother that day, but it was so frightening that I will never forget it.

1 ....✓.................................
2 .....used to live / lived.....
3 ....
4 ....

5 ....
6 ....
7 ....
8 ....
9 ....
10 ....

11 ....
12 ....
13 ....
14 ....
15 ....
16 ....

Academic Reading

*You should spend about 20 minutes on **Questions 1–13** which are based on the Reading Passage below.*

Jumping spiders

Peter Aldhons examines how Portia spiders catch their prey

A

For a stalking predator, the element of surprise is crucial. And for jumping spiders that sneak onto other spiders' webs to prey on their owners, it can be the difference between having lunch and becoming it. Now zoologists have discovered the secret of these spiders' tactics: creeping forward when their prey's web is vibrating.

B

The fifteen known species of Portia jumping spiders are relatively small, with adults being about two centimetres long (that's smaller than the cap on most pens). They habitually stay in the webs of other spiders, and in an area of these webs that is as out-of-the-way as possible. Portia spiders live mostly in tropical forests, where the climate is hot and humid. They hunt a range of other spiders, some of which could easily turn the tables on them. 'They will attack something about twice their own size if they are really hungry,' says Stimson Wilcox of Binghamton University in New York State. Wilcox and his colleague, Kristen Gentile of the University of Canterbury in Christchurch, New Zealand, wanted to find out how Portia spiders keep the upper hand.

C

All jumping spiders have large eyes that look like binocular lenses, and they function pretty much the same way. Most jumping spiders locate their prey visually, and then jump and capture from one centimetre to over ten centimetres away. Only a few species of jumping spiders invade the webs of other spiders, and the Portia spider is among them. Jumping spiders, including Portia spiders, prey on insects and other arthropods by stalking. Sometimes the spiders lure their victims by vibrating the web to mimic the struggles of a trapped insect. But many web-weaving spiders appear to be wise to these tricks, so stalking is often a better strategy. Sometimes, the researchers found, Portia spiders take advantage of the vibrations created in the web by a gentle breeze. But, if necessary, they will make their own vibrations.

D

The researchers allowed various prey spiders to spin webs in the laboratory and then introduced Portia spiders. To simulate the shaking effect of a breeze the zoologists used either a model aircraft propeller or attached a tiny magnet to the centre of the web which could be vibrated by applying a varying electrical field. The researchers noticed that the stalking Portia spiders moved more when the webs were shaking than when they were still, and they were more likely to capture their prey during tests in which the webs were periodically shaken than in those where the webs were undisturbed. If the spiders were placed onto unoccupied webs, they would make no attempt to change their movements.

E

It is the Portia spider's tactic of making its victims' webs shake that has most intrigued the researchers. They noticed that the spiders would sometimes shake their quarry's web violently, then creep forwards up to five millimetres before the vibrations died down. 'They'd make a big pluck with one of their hind legs,' says Wilcox. These twangs were much more powerful than the gentler vibrations Portia spiders use to mimic a trapped insect, and the researchers were initially surprised that the prey spiders did not respond to them in any way. But they have since discovered that the violent twanging produces a pattern of vibrations that match those caused by a twig falling onto the web.

F

Other predators make use of natural 'smokescreens' or disguises to hide from their prey: lions hunting at night, for example, move in on their prey when clouds obscure the moon. 'But this is the first example of an animal making its own smokescreen that we know of,' says Wilcox. 'Portia spiders are clearly intelligent and they often learn from their prey as they are trying to capture it. They do this by making different signals on the web of their prey until the prey spider makes a movement. In general, Portia spiders adjust their stalking strategy according to their prey and what the prey is doing. Thus, Portia spiders use trial-and-error learning in stalking. Sometimes they will even take an indirect route to reach a prey spider they can see from a distance. This can sometimes take one to two hours following a predetermined route. When it does this, the Portia spider is actually solving problems and thinking ahead about its actions.'

Questions 1–9

The Reading Passage has six paragraphs labelled **A–F**.

Which paragraph contains the following information?

*Write the correct letter **A–F** next to Questions 1–9.*

NB *You may use any letter more than once.*

1 the reaction of the Portia spider's prey to strong web vibrations

2 a description of how the researchers set up their experiment

3 a comparison between Portia spiders and another animal species

4 an explanation of how the researchers mimicked natural conditions

5 a comparison between Portia spiders and their prey

6 the reason why concealment is important to Portia spiders

7 a description of the Portia spider's habitat

8 the number of species of Portia spiders

9 an example of the Portia spider's cleverness

Questions 10–13

*Choose the correct letter, **A, B, C** or **D**.*

10 In their laboratory experiments, the researchers found that the Portia spiders moved most when the web was

    A vibrating.
    B motionless.
    C undisturbed.
    D unoccupied.

11 What discovery did the researchers make about Portia spiders?

    A They make very strong vibrations with one leg.
    B They move 5 mm at a time on a still web.
    C They move slowly when vibrations stop.
    D They use energetic vibrations to mimic a trapped insect.

12 Portia spiders are the only known animal to

    A use the weather to disguise themselves.
    B mimic other prey-eating animals.
    C create their own smokescreen.
    D stalk using 'trial and error'.

13 The Portia spider demonstrates 'thinking ahead' when it

    A chooses prey that is a short distance away.
    B takes a longer route to reach its prey.
    C reaches its prey in a short time.
    D solves the problem of locating its prey.

Grammar focus task

Look at the underlined verbs in these sentences from the text. Match the sentences (1–3) to the explanations (a–c).

1 The researchers allowed various prey spiders to spin webs in the laboratory and then introduced Portia spiders.
2 Portia spiders moved more when the webs were shaking than when they were still.
3 They noticed that the spiders would sometimes shake their quarry's web violently.

a a series of single past completed actions
b a repeated action in the past
c a background scene and an action

17

Present perfect
present perfect simple and continuous

A Context listening

1 You are going to hear two university students, Carl and Sue, talking about an assignment. Before you listen, look at the list of activities (A–F). Put the activities in the order which you think is best when writing an assignment.

> A make notes
> B start to write
> C do research
> D make a plan
> E re-read books
> F get a book list

2 🎧 3 Listen to the first part of the conversation. Which five activities does Sue mention? Write the letters A–F in the correct order in boxes 1–5 on the flowchart.

3 🎧 3 Listen to the second part of the conversation and fill in the gaps.

1 Sue: I .... plenty of information for the assignment.

2 Sue: When I was in the library last week, I .... those leaflets.

3 Carl: I .... tired since I started this course!

4 Carl: I .... and I'm already tired.

4 Look at your answers to Exercise 3 and find examples of each of the following:

a something that only happened recently ....

b something that happened at some time before now, but we do not know when ....

c an action + the length of time it has been going on ....

d something that happened at a stated time in the past ....

Which tense is used in each of the examples a–d above?

B Grammar

现在完成时用于连接现在和过去。

1 Present perfect simple（现在完成时）

+	have/has + past participle	She's **started** the assignment.
−	have/has not + past participle	I **haven't started** the assignment.
?	have/has ... + past participle?	**Have** you **started** the assignment?

现在完成时用于：

◆ 到现在（如 *today*, *this week*）为止仍未结束的一段时间：
I've written a rough plan this morning. (it is still morning)

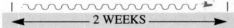

I've written a rough plan　　NOW

THIS MORNING

◆ 现在之前的过去某个时间点已经发生的事情。句中不需要指出具体发生的时间：
I've collected plenty of information. (at some point before now and I will use it to write my essay)

经常使用以下表示时间的单词和短语：*ever, never, before, up to now, still, so far*。
It's the longest I've ever had to write. (at any point before now)

⚠ 注意：如果强调的只是某件事情在某时发生了，使用一般过去时。
I wasted a lot of time last week. (**not** *I have wasted a lot of time last week*)

◆ 起源于过去，并延续到现在的某种状态，通常和 *for*、*since* 连用：

I've worked really hard
for the last two weeks　　NOW

— 2 WEEKS —

I've worked really hard for the last two weeks. (I've worked hard till now)
for 指某个时间段，例如 *for two hours, for three days, for six months*，*since* 指某个时间点，例如
since 2001, since Monday, since ten o'clock, since I was four, since I started the course。

◆ 过去未提及的时间里发生的、与现在情况有联系的事情：
I've read all the books on the reading list. (I have the notes now)

通常使用以下表示时间的单词和短语：*recently, just, already, yet*。
I've just got up.
Have you written your assignment yet?

现在完成时与一般过去时的比较：

现在完成时

◆ 连接过去和现在
I've made quite a lot of notes. (at some point before now and I may make more notes)

◆ 不关注过去某个具体的时间点
Have you read the leaflet? (at some time before now)

◆ 使用说明时段仍未结束的时间表达
I've read six articles this week. (the week isn't finished)

一般过去时

◆ 仅仅谈论过去
I made notes on the most important things. (when I did the reading and I've finished making notes)

◆ 说明过去的一个具体时间或者过去时间是可推知的
I read the leaflets when I was in the library. (I'm not in the library now and the reading is finished)

◆ 使用说明时段已经结束的时间表达
I read five books last week. (last week has finished)

注意：下列时间表达在现在完成时中的位置：

◆ 在助动词和主动词之间：（如 *recently*, *already*, *always*, *ever*, *just*, *never*）
*I've **already** written the notes.*
*I've **just** finished my essay.*

ever 通常用于疑问句或否定句中：
*Have you **ever** been to Buenos Aires?*

◆ 在主动词之后：（如 *all my life*, *every day*, *yet*, *before*, *for ages*, *for two weeks*, *since 2003*, *since I was a child* 等）
*I've felt tired **for weeks**.*
*I haven't flown **before**.*

如果句子中有宾语从句，时间表达放在句尾：
*I've gone to bed early **every night since then**.*
*I've written more than ten assignments **since I started this course**.*

2 Present perfect continuous （现在完成进行时）

+	have/has been + verb + -ing	*I've **been studying** really hard.*
–	have/has not been + verb + -ing	*He **hasn't been studying** really hard.*
?	have/has ... been + verb + -ing?	***Have** you **been studying** really hard?*

描述某种状态或动作持续了多久，可以使用现在完成时或现在完成进行时 (通常和 *for* 或 *since* 连用)：
*I've **felt** tired **for** weeks.*
*I've **been feeling** tired **since** I started this course.*
*I've **worked** at the restaurant **since** I moved here.*
*I've **been working** at the restaurant **for** three years.*

现在完成进行时与现在完成时比较：

现在完成进行时	现在完成时

现在完成进行时

- 强调状态或行为持续了多久：
  I've been reading for the past two weeks.

- 关注行为本身（而不是关注这个行为是否已经完成）：
  I've been writing my essay. (we don't know if the essay is finished or not)

现在完成时

- 强调已经完成的次数：
  I've read three articles.

- 关注行为的结果或完成情况：
  I've written my essay. (the essay is finished but we don't know when)

What have you been doing? (the boy's mother is interested in the activity that made him so dirty now)

What have you done? (the boy's mother is interested in the result of the action: the broken window)

⚠ 注意：状态动词（见Unit 1）通常没有进行时态：
I've known them since I was a child. (**not** ~~I've been knowing them since I was a child~~)

Grammar extra: *This is the first time* etc.

在以下的句型中使用现在完成时态：*it/this/that is the first / the second / the best / the only / the worst ...*

It's the first time I've ever had to write such a long assignment.

Is this the only time you've travelled abroad?

That's the sixth cup of coffee you've had today.

C Grammar exercises

1 Tick (✓) the correct <u>underlined</u> verbs, and correct the verbs that are wrong.

I would like to be considered for your degree course in Zoology, starting in October next year. I feel I am a good candidate for this course as I **1** <u>have always been</u> interested in natural history and even as a child I **2** <u>have enjoyed</u> studying animals and insects in my garden. Your science faculty has a good reputation and I would very much like to be part of it.

As you **3** <u>already saw</u> in Section A of this application, I have a good academic record and I **4** <u>just received</u> the results of my recent exams, all of which **5** <u>have been</u> excellent.

In addition, your university attracts me because I enjoy sports and I **6** <u>have read</u> in your prospectus about the large number of sports on offer. Last year I **7** <u>have represented</u> my school at badminton and I **8** <u>played</u> in football teams since I was eleven. I **9** <u>have recently joined</u> a basketball team which competes at a national level.

I **10** <u>did not travel</u> abroad much yet, although as a young child I **11** <u>have been</u> to Singapore and Hong Kong with my family. I realize that I **12** <u>have not spent</u> much time away from home up to now, but am keen to become more independent.

1 ....✓.......
2 ...enjoyed...
3 ....
4 ....
5 ....
6 ....
7 ....
8 ....
9 ....
10 ....
11 ....
12 ....

2 Look at the chart and fill in the gaps with the past simple or present perfect simple of the verbs in brackets to make true sentences.

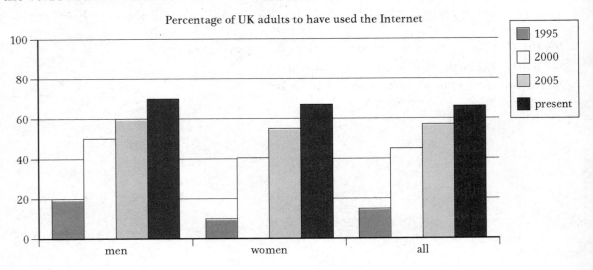

Percentage of UK adults to have used the Internet

1 The chart shows the percentage of British adults who ......*have used*...... (*use*) the Internet since 1995.

2 The number of women who have ever used the Internet *has increased*. (*increase*) by more than 60% since 1995.

3 The percentage of men who have accessed the Internet ...*has rised*...... *rose* (*rise*) to 60% in 2005.

4 The number of women to have accessed the Internet ....*rises* *has risen*........ (*rise*) each year.

5 The percentage of men who used the Internet ....*was*............... (*be*) greater than the percentage of women from 1995 to 2005.

6 However, British women ...*have overtaken*... (*overtake*) British men in Internet usage since 2005.

7 The total number of people accessing the Internet *has grown*......... (*grow*) each year although the most significant rise ...*occured*........ (*occur*) between 1995 and 2000.

3 Underline the correct form of the verbs.

To: Paul Johnson

From: Sunita Soh

Subject: Seminar presentation on Friday

Dear Paul

1 *I've just received* / *I've just been receiving* your message to us all about the seminar on Friday. 2 *I've worked* / *I've been working* on my presentation for the last week, and 3 *have now finished* / *now finished* it, so I am happy to be one of the first to present it. However, 4 *I've made* / *I made* an appointment to see the university careers advisor immediately after the seminar, so I will need to leave on time.

I'd like some advice about my presentation. At last week's lecture 5 *you've said* / *you said* that we should use visual aids as much as possible. 6 *I haven't found* / *I didn't find* anything to use. Is it essential? 7 *I've done* / *I did* lots of presentations before, and I feel OK about this one. In my last presentation 8 *I used* / *I have been using* the overhead projector, and I want to do this again – does this count as a visual aid?

One last question: 9 *I've been* / *I went* to Professor Russell's lecture yesterday, and 10 *have been learning* / *learnt* quite a lot that is relevant to this course. Is it okay to refer to another course in my presentation? 11 *I've been wondering* / *I wondered* about this – maybe it is better to stick to the materials and references 12 *you've given* / *you've been giving* us. I hope you can let me know.

Thanks for your help.

Sunita

---

4 Fill in the gaps with a verb from the box in the present perfect simple or present perfect continuous. You will need to use some verbs more than once.

| be | do | feel | have | live | pass | study | start | take | travel | want | work |

Interviewer: How long .....have you been living.. (**1** *you*) here?

Student: I .... (**2**) in London for the past three years. I come from Japan originally. I .... (**3**) at a college here since I arrived.

Interviewer: .... (**4** *you*) any travelling over the past three years?

Student: Yes, I .... (**5**) really lucky. I have long holidays so I .... (**6**) all over Europe. I especially liked Spain.

Interviewer: What is the most interesting thing you .... (**7**) recently?

Student: Well, I .... (**8**) to play tennis, and I .... (**9**) singing lessons for a few months now too. But the thing that I am most proud of is that I .... (**10** *just*) my driving test. It's the first time I .... (**11**) it so I'm really pleased but I .... (**12** *never*) so nervous in all my life!

Interviewer: How do you think English will be useful in your life?

Student: I .... (**13**) a Hospitality and Tourism course over here, so I need English for my studies and my job. I .... (**14** *always*) to work in the tourist industry because I .... (**15** *always*) interested in history and cultural sites, and I .... (**16** *already*) as a tour guide in my home town.

Now answer these questions about yourself.

17 How long have you been studying English?

....

18 Have you studied any other languages? (Which ones? For how long?)

....

19 Have you travelled very much? (Where have you been to?)

....

20 What have you been doing to prepare for this exam?

....

21 How has your life changed over the past ten years?

....

General Training Writing Task 1

You should spend about 20 minutes on this task.

> *You have seen an advertisement for a weekend job as a local tour guide showing visitors around your city.*
>
> *Write a letter of application to the tourism office. In the letter*
>
> * *give your reasons for wanting the job*
> * *explain why you think you can do the job*
> * *describe any relevant experience you have*

Write at least 150 words.

You do **NOT** need to write any addresses.

Begin your letter as follows:

Dear Sir or Madam,

Look at the model answer. Find one example each of:

1 a sentence which uses the present perfect simple to show something which started in the past and is still going on

2 a sentence which uses the present perfect continuous to show something which started in the past and is still going on

3 a sentence which uses the present perfect simple to show something happened at an unstated time in the past but has a present result

Dear Sir or Madam,

I am writing to apply for the post of tour guide advertised on your website. I believe I fulfil all the necessary criteria, and very much hope that you will consider my application.

I have lived in this town all my life, and therefore know all about the places of interest and their history. I have visited the castle and the cathedral many times and I have read many guide books full of interesting historical facts. I therefore feel that I am in a good position to lead visitors around these sites. I have always been interested in history and over the past few years I have regularly participated in activities at the castle and at other sites.

Recently I have been working as a receptionist at a local hotel in the evenings, so I have experience of dealing with overseas visitors, and I enjoy talking to them.

I do hope you will consider me for this post, and I look forward to hearing from you.

Yours sincerely,

A Context listening

1 You will hear a woman giving a talk on the famous composer, Mozart. Before you listen match the words (1–10) with the correct meanings (a–j).

1	extraordinary	a	brother or sister
2	sibling	b	reach a high level in something
3	achievement	c	part of a piano or computer
4	keyboard	d	amazing
5	demand	e	status
6	master (*verb*)	f	success
7	gifted	g	very talented
8	in rapid succession	h	ask in a forceful way
9	reputation	i	fast development at a very early age
10	precocious	j	quickly one after another

2 🎧 4 Now listen and complete the notes below.

Name:

Wolfgang Amadeus Mozart

Date of birth:

1 ....

Number of surviving brothers and sisters:

2 ....

Profession of father:

3 ....

Wrote first composition before the age of:

4 ....

Taught self to play:

5 ....

3 **4 ◄◄** **Listen to the text again and fill in the gaps.**

1 However, when Mozart .... five of his siblings .... in infancy or early childhood.

2 Mozart's father, Leopold, ... a composer, and his grandfather .... a musician.

3 In just 30 minutes Mozart .... the piece of music, which his father .... into Nannerl's notebook.

4 By the time he .... six, the little boy .... a composition of his own.

5 They .... to Vienna and .... sensational reports of Mozart's talent.

6 His family .... richer than they .... before.

For each sentence <u>underline</u> which event happened first.

4 **Look at your answers to Exercise 3 and answer these questions.**

1 Which tense is used in sentence 5 to show that the events took place in chronological order? ....

2 Which tense is used in the other sentences to show that the second event the speaker mentioned actually happened first? ....

B Grammar

1 Past perfect simple（过去完成时）

+	*had* + past participle	*They **had listened** to his music.*
−	*had not* + past participle	*They **hadn't listened** to his music.*
?	*had ... + past participle?*	***Had** they **listened** to his music?*

过去完成时用于：

◆ 表示过去某时前某事已经发生（过去的过去）
*His father was a composer and his grandfather **had** also **been** a musician.* (Mozart's grandfather was a musician and then later his father became a composer)
有时会使用诸如 *just*、*already* 等词语。需要注意的是，这些副词出现在助动词和主动词之间：
*By the time he was 17, Mozart's reputation **had already begun** to spread through Europe.*

⚠ 注意：在事件按照年代顺序出现时，使用一般过去时。
*His grandfather **was** a musician and his father **was** also a composer.*

◆ 由时间状语（如 *when, as soon as, by the time, after*）引出以说明事件的顺序：
***When** Mozart was born, five of his siblings **had** already **died**.* (Mozart's siblings died first, then Mozart was born)

⚠ 注意：以下两个句子中的意义差别：
*When I got home, my husband **cooked** dinner.* (= I got home and then my husband cooked dinner)

*When I got home, my husband **had cooked** dinner.* (= my husband cooked dinner before I got home)

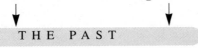

◆ 表示在过去某个确定的时间点之前的不明确时间，句中通常会出现 *always*，*sometimes*，*never*，*before* 或 *by* + 固定时间：
*His family were richer than they **had ever been before**.* (= they were not as rich at any time before this point in the past)
***By the time** he was six, the little boy **had written** a composition of his own.*

◆ 使用引出间接引语的动词来（见 Unit 15）陈述过去发生的事情：
*The man told me he **had met** my father a long time before.*

2 Past perfect continuous（过去完成进行时）

+	*had been* + verb + *-ing*	*She'd been studying for ages.*
−	*had not been* + verb + *-ing*	*He hadn't been studying for long.*
?	*had ... been* + verb + *-ing?*	*Had you been studying for long?*

过去完成进行时关注的是某一动作持续时间的长短或该动作本身：

*Times were hard and the family **had been struggling for some time**.* (to show how long)

*Mozart's sister was extremely gifted at the keyboard and she **had been making excellent progress**.* (focus on the activity)

⚠️ 过去完成进行时不能表示某事过去发生的次数：

*I knew the way as I **had visited** her several times before.* (**not** *I knew the way as I had been visiting her several times before.*)

⚠️ 状态动词（见Unit 1）通常没有进行时态。

Grammar extra: Unfulfilled hopes

在描述过去的失望或者没有按预期发生的事情时，用过去完成时：

*The politician **had expected** to be re-elected, but in the end she only got ten per cent of the vote.*

*I **had been hoping** to go with my brother on his trip but I was too sick to go.*

C Grammar exercises

1 Fill in the gaps with the past perfect simple of the verbs in brackets in the positive or negative.

According to Dr Ken Winkle, Australia's Red-back spider is colonising the world.
Dr Winkle, a venom expert from the University of Melbourne, said that authorities
1 ......*had found*..... (*find*) Red-back spiders in Japan and Belgium. They suspected that
spiders or their eggs 2 .... (*enter*) these countries along with Australian
trading goods. Furthermore, it was extremely likely that the spiders 3 ....
(*make*) their way into other nations around the world but that people 4 ....
(*discover*) them yet. Dr Winkle said the spiders 5 .... (*also/turn up*) in the
port city of Osaka (which receives a variety of Australian trade goods) in the late 1990s
and 6 .... (*multiply*) quickly. He said Australian spider experts were
collaborating with Japanese officials to find a way to stop the venomous invader.

2 Complete the report with the past simple or past perfect simple of the verbs in brackets.

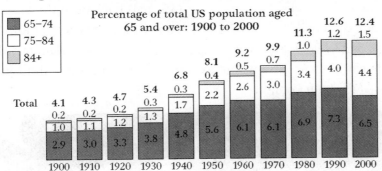

Percentage of total US population aged 65 and over: 1900 to 2000

The chart shows the percentage of people aged 65 and over in the United States between 1900 and
2000. In the year 1900 just over 4% of the population 1 ....*was*.............. (be) aged over 65. However,
by 1960 this figure 2 .... (double).

The number of people aged between 75 and 84 3 .... (remain) fairly steady between
1900 and 1930, making up only 1–1.3% of the population. The figure 4 .... (begin) to rise
more significantly in 1940 and by 1970 it 5 .... (triple) to reach 3% of the population.

Although there 6 .... (be) no change in the number of people aged 65–74 between 1960
and 1970, the number of people aged 75 and over 7 .... (increase) during this time. By the
year 2000, 12.4% of the US population 8 .... (reach) the age of 65 or more, although this
was slightly lower than in 1990 when it 9 .... (peak) at 12.6%.

The chart shows that today people in the United States can expect to live longer than in 1900. By the
year 2000 more than 12% of the population 10 .... (manage) to live to the age of 65 and
over compared to only 4.1% in 1900.

4

3 Fill in the gaps with the past simple, past perfect simple or past perfect continuous of the verbs in brackets.

Last year my friends ......*arranged*...... (**1** *arrange*) for us to try fire-walking, which is when you walk on hot coals. I .... (**2** *always/be*) fascinated by it and I .... (**3** *hear*) people say it was an unforgettable experience. I was very excited when I .... (**4** *arrive*) on the day, although beforehand I .... (**5** *feel*) a little frightened! My friends and I .... (**6** *come*) in the hope that by the end of the day we would be able to say we .... (**7** *walk*) across hot, burning coals.

Our teacher was very good, and by teatime we .... (**8** *learnt*) a great deal and .... (**9** *prepare*) the fires. I .... (**10** *expect*) to be terrified when the time came to walk, but as I .... (**11** *take off*) my shoes and socks I .... (**12** *not/feel*) afraid. I .... (**13** *approach*) the coals as all my friends before me .... (**14** *do*), and started walking! I could feel the heat, but as I .... (**15** *step*) back onto the grass at the other end I knew the coals .... (**16** *not/burn*) my feet at all. As I .... (**17** *hope*), all my friends .... (**18** *manage*) the walk and none of us were burnt. The whole experience was amazing, and I just wished I .... (**19** *do*) it sooner.

4 Fill in the gaps with a verb from the box in the past simple, past perfect simple or past perfect continuous tense. Use each verb once.

> be   buy   decide   develop   discuss   feel   like   make
> phone   run   start   stay   take   visit   wait   ~~work~~

1 She _'d been working_ as a waitress for five years when he met her.

2 The lecture .... by the time they got there.

3 In the supermarket he .... all the ingredients he needed and then went home to make her birthday cake.

4 Holly did very well in her exam, which was a shock because she .... (*never*) an exam before.

5 They went on a big tour of Britain. First they .... in London for a few days. Then they .... Cambridge, York, and Edinburgh, and then Bath. They .... to Bath before, but they .... it so much that they .... to go back again.

6 Scientists announced the launch of the new drug last week. They .... it for five years.

7 By the time I got to the meeting they .... (*already*) the important issues and they .... the big decisions without me. I .... from my mobile to tell them the train was late and I .... annoyed that they .... (*not*) for me.

8 I looked terrible when I saw Joe last night because I .... for over an hour and I was exhausted.

Academic Reading
Questions 1–12

Read the passage below and answer Questions 1–12.

The history of the biro

A

One chilly autumn morning in 1945, five thousand shoppers crowded the pavements outside Gimbels Department Store in New York City. The day before, Gimbels had taken out a full-page newspaper advertisement in the *New York Times*, announcing the sale of the first ballpoint pens in the United States. The new writing instrument was heralded as "fantastic... miraculous... guaranteed to write for two years without refilling!" Within six hours, Gimbels had sold its entire stock of ten thousand ballpoints at $12.50 each – approximately $130 at today's prices.

B

In fact this 'new' pen was not new after all, and was just the latest development in a long search for the best way to deliver ink to paper. In 1884 Lewis Waterman had patented the fountain pen, giving him the sole rights to manufacture it. This marked a significant leap forward in writing technology, but fountain pens soon became notorious for leaking. In 1888, a leather tanner named John Loud devised and patented the first "rolling-pointed marker pen" for marking leather. Loud's design contained a reservoir of ink in a cartridge and a rotating ball point that was constantly bathed on one side with ink.

Loud's pen was never manufactured, however, and over the next five decades, 350 additional patents were issued for similar ball-type pens, though none advanced beyond the design stage. Each had their own faults, but the major difficulty was the ink: if the ink was thin, the pens leaked, and if it was too thick, they clogged. Depending on the climate or air temperature, sometimes the pens would do both.

C

Almost fifty years later, Ladislas and Georg Biro, two Hungarian brothers, came up with a solution to this problem. In 1935 Ladislas Biro was working as a journalist, editing a small newspaper. He found himself becoming more and more frustrated by the amount of time he wasted filling fountain pens with ink and cleaning up ink smudges. What's more, the sharp tip of his fountain pen often scratched or tore through the thin newsprint paper. Ladislas and Georg (a chemist) set about making models of new pen designs and creating better inks to use in them. Ladislas had observed that the type of ink used in newspaper printing dried rapidly, leaving the paper dry and smudge-free. He was determined to construct a pen using the same type of ink. However, the thicker ink would not flow from a regular pen nib so he had to develop a new type of point. Biro came up with the idea of fitting his pen with a tiny ball bearing in its tip. As the pen moved along the paper, the ball bearing rotated and picked up ink from the ink cartridge which it delivered to the paper.

D

The first Biro pen, like the designs that had gone before it, relied on gravity for the ink to flow to the ball bearing at the tip. This meant that the pens only worked when they were held straight up, and even then the ink flow was sometimes too heavy, leaving big smudges of ink on the paper. The Biro brothers had a rethink and eventually devised a new design, which relied on capillary action rather than gravity to feed the ink. This meant that the ink could flow more smoothly to the tip and the pen could be held at an angle rather than straight up. In 1938, as World War II broke out, the Biro brothers fled to Argentina, where they applied for a patent for their pen and established their first factory.

E

The Biros' pen soon came to the attention of American fighter pilots, who needed a new kind of pen to use at high altitudes. Apparently, it was ideal for pilots as it did not leak like the fountain pen and did not have to be refilled frequently. The United States Department of War contacted several American companies, asking them to manufacture a similar writing instrument in the U.S. Thus fortune smiled on the Biro brothers in May 1945, when the American company 'Eversharp' paid them $500,000 for the exclusive manufacturing and marketing rights of the Biro ballpoint for the North American market. Eversharp were slow to put their pen into production, however, and this delay ultimately cost them their competitive advantage.

F

Meanwhile, in June 1945 an American named Milton Reynolds stumbled upon the Biro pen while on vacation in Buenos Aires. Immediately seeing its commercial potential, he bought several pens and returned to Chicago, where he discovered that Loud's original 1888 patent had long since expired. This meant that the ballpoint was now in the public domain, and he therefore wasted no time making a copy based on the Biro design. Establishing his pen company with just $26,000, Reynolds quickly set up a factory with 300 workers who began production on 6th October 1945, stamping out pens from precious scraps of aluminum that hadn't been used during the war for military equipment or weapons. Just 23 days later, it was Reynolds' ballpoint pen that caused the stampede at Gimbels Department Store. Following the ballpoint's debut in New York City, Eversharp challenged Reynolds in the law courts, but lost the case because the Biro brothers had failed to secure a U.S. patent on their invention.

4

Questions 1–6

The reading passage has six paragraphs **A–F**.

Choose the most suitable heading for each paragraph from the list of headings below.

Write the correct number *i–ix* in the space provided.

List of Headings
i   Fountain pens are history
ii   Fame at last for the Biro brothers
iii A holiday helps bring the biro to America
iv   A second design and a new country
v   War halts progress
vi   Dissatisfaction leads to a new invention
vii Big claims bring big crowds
viii A government request brings a change of ownership
ix   Many patents and many problems

1 Paragraph A ....
2 Paragraph B ....
3 Paragraph C ....
4 Paragraph D ....
5 Paragraph E ....
6 Paragraph F ....

Questions 7–9
Choose the correct answer, **A, B, C** or **D**.

7 The problem with the ballpoint pens invented between 1888 and 1935 was that
   A they cost a great deal of money to manufacture.
   B the technology to manufacture them did not exist.
   C they could not write on ordinary paper.
   D they were affected by weather conditions.

8 The design of the Biro brothers' first pen
   A was similar to previous pens.
   B was based on capillary action.
   C worked with heavy or light inks.
   D worked when slanted slightly.

9 Milton Reynolds was able to copy the Biro brothers' design because
   A the Biro brothers' original patent was out of date.
   B it was legal to copy other designs at the time.
   C they did not have a patent for North America.
   D the Biro brothers gave him permission.

Questions 10–12

Answer the questions below using **NO MORE THAN TWO WORDS AND/OR A NUMBER** for each answer.

Write your answers in the spaces provided.

10 What material was the first ballpoint pen designed to write on? ....

11 Where did the Biro brothers open their first factory? ....

12 In what year did the first American biro factory begin production? ....

Grammar focus task

Look at the extracts from the text. Without looking back at the text, fill in the gaps with the correct form of the verbs in brackets.

1 The day before, Gimbels .... (*take out*) a full-page newspaper advertisement in the *New York Times*, announcing the sale of the first ballpoint pens in the United States... Within six hours, Gimbels .... (*sell*) its entire stock of ten thousand ballpoints at $12.50 each – approximately $130 at today's prices.

2 In 1884 Lewis Waterman .... (*patent*) the fountain pen, giving him the sole rights to manufacture it. This marked a significant leap forward in writing technology, but fountain pens .... (*soon/become*) notorious for leaking.

3 Ladislas .... (*observe*) that the type of ink used in newspaper printing dried rapidly, leaving the paper dry and smudge-free.

4 Immediately seeing its commercial potential, he .... (*buy*) several pens and .... (*return*) to Chicago, where he .... (*discover*) that Loud's original 1888 patent .... (*long since/expire*).

5 Following the ballpoint's debut in New York City, Eversharp .... (*challenge*) Reynolds in the law courts, but .... (*lose*) the case because the Biro brothers .... (*fail*) to secure a U.S. patent on their invention.

5

Future 1
plans, intentions and predictions:
present continuous; *going to*; *will*

A Context listening

1 You are going to hear Tim, a sports team
coach, talking to Amanda, a player in the
team, about a trip they are going to make.
Before you listen look at the pictures.
Which sport does the team play? Which
two countries will they visit?

2 🎧 **5** Listen and complete the table below. Write no more than two words or a number
for each answer.

Country	Number of matches	Number of free days	Accommodation	Other plans
1	2	3	stay in a 4	do lots of walking
5	6	7	8	visit some 9 ....

3 **5** ◄◄ Now listen again and write

    A if Tim makes this statement

    B if Amanda makes this statement

    C if both Tim and Amanda make this statement

1 We're travelling to Scotland by plane. ....

2 We'll have fun even if the weather is bad. ....

3 The team will be pleased with the accommodation in Athens. ....

4 The two countries are going to provide very different experiences. ....

5 The team manager is holding a party on our return. ....

4 **Look at the statements in Exercise 3 and answer these questions.**

1 Which tense is used in statements 1 and 5? ....

2 Which structure is used in statements 2 and 3 to refer to the future? ....

3 Which structure is used in statement 4 to refer to the future? ....

4 Which statements talk about a fixed arrangement? ....

5 Which statements are predictions? ....

B Grammar

1 Present continuous（现在进行时）

现在进行时谈论的是针对将来的计划或明确的安排。

We're staying in a small hotel. (we have made the arrangements)

注意句子中使用的或从上下文推知的时间表达是用来谈论将来的，而非现在。

The manager is having a party just after we get back. (time expression given)

We're playing four matches there. (future time expression understood)

2 *Will*

+	*will* + verb	*We'll enjoy it.*
-	*will not (won't)* + verb	*He won't enjoy it.*
?	*will ...* + verb?	*Will they enjoy it?*

will 用于

◆ 做出预测，而这种预测通常是基于个人观点或过去的经验：

I think it'll be extremely hot there.

◆ 表达目前尚未安排将来有可能发生的事情：

We'll probably stay in some sort of mountain lodge there.

◆ 表达将来可能发生的非主观的事情或事实：

The best player on the tour will get a special trophy.

The prime minister will open the debate in parliament tomorrow.

◆ 表达说话者在说话间决定要做的事情：

Tell me all about it and I'll pass on the information to the rest of the team.

*will*常用来提供帮助、做出承诺或给予建议。

Don't worry, I'll let everyone know. (a promise)

3 *Going to*

+	*am/is/are* + *going to* + verb	*We're going to hire a bus.*
-	*am/is/are not* + *going to* + verb	*He's not going to hire a bus.*
?	*am/is/are ...* + *going to* + verb?	*Are they going to hire a bus?*

*Going to*通常相当于现在进行时和*will*。

*going to*用于

◆ 表达已经考虑过并打算实施的将来的某种行为：

We're going to hire a bus. (we intend to go, but we haven't made the arrangements yet)

We're going to get a boat to a couple of the islands.

◆ 根据目前事实做出的预测：

Well, we're certainly going to have a varied trip. (I am judging this from what I know about the plans)

Going to 和 *will* 跟在 *think*，*doubt*，*expect*，*believe*，*probably*，*certainly*，*definitely*，*be sure* 这些单词和短语后面，表达了关于将来的某种看法。

*I **think** it's **going to be** a great trip.*
*I'm **sure** we'll **enjoy** it whatever the weather.*
*It'll **probably rain** every day.*

在谈论同一个将来状态的时候，经常可以选择不同的将来形式。而使用何种将来形式则取决于说话者关于这个状态的主观想法。

Present continuous or *going to*?

*The manager **is having** a party when we get back.* (definite arrangement)

*We're **going to hire** a bus and then drive through the mountains.* (less definite arrangement – we haven't booked the bus yet)

Going to or *will*?

*I'm **sure** we'll **enjoy** it.* (prediction based on my guess)

*We're **going to have** a very varied trip!* (prediction based on what I know about the weather)

在表达对未来的预测时，*going to* 和 *will* 之间几乎没有区别。

Grammar extra: Making predictions using words other than *will*

在正式写作中，我们经常使用一些短语来预测未来，而不是使用 *will*。此类短语包括 *be likely to*，*be predicted to*，*be estimated to*，*be certain to* 等：

*The population **is likely to** increase to 22 million in 2011.*
*The average annual rainfall **is predicted to** be ten per cent lower than today's figures.*

C Grammar exercises

1 Fill in the gaps in the second half of this model answer with phrases from the box.

Thanks to modern technology, there have been enormous changes in the workplace over the past 100 years.

What are the most significant changes that have occurred and what changes do you foresee in the next 100 years?

are going to feel	are going to happen	are likely to lead to
~~are likely to occur~~	are predicted to work	is likely to become
will be	will continue	will develop
will find	will have	will result

... So, now let us consider the changes that **1** _are likely to occur_ in the next 100 years. Unfortunately, I believe that not all changes **2** .... for the better. For example, in the future more and more people **3** .... from home and so they **4** .... more isolated from their colleagues. On the other hand, they **5** .... (certainly) greater freedom to choose their working hours.

A further possible change is that handwriting **6** .... obsolete. We are already so used to using a keyboard that today's children are losing the ability to spell without the aid of a word processor.

Without a doubt, even greater changes **7** .... in technology used in the workplace. Computers **8** .... (undoubtedly) to grow even more powerful and this **9** .... (probably) in an even faster pace of life than we have now. Let us hope that our employers **10** .... a way to reduce the stress on workers this fast pace can bring.

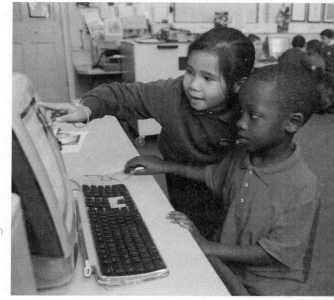

I also think these improvements in technology **11** ...., even more globalisation than now and companies **12** .... very strong international links.

2 <u>Underline</u> the most suitable form of the verbs.

Dear Paul and Claire

We're having a wonderful time here in France. The weather is beautiful and we've got lots of plans for how to spend the next couple of weeks. Tomorrow 1 <u>we're going out</u> / we will go out on a glass-bottomed boat to look at the wonderful sea life, and then on Wednesday we think 2 we're taking / we'll take a tour of the old town. Ollie's aunt lives quite close, so 3 we're visiting / we're going to visit her too if we have time.

The hotel is lovely and lively and has lots of good night life. Tonight 4 they're holding / they'll hold an international evening, with lots of food from different countries.

As you know, we're here with our friends, John and Wendy, but 5 they aren't staying / they won't stay as long as us, so 6 we're probably doing / we'll probably do the really 'touristy' things with them, and be lazy in our second week. You can hire small sailing boats for the day, so we think 7 we're doing / we're going to do that next week, and 8 we're also going to try / we're also trying to have time to do some shopping!

I hope you are ready for your big trip. 9 You're loving / You'll love Australia. In fact 10 you're going to probably end up / you'll probably end up staying there much longer than you've planned.

Have a great time, and 11 we're going to see / we'll see you when you get back.

Love Kath and Ollie

3 Fill in the gaps with the present continuous or *will*-future form of the verbs in brackets.

Kirsty: Hi Elaine. It's Kirsty, here.

Elaine: Hello, how are you?

Kirsty: Fine. Listen, I know this is very short notice but _are you doing_ (**1** *do*) anything tonight?

Elaine: Nothing why?

Kirsty: Well I .... (**2** *take*) my class to the theatre, but one of them can't go. Would you like to come?

Elaine: I'd love to. What's the play about?

Kirsty: Oh, I .... (**3** *tell*) you all about that a little later. I .... (**4** *pick*) you up at 6.30 – is that okay?

Elaine: Yes, OK. Or how about meeting a bit earlier? We could have a coffee beforehand.

Kirsty: Well, I .... (**5** *see*) the school principal at four, but I suppose I could come after that. My meeting .... (**6** *probably/finish*) at about 5.30. Is that okay?

Elaine: Yes, of course. What time does the play actually start?

Kirsty: At 7.30, although we .... (**7** *need*) to be there before as I .... (**8** *meet*) my students at the theatre at seven. Afterwards they .... (**9** *probably/want*) to talk about the play for a little while. But I hope that .... (**10** *not/go on*) for too long. There .... (**11** *be*) plenty of time for us to discuss it at tomorrow's lesson.

Elaine: That's fine. I .... (**12** *see*) you at 5.30!

4 Write sentences about yourself.

1 Write two **intentions** about your future.

....
....

2 Write three **plans** or **arrangements** for your future.

....
....
....

3 **Predict** three things that you think will happen to the workplace in the future.

....
....
....

General Training Reading
Questions 1–9

Read the passage below and answer Questions 1–9.

How to choose a university course

How do I choose a course?

You've decided you want to do a course. Whether you would like a career change, a better job or simply to learn something new, it's a good idea to think carefully first. Here's a guide to help you.

Qualifications – why do I need them?

Qualifications prove you've acquired knowledge or developed skills. For some careers like medicine and law, it's essential you have specific qualifications. For others, such as journalism, it helps to have a particular qualification.

Most universities set entry requirements for degree courses. Mature entrants don't always need formal qualifications, but need evidence of recent study, relevant work experience or professional qualifications. Professional bodies may grant you membership if you have certain qualifications. It's not always essential to have a qualification. Working knowledge, such as being able to use computer software, can be just as important.

What type of course should I do?

Your motives will help you choose the best course for your aims and goals. If you are career-driven, you'll need a course relevant to your profession. If you are interested in self-development and meeting people, you should find out who else will be on the course.

There are work-related (vocational) and academic courses. Further education colleges offer academic courses and work-related courses. Universities offer higher education qualifications, such as academic first degrees and higher degrees and the more vocational diplomas.

For a career in plumbing, a vocational course is essential. For teaching, you need a degree. However, for many jobs, you have a choice between academic and vocational courses. A vocational course is better if you like doing things with your hands and working manually. You might prefer an academic course if you like researching, analysing and presenting arguments.

Which type of study would suit me best?

Do you prefer on-the-job training, or do you prefer to research and gather facts? Do you like working in a group covering the same topics and working towards the same goal? If you prefer to work on your own, at your own pace, an open or distance learning course might suit you. You study from home, with the help of tuition packs, computers and tutor support via telephone or email. You can speed through the course or take your time. But you do need self-discipline and motivation.

What about my personal circumstances?

You might prefer an open or distance learning course if:
- you're working and you don't know how much time a week you can commit to
- you work irregular hours
- you're at home looking after pre-school children.

Many colleges and training centres now offer flexible open-learning courses, where you can study at your own pace.

How do I know if it's a good course?

You've decided which subject and type of course you want, and how to study it. You now need to choose between different course titles and providers. There are many courses and they aren't of equal value. The only way to assess the quality and value of a course is by research. Read prospectuses (course guides) carefully and note if a course is accredited or validated by a recognised body (this might be an awarding body or a professional body). This can add extra weight to your qualification.

Don't take everything you read at face value; check out the facts about each course yourself. Ask course tutors as many questions as you want.

How can I be sure I'm making the right choice?

Be clear of your goal. If you've decided on a particular job, get an idea of what the job's about and if you'll like it. Read careers information, buy trade magazines, and speak to people currently working in the job. This research is well worth it. It's better to take your time rather than do a course that leads to a job you might not really want. You'll ensure that you don't waste any time or money.

What am I going to do after the course?

Plan for when you finish. If you're aiming for a particular job, do voluntary work while studying. If you're doing an English course and want to be a journalist, you could write for the student newspaper or work on the radio. Having a plan will help you make the most of the opportunities that come your way when you're on the course.

5

Questions 1–5

Complete each sentence with the correct ending A–F from the box below.

Write the correct letter A–F next to Questions 1–5.

1 Students who want to do law ....
2 Mature students ....
3 Students who are motivated by self-development ....
4 Students who have young children ....
5 Students who choose a career in journalism ....

> A will not need any experience to start a course
> B will benefit from open-learning courses
> C could get relevant work experience while they study
> D can be accepted onto a course without qualifications
> E should enquire about the other students on their course
> F must have certain qualifications

Questions 6–9

Classify the following statements as applying to
    A academic courses
    B vocational courses
    C both academic and vocational courses

Write the correct letter A–C next to Questions 6–9.

6 These courses are available through further education colleges. ....
7 You must take this kind of course if you wish to have a career in plumbing. ....
8 You will learn research methods on this type of course. ....
9 You will learn practical skills on this course. ....

Grammar focus task

These are extracts from the text. Without looking back at the text, fill in the gaps with the correct form of the verbs in brackets and then answer the questions that follow.

1 Your motives .... (*help*) you choose the best course for your aims and goals.

2 If you are career-driven, you .... (*need*) a course relevant to your profession.

3 You .... (*ensure*) that you don't waste any time or money.

4 What .... (*I/do*) after the course?

5 Having a plan .... (*help*) you make the most of the opportunities that come your way when you're on the course.

Which future forms are used? ....

Why? ....

Future 2

present simple; *be about to*;
future continuous; future perfect

1 Janet is a university lecturer. She gets nervous when she gives talks at conferences. Look at the pictures. Which do you think would help Janet feel more confident and relaxed?

2 🎧 **6** Listen to Janet's conversation with her colleague, Phil. What advice does Phil give her?

3 **6** ◀◀ Listen again and complete the sentences below. Write no more than three words for each answer.

1 Janet .... on the report all next week.

2 By the end of the year, Janet .... the same talk at six conferences.

3 When she gets to Rome, Janet .... very nervous.

4 Before he gives his talk in London, Phil .... it at least ten times.

5 Janet is in a hurry because the train to the airport .... in 20 minutes.

4 Look at the sentences used in Exercise 3 and answer these questions.

1 Which sentences talk about events that will be over before a time in the future?
   ....

2 Which sentences talk about events or situations in progress at a particular time in the future? ....

3 Which sentence talks about a scheduled event? ....

B Grammar

1 Present simple （一般现在时）

具有将来意义的一般现在时的用法：

◆ 谈论时间表或日程：
*The conference only **lasts** three days.*
*The train to the airport **leaves** in 20 minutes.*

◆ 跟在 *when*，*as soon as*，*after*，*before*，*until*，*as long as* 等连词后面：
*I'll be feeling really nervous **when I get** to Rome.* (**not** ~~when I will get to Rome~~)
*Can you do it **before** we **have** the departmental meeting?* (**not** ~~before we will have the meeting~~)
注意：其他的现在时态也能表达将来意义：
*I won't be able to relax **until** I'm actually **giving** my talk.*

2 *Be about to*

+	*am/is/are about to* + verb	*I'm **about to** go to Rome.*
−	*am/is/are not about to* + verb	*I'm not **about to** go to Rome.*
?	*am/is/are ... + verb?*	*Are you **about to** go to Rome?*

be about to 用于表示即将可能发生的事情：
*I'm **about to** go to Rome for a conference.* (I will be leaving very soon)

⚠ 注意：*be about to* 的否定形式表示说话者没有意图做某事：
*I'm **not about to** cancel my trip.* (= I have no intention of cancelling my trip)

3 Future continuous （将来进行时）

+	*will be* + verb + *-ing*	*I'll **be feeling** nervous.*
−	*will not (won't) be* + verb + *-ing*	*She **won't be feeling** nervous.*
?	*will ... be* + verb + *-ing?*	***Will** you **be feeling** nervous?*

将来进行时用于：
◆ 描述或预测在将来某一特定时间或某一段时间持续发生的事情或状态：
*I'll **be working** on the report all next week.*
*I'll **be thinking** of you in Rome.*

*I'll **be working** on the report*

| NOW | N E X T   W E E K |

*By the year 2015 it is estimated that well over one billion people **will be learning** English.*

◆ 谈论已经计划好的事情或已经决定了的事情（此种用法类似于表将来安排的现在进行时）：
*I'll **be seeing** Sarah at lunch.*

4 Future perfect simple（将来完成时）

+	will have + past participle	I'll have done it by then.
–	will not (won't) have + past participle	We won't have done it by then.
?	will ... + have + past participle?	Will you have done it by then?

将来完成时表示在将来某一时间之前完成的动作，通常句中会出现 *before*，*by* + 固定时间，*in* + 某段时间：

*By the end of the year I **will have given** the same talk at 6 conferences!*
*I'**ll have finished** it by next Friday.*
*In a week's time I'**ll have written** the report.*

5 Future perfect continuous（将来完成进行时）

+	will have been + verb + -ing	I'll have been studying here for three months.
–	will not (won't) have been + verb + -ing	We won't have been studying here for long.
?	will ... + have been + verb + -ing?	How long will you have been studying here?

将来完成进行时表示在将来某一时间之前某个动作或状态存在了多久。句中通常会提到时间的长度：
*By the end of the month I'**ll have been working** here for three years.*

Grammar extra: The future in the past

在表达过去计划过的事情没有发生或不会发生时，使用*was / were going to, was / were planning to, was / were about to* +动词。
*I **was going to leave** this morning but they cancelled my flight.*
*We **were about to leave** when the phone rang.*

C Grammar exercises

1 The following chart shows the results of a class survey about planned activities for Saturday afternoon. Complete the sentences using the future continuous tense.

Class plans for Saturday afternoon

1 Twelve students _will be watching TV_ on Saturday afternoon.
2 The students .... books on Saturday.
3 The largest group of students .... this Saturday afternoon.
4 A similar number of students .... and .... this weekend.
5 A very small number of students .... this weekend.
6 Approximately 15 students .... this weekend.

Write what you will be doing at the following times.

7 At six o'clock tomorrow I'll ....
8 Next Saturday afternoon I won't ....
9 On Sunday morning ....
10 In a year's time ....

2 Read the following projections about the future population of Australia.

Population projections

According to the latest available projections (which are based on several combinations of assumptions reflecting past trends in births, deaths and migration), the total population of Australia is likely to have increased to between 22.3 and 23.3 million by 2021.

The projected population will increase at a declining rate. The average annual growth rate is predicted to be between 0.5 and 0.8 during 2011–2021. Without overseas migration, the projected total population should peak at about 23.3 million in 2041, and then start to decline marginally.

Age distribution
The projected population will age progressively due to the increasing proportion of the elderly (aged 65 years or more) and the decreasing proportion of children (aged under 15 years). In brief, the number of persons aged under 15 is projected to be between 3.7 and 4.1 million in 2031; the population of working age (15–64 years) is projected to increase to between 14.4 and 15.0 million in 2031; and the number of persons aged 65 years or more is projected to increase to between 2.94 and 2.98 million in 2031. The projections also show significant increases in the number of persons aged 80 years or more.

Write the verbs in brackets in the future perfect tense. Then choose the correct ending for each sentence.

1 By the year 2021 the population of Australia _will have reached_ (reach)

2 The population of Australia .... (peak)

3 By the year 2031 the number of children aged under 15 .... (rise)

4 By 2031 the number of people of working age in Australia .... (grow)

5 By 2031 the number of people aged 65 and over .... (go up)

6 By the year 2031 the number of people aged over 80 .... (increase)

a by the early 2040s.

b to almost 2.98 million.

c a maximum of 23.3 million.

d to between 3.7 and 4.1 million.

e significantly.

f to around 15 million.

3 In six of these sentences there is a verb in the wrong tense. <u>Underline</u> each mistake and write the correction.

1 When <u>I'll find</u> the answer I'll let you know. .... I find ....

2 My exams finish on 27th June. ....

3 I'll be fine in the interview as long as they won't ask me technical questions. ....

4 What time is your meeting about to start tomorrow? ....

5 I'll hand in my notice for this job after I'll get the contract for my new one. ....

6 I'll text you before we set off. ....

7 The bus doesn't arrive until 7.30 in the evening. ....

8 I've got my schedule for the Japan trip. We're about to fly to Tokyo at 10 am on Monday, and then travel by train to Kyoto for one night. ....

9 The moment I'll receive my results I'll phone you. ....

4 Fill in the gaps with a future form from this unit and the verbs in brackets.

Teacher: What ..will you be doing.. (**1** *you/do*) this time next year?

Student 1: Well, that's difficult to say but I hope that I .... (**2** *travel*) round the world. Before then I .... (**3** *hopefully/save up*) enough money for the ticket. I plan to end up in Australia and when I .... (**4** *get*) there I'll get a job and earn some money. So, in a year's time I .... (**5** *probably/travel*) for a few months already. I hope that I .... (**6** *visit*) quite a lot of different countries by then too.

Teacher: What do you plan to do when you graduate?

Student 2: Well, my plans have changed a bit. I .... (**7** *do*) a journalism course, but I didn't get accepted. So I've sorted something else out and I .... (**8** *start*) a hospitality course tomorrow, actually. It's for six months, so I .... (**9** *not/finish*) in time to go travelling next spring, unfortunately. However, as soon as I .... (**10** *find out*) if I've passed the course, I can apply for a job in a hotel in Australia.

D Test practice

Academic Writing Task 2

You should spend about 40 minutes on this task.

Write about the following topic:

> *The birth rate in most developed countries is predicted to begin to fall over the next 50 years. By 2030 it is estimated that over one third of the population in most developed countries will be aged 65 and over.*
>
> *What effects will these predictions have on developed countries if they prove true? What can be done now to deal with this situation?*

Give reasons for your answer and include any relevant examples from your own knowledge or experience.

You should write at least 250 words.

Grammar focus task

Look at the extract from a model answer below. Fill in the gaps with the verbs in the box in the correct future tense.

be	pay	rise	work

... By 2030 the percentage of the population aged 65 or older **1** .... significantly, to more than 30%. This means that fewer people **2** ...., and therefore fewer people **3** .... income tax. In the future it may be necessary for governments to increase the official retirement age to 70 or even older. When today's 30-year-olds **4** .... in their sixties it is unlikely that they will enjoy the relaxed lifestyle that today's older generation can expect when they give up work.

Countable and uncountable nouns
countable and uncountable nouns; quantity expressions
(*many, much, a lot of, some, any, a few, few, no*)

7

A Context listening

1 You are going to hear Alan and Sara talking about advertising a spare bedroom to rent. Before you listen look at the types of furniture below. Tick the furniture you think might be in the room.

☐ shelves   ☐ a wardrobe   ☐ a lamp   ☐ a bedside table

☐ a filing cabinet   ☐ a bed   ☐ a desk   ☐ a mirror

☐ a sofa   ☐ a towel rail   ☐ a coffee table   ☐ a rug

2 🎧 **7** Listen and answer the questions below.

1 Which three pieces of furniture are in the room?

A a bed   C a desk   F a mirror

B a bedside table   E a lamp   G a wardrobe

2 What does the desk look like?

A   B   C

3 **7◀◀** Listen again and fill in the gaps in the advertisement. Write no more than one word or a number for each answer.

> **Accommodation for rent**
>
> Small, furnished 1 .... available. Sunny with a nice view of the 2 .... Good location close to two types of 3 ....
> Rent 4 £................... per 5 .... Rent includes 6 .... and all other bills.

4 Look at the two groups of nouns in the table below. How are they different? Add the nouns from Exercises 2 and 3 into the table in the correct group.

Group 1	Group 2
advertisement *newspaper* *windows*	*money* *news* *accommodation*

B Grammar

1 Countable and uncountable nouns （可数名词和不可数名词）

Countable nouns

◆ 通常有单数和复数形式：
a window, *lots of windows*
⚠ 注意：有些可数名词只有一个复数形式：
clothes, *trousers*, *jeans*, *scissors*

◆ 和动词一起使用时，动词也分单复数形式：
*The window **is** big. The windows **are** big.*

◆ 能被单数或复数代词指代：
*I'd like that **desk**; **it's** better than mine.*
*It's got **shelves** as well. **They**'re really handy.*

◆ 能用表示重量、尺寸或数量的词计量：***two kilos** of potatoes*
or numbers: *It's got **three** drawers.*

◆ 能与*a / an* 冠词连用：
a desk, an apple

Uncountable nouns

◆ 没有复数形式：*advice* (**not** ~~advices~~), *furniture* (**not** ~~furnitures~~), *data*
⚠ 注意：有些不可数名词看上去像是复数形式，实则不是：*news, economics, physics*

◆ 只和单数动词一起使用：
*The natural light **is** really nice.*

◆ 可以被一个单数代词指代：
*'What shall we say about **the furniture**?'*
*'Well, **it's** not luxurious but **it** is very comfortable.'*

◆ 能用表示重量、尺寸或诸如*a piece of*, *cup of*, *bit of*, *slice of* 等短语计量：***a piece of** information*

◆ 不能与*a / an* 连用：
information (**not** ~~an information~~)

2 *Some* and *any* （Some和any）

Some

◆ 通常用于肯定句中：*There are **some** shelves above the desk.*

◆ 也可以用于疑问句中。在表示建议、反问或请求的疑问句中，或期望得到肯定的回答时，用*some*。
*Would you like **some** biscuits?*

◆ 表示"不明确（不是很多）的数量"：
*It would be great to get **some money** to help with the rent.* (we don't know how much money)

⚠ 注意：*some of*加其他限定词（如*my*，*the*，*these*）表示某一特定群体：
***Some of my** students have part-time jobs.*

Any

◆ 通常用于否定句和疑问句中：
*My desk **hasn't** got **any** drawers.*   *Has your desk got **any** drawers?*

◆ 也可用于表肯定的陈述句中，表示"无论谁 / 哪个 / 什么地点 / 什么时间、什么事"：
*Call me **any time** if you need further help.* (= it doesn't matter when you call)

⚠ 注意：*no* ＋名词等同于*not...any*：
*My desk has got **no** drawers.* (= my desk hasn't got any drawers)
当该名词是主语时，通常使用*no*：
***No applicants** had the necessary experience for the job.* (**not** ~~Not any applicants~~)

类似于*something / anything*，*somebody / anybody*之类的词遵循*some* 和*any* 的使用规则。

3 Quantities（量词）

可以使用下列词来表达数量或程度的多少：

	Plural countable nouns	Uncountable nouns
everything	*all* (*of*)	*all* (*of*)
large quantities	*lots of* / *plenty of* / *a lot of* *many* (*of*) *most* (*of*) *a large/considerable/substantial number of*	*lots of* / *plenty of* / *a lot of* *much* (*of*) *most* (*of*) *a large/considerable/substantial amount of*
medium quantities	*some* (*of*)/*a certain number of*	*some* (*of*)/*a certain amount of*
small quantities	(*a*) *few* (*of*) *a small/limited/tiny number of*	(*a*) *little* (*of*) *a small/limited/tiny amount of*
nothing	*no* / *not any* / *none of*	*no* / *not any* / *none of*

*A few*和*a little*不同于*few* 和*little*。对比：
Few rooms have such good natural light. (= not many, so you are lucky)
*We have **a few** rooms available with a sea view.* (= a small number)

Little research has been done in this area. (= not enough)
A little research has already been carried out in this area. (= a small amount)

⚠ 注意：*a few of* 和其他限定词（如 *my*, *the*, *these*）使用时表一个特殊的群体。
A few of the rooms have a sea view.

Lots of / *a lot of* 相对 *much*/*many* 不是很正式：
*There are **lots of** advertisements for accommodation in the paper.*
Many scientists believe that global warming is having a negative impact on our climate.

⚠ 注意：*lots of* 通常不用于否定陈述句：
*We don't have **a lot of**/**much** time so we'll have to be quick.* (**not** ~~we don't have lots of time~~)

⚠ *Much* 通常不用于肯定陈述句。
*I found **a lot of** information on the Internet.* (**not** ~~much information~~)

Grammar extra: Nouns that can be both countable and uncountable

有时，根据意思的不同，同一个名词既可做可数名词，也可做不可数名词，如 *light*, *room*, *cake*, *time*。表材料和液体的名词也可以两者皆可，如 *glass*, *paper*, *coffee*, *wine*。对比：
The natural light is really nice. (uncountable)
Both of the lights in the ceiling are really old. (countable)
There isn't much room for a desk. (uncountable = space)
We have two spare rooms. (countable = rooms in a house)
Do you drink much coffee? (uncountable = in general)
I'd like to order a coffee, please. (countable = a cup of coffee)

C Grammar exercises

1 **Fill in the gaps with a word from the box below in the correct form. If the word is countable, you may need to change it to a plural form.**

| advice | cake | ~~challenge~~ | electricity | information | situation | size |

1 I've faced many __challenges__ in my life, but none as difficult as this.

2 Some of the best .... I heard while I was a student was to take regular breaks when studying so that you don't lose concentration.

3 A dictionary is a wonderful source of ....

4 I've made some little .... for Claire's birthday party.

5 One hundred years ago cars all looked the same but these days they come in lots of different shapes and ....

6 My job as a journalist means I can find myself in difficult .... at times, but at least it's never boring.

7 There was no .... in the remote cottage, so they had to cook over the fire.

2 **Underline the correct form of the verbs.**

1 Despite the recent improvement in the economy, unemployment *has continued* / *have continued* to rise.

2 Our company hasn't changed its products for over 30 years but now the time *has come* / *have come* for a rethink.

3 The ideas in the report *was* / *were* presented in a very clear way.

4 The data *show* / *shows* that the numbers of people buying mobile phones has remained stable for the past two years.

5 Transport to and from the airport *is included* / *are included* in the price.

6 There *was* / *were* no facilities like running water or electricity in the village.

7 All the information *is* / *are* interesting and well presented, but we need to consider the whole situation very carefully before we reach a decision.

8 There *was* / *were* some important news about the proposed new hospital in the local paper today.

3 Fill in the gaps with *amount, number, few, little, many* or *much*.

How much sleep do we need?

The 1 ..amount.. of sleep each person needs depends on 2 .... factors, including age. Infants generally require about 16 hours a day. For most adults, seven to eight hours a night appears to be the ideal 3 .... of sleep, although a 4 .... people may need as 5 .... as five hours' sleep or as 6 .... as ten hours' sleep each day. Getting too 7 .... sleep creates a sleep debt, and eventually, your body will demand that the debt be repaid.

A large 8 .... of people over 65 have frequent sleeping problems, such as insomnia, and deep sleep stages in 9 .... elderly people often become very short or stop completely. Microsleeps, or very brief episodes of sleep in an otherwise awake person, are another mark of sleep deprivation. In 10 .... cases, people are not aware that they are experiencing microsleeps. The widespread practice of burning the candle at both ends in western industrialized societies has created so 11 .... sleep deprivation that what is really abnormal sleepiness is now almost the norm.

4 Read the extract from a talk about a holiday destination. Decide if the <u>underlined</u> quantity expressions are correct or not. Tick (✓) them if they are right and correct them if they are wrong.

The island is beautiful. Don't be dismayed when you get off the plane and find yourself in a large, rather ugly city with **1** <u>a little</u> sense of the old way of life you have read about. Just a short car ride away is the island you have been promised with its small villages and slow pace of life. And there really is **2** <u>anything</u> for everyone. For those that like sunbathing, it has **3** <u>some</u> of the most beautiful beaches in the world. If you like walking, the paths take you through some breathtaking scenery. **4** <u>Little</u> other places can match the stunning landscape of this island. For water sports enthusiasts, there are **5** <u>any</u> unusual activities such as diving for pearls or turtle spotting, along with **6** <u>few</u> of the more common sports such as waterskiing or windsurfing. If history is your thing, don't worry. There's **7** <u>much</u> history round every corner. Ruins from the ancient civilisations that lived here over 3000 years ago are everywhere, and although **8** <u>a lot of</u> people come here just to see the palace, you can find some lesser remains scattered around the surrounding hills.

Visit it **9** <u>some</u> time of the year and you will not be disappointed. Not **10** <u>many</u> places in the world can offer so much. **11** <u>Not any</u> holiday will ever match this one – our island has got it all!

1 .a little.
2 ....
3 ....
4 ....
5 ....
6 ....
7 ....
8 ....
9 ....
10 ....
11 ....

Academic Reading

*You should spend about 20 minutes on **Questions 1–14** which are based on the Reading Passage below.*

Dressed to dazzle

As high-tech materials invade high-street fashion, prepare for clothes that are cooler than silk and warmer than wool, keep insects at arm's length, and emit many pinpricks of coloured light.

The convergence of fashion and high technology is leading to new kinds of fibres, fabrics and coatings that are imbuing clothing with equally wondrous powers. Corpe Nove, an Italian fashion company, has made a prototype shirt that shortens its sleeves when room temperature rises and can be ironed with a hairdryer. And at Nexia Biotechnologies, a Canadian firm, scientists have caused a stir by manufacturing spider silk from the milk of genetically engineered goats. Not surprisingly, some industry analysts think high-tech materials may soon influence fashion more profoundly than any individual designer.

A big impact is already being made at the molecular level. Nano-Tex, a subsidiary of American textiles maker Burlington, markets a portfolio of nanotechnologies that can make fabrics more durable, comfortable, wrinkle-free and stain-resistant. The notion of this technology posing a threat to the future of the clothing industry clearly does not worry popular fashion outlets such as Gap, Levi Strauss and Lands' End, all of which employ Nano-Tex's products. Meanwhile, Schoeller Textil in Germany, whose clients include famous designers Donna Karan and Polo Ralph Lauren, uses nanotechnology to create fabrics that can store or release heat.

Sensory Perception Technologies (SPT) embodies an entirely different application of nanotechnology. Created in 2003 by Quest International, a flavour and fragrance company, and Woolmark, a wool textile organisation, SPT is a new technique of embedding chemicals into fabric. Though not the first of this type, SPT's durability (evidently the microcapsule containing the chemicals can survive up to 30 washes) suggests an interesting future. Designers could incorporate signature scents into their collections. Sportswear could be impregnated with anti-perspirant. Hayfever sufferers might find relief by pulling on a T-shirt, and so on.

The loudest buzz now surrounds polylactic acid (PLA) fibres – and, in particular, one brand-named Ingeo. Developed by Cargill Dow, it is the first man-made fibre derived from a 100% annually renewable resource. This is currently maize (corn), though in theory any fermentable plant material, even potato peelings, can be used. In performance terms, the attraction for the 30-plus clothes makers signed up to use Ingeo lies in its superiority over polyester (which it was designed to replace).

As Philippa Watkins, a textiles specialist, notes, Ingeo is not a visual trend. Unlike nanotechnology, which promises to transform what clothes can do, Ingeo's impact on fashion will derive instead from its emphasis on using natural sustainable resources. Could wearing synthetic fabrics made from polluting and non-renewable fossil fuels become as uncool as slipping on a coat made from animal fur? Consumers should expect a much wider choice of 'green' fabrics. Alongside PLA fibres, firms are investigating plants such as bamboo, seaweed, nettles and banana stalks as raw materials for textiles. Soya bean fibre is also gaining ground. Harvested in China and spun in Europe, the fabric is a better absorber and ventilator than silk, and retains heat better than wool.

Elsewhere, fashion houses – among them Ermenegildo Zegna, Paul Smith and DKNY – are combining fashion with electronics. Clunky earlier attempts involved attaching electronic components to the fabrics after the normal weaving process. But companies such as SOFTswitch have developed electro-conductive fabrics that behave in similar ways to conventional textiles.

Could electronic garments one day change colour or pattern? A hint of what could be achieved is offered by Luminex, a joint venture between Stabio Textile and Caen. Made of woven optical fibres and powered by a small battery, Luminex fabric emits thousands of pinpricks of light, the colour of which can be varied. Costumes made of the fabric wowed audiences at a production of the opera *Aida* in Washington, DC, last year.

Yet this ultimate of ambitions has remained elusive in daily fashion, largely because electronic textiles capable of such wizardry are still too fragile to wear. Margaret Orth, whose firm International Fashion Machines makes a colour-changing fabric, believes the capability is a decade or two away. Accessories with this chameleon-like capacity – for instance, a handbag that alters its colour – are more likely to appear first.

Questions 1–6

Look at the following list of companies (1–6) and the list of new materials below.

Match each company with the correct material.

Write the correct letter **A–H** next to the companies 1–6.

NB You may use any answer more than once.

1 Corpe Nove ....
2 Nexia Biotechnologies ....
3 Nano-Tex ....

4 Schoeller Textil ....
5 Quest International and Woolmark ....
6 Cargill Dow ....

New materials

A material that can make you warmer or cooler
B clothing with perfume or medication added
C material that rarely needs washing
D clothes that can change according to external heat levels
E material made from banana stalks
F material that is environmentally-friendly
G fibres similar to those found in nature
H clothes that can light up in the dark

Questions 7–14

Complete the summary below.

Write **NO MORE THAN TWO WORDS** from the Reading Passage for each answer.

Major changes in fabrics

Using plants

Nanotechnology will bring changes we can see, while the brand called **7** .... will help the environment. Fibre made from the **8** .... plant has better qualities than silk and wool.

Electronics

In first attempts to use electronics, companies started with a material made by a standard **9** .... method and then they fixed **10** .... to the material.
Luminex fabric
• needs a **11** .... to make it work.
• has already been used to make stage **12** ....
• is not suitable for everyday wear because it is too **13** ....
The first products that can change colour are likely to be **14** ....

Which of these nouns from the text are countable (C) and which are uncountable (U)? Which is an example of a noun that can be both countable and uncountable? How is it used in the text?

1 materials (paragraph 1) ....C....

2 shirt (paragraph 2) ....

3 heat (paragraph 3) ....

4 technique (paragraph 4) ....

5 sportswear (paragraph 4) ....

6 fibre (paragraph 5) ....

7 clothes (paragraph 6) ....

8 choice (paragraph 6) ....

8

Referring to nouns
articles; other determiners (demonstratives, possessives, inclusives: *each, every, both, all, either, neither* etc.)

A Context listening

1 You are going to hear a speaker at an environmental awareness conference talking about a European satellite called Envisat. Before you listen, put the words below into two groups: *the environment* and *satellites*.

climate	fully-equipped	global warming	instrument
launch	monitoring	observation	operational costs
outer space	ozone depletion	precise	

2 **⌂ 8a** Now listen to the talk and complete the notes below. Write no more than two words or a number for each answer.

> Envisat satellite
> - Envisat was launched **1** ....
> - Envisat has **2** .... instrument systems.
> - In 1990s ESA launched **3** .... and **4** ....
> - ESA will spend 2.3 billion euros over **5** ....
> - This is the same as **6** .... of coffee per person per year.

3 Underline the correct words. **8a◀◀** Listen again to check your answers.

1 Envisat is *a/the* fully equipped observation satellite.

2 *A/The* satellite was launched in 2002.

3 With its ten instrument systems it is equipped with *–/the* best eyes possible and offers everything that *–/the* scientists could wish for.

4 The total cost of the Envisat Programme is 2.3 billion euros over 15 years. Included in *that/this* sum is development and construction of the instruments.

5 *Neither/None* of our countries can afford to let down their environmental guard.

4 Look at your answers to Exercise 3 and answer these questions.

1 Why do we say *a satellite* in sentence 1 and *the satellite* in sentence 2?

2 In sentence 3, why do we use an article before *best*? Why don't we use an article in front of the word *scientists*?

3 In sentence 4, what does *this sum* refer to?

4 In sentence 5, why can't we use *neither*?

B Grammar

1 Articles（冠词）

a/an

a / an 用于以下情况：

◆ 第一次提到的事物：
*I'd like to talk to you today about **an exciting development**.*

◆ 几个为一组中的任意一个：
*Climate protection is **a challenge** for our entire society.* (one of many challenges)

◆ 将人或事物分类归到一个组：
*Envisat is **a fully-equipped observation satellite**.* (there are different kinds of satellite)

◆ 谈论职业：
*My brother is **an engineer**.*

⚠ 在单数可数名词前只能用 *a / an*。

the

the 用于以下情形：

◆ 当听众／读者知道所指的是哪件事时（此事可能前面已经提到过）：
*Envisat is **a fully-equipped observation satellite** ... **The satellite** was launched in 2002.*
或了解所指的事：
*As part of **the conference** on environmental awareness ...* (we are at the conference now so it is clear which one I mean)
比较：
*I went to **a conference** on Environmental awareness last week.* (the person I am talking to does not know which conference I am talking about)

◆ 当该事物为独一无二时：
the earth, the sun, the twentieth century, the sixties, the Government, the Prime Minister (there is only one government and one prime minister in each country)

◆ 最高级（见Unit 11）：
*It is equipped with **the best eyes** possible.*

◆ 谈论演奏乐器：
*He plays **the piano** and she plays **the guitar**.*

◆ 与特定的专有名词连用：
nationalities (*the British, the Chinese, the Egyptians*)
rivers (*the Thames, the Yangtze, the Nile*)
island groups (*the Maldives, the Philippines, the Seychelles*)
mountain ranges (*the Alps, the Himalayas*)
seas and oceans (*the Black Sea, the Mediterranean, the Pacific*)
country names that represent a group (*the United Kingdom, the United States of America*)
many famous/historical buildings (*the White House*)
noun phrases with *of* (*the Great Wall of China, the Temple of Heaven*)

⚠ 与大学名称连用时，可以说 *the university of Bath* 或 *Bath University*。

No article

下列情况不用冠词：

◆ 用来概述事情的复数名词或不可数名词：
*It will deliver **information** about our changing environment.*
*It offers everything that **scientists** could wish for.* (scientists in general not a specific group of scientists)

◆ 特定的专有名词：
continents (*Europe*, *Asia*)
countries (*Australia*, *China*)
states or counties (*Michigan*, *Cambridgeshire*)
towns and cities (*Tokyo*, *Jeddah*)
mountains (*Everest*, *Kilimanjaro*)
lakes (*Lake Superior*)
companies (*Microsoft*, *Sony*)
buildings and places with the name of a town (*Heathrow Airport*)

◆ 进餐时间：
*I have **lunch** at 12.30.*

◆ 介词后的习惯性表达：
to/at school/university; to/in class; in prison/hospital/bed

⚠ 如果特指某物，可以用*the / a*：
*When I was a child I used to walk **to school**.*
*When I was a child I went **to the school on the other side of town**.*

但是，冠词不能用于下列表达中：
at home; at/to work; at night; by bus/bicycle/car/train/plane; on foot

2 Demonstratives（指示代词）: *this, that, these, those*

使用这些词可以表达某事物在时间或空间上的远或近：

	near	remote
time	*I'd like to talk to you **this morning** about an exciting development.* (today)	*My mother called me later **that day**.* (I am telling you this on a different day)
place	*I like **these** pictures.* (here)	*Oh, I prefer **those** pictures.* (over there)

可以用 *this / that / these / those* 指前文中已经提到的事物：
*The total cost of the Envisat programme is 2.3 billion euros over 15 years. Included in **this sum** ...* (this sum = 2.3 billion euros)

可以用 *this* 和 *that* 指前面提到的整句话或观点：
*Seeing the earth from outer space highlights how tiny and fragile our planet is. Envisat helps people to understand **that**.* (= understand how tiny and fragile our planet is)

这样使用的时候，*this* 和 *that* 之间几乎没有差别，所以可以说：
*Envisat helps people to understand **this**.*

3 Possessives（物主代词）

当告知某物属于什么或属于谁时，可以使用各种表所属关系的限定词（*my/your/his/her/our/their*）。
our blue planet; *their* children

⚠ 注意：不能在一个限定词（如 *a, the*）后使用表所属关系的限定词。一般用如下形式：限定词 +
名词 + *of* + 物主代词：
this planet of ours (**not** ~~this our planet~~)

表所有关系时，可在单数名词或不规则复数名词后加's；在规则复数名词后需加 s'：
Europe's technological showpiece; the children's toys; my parents' house

当所指非人非物时，一般用名词 + *of* 形式，而不用's 形式：
the price of the hotel (**not** ~~the hotel's price~~)

4 Inclusives（不定代词）

each, every

Each 和 *every* 与单数名词和动词连用：

Each 用于两个或更多为一个群体中的事物或人，侧重点是群体中的个体：

Each European citizen has therefore invested seven euros in the environment.

Every 用于三个或三个以上的事物，侧重点是群体。通常 *each* 和 *every* 之间侧重点的差别很小：

Every citizen will have access to precise information about changes in the environment (= *Each citizen* ...)

可以用 *each*（不能用 *every*）+ *of* + 名词 / 代词：
Each of the students gave the teacher a present. (**not** ~~every of the students~~)

all, most, some

可以用 *all* / *most* / *some* + 复数名词和动词来概述事物：
Most children like sweets.
Some people believe space exploration is a waste of money.

可以用 *all* / *most* / *some* + *of* + 代词或限定词 + 名词来指某特定群体：
Most of the children at my school play football.

⚠ 不需要在一个名词前用 *all* + *of* 形式，但在代词前需用 *of*：
All the children at my school play a musical instrument.
All of them like music. (**not** ~~all them~~)

⚠ 当 *all* 后面跟的是指时间的单数名词时，其意义不同。比较：
I worked hard all day. (= I worked hard for one whole day)
I worked hard every day. (= I regularly worked hard)

Both, neither, either, none

Both，*neither* 和 *either* 指两个人或物。可以用 *both* + 复数名词或 *either* / *neither* + 单数名词形式：
Both satellites were launched in the 1990s.
Neither person knew very much about Envisat before the conference. (= not one or the other)
I don't mind where we go. Either restaurant is fine. (= one or the other is fine)

⚠ 可以用 *both* + *of* + 限定词 + 复数名词（或代词）+复数动词形式。也可以用 *either* / *neither* + *of* + 限定词 + 复数名词（或代词）+单数或复数动词形式：
Neither of my sisters lives/live in the same town as me.
Both of them are married. (**not** ~~Both of them is married.~~)

None 的意思是（群体中）"没有一个"。它的后面可以跟单数动词或复数动词：
None of our countries is/are able to ignore the implications of global warming.

C Grammar exercises

1 In some of these sentences there is a mistake with articles. <u>Underline</u> each mistake and write the correction.

1 My father likes <u>the classical music</u> and listens to it all the time. ..~~the~~ ~~classical~~ ~~music~~...

2 I saw a man sitting in a restaurant. A woman came and joined him, but the man got up and left without speaking to her! ....✓................

3 Sun was shining and it was a lovely day. ....

4 I can play piano. ....

5 I come from United Arab Emirates. ....

6 I've applied to study at the University of Edinburgh. ....

7 I usually go to work by the bus. ....

8 My husband is doctor. ....

9 Sorry I'm late – car wouldn't start this morning. ....

10 I'm going to take a cruise down river Nile. ....

11 I once saw a cat wearing a pink coat and boots! ....

12 My husband collects the antiques. He's always going to auctions. ....

2 Fill in the gaps with *a/an* or *the* or put a cross (✗) if no article is needed.

BORNEO BORN AND BRED

1 .....X...... Local legends say that 2 .... Borneo's few thousand wild elephants are descendants from those brought to 3 .... island from India or Malaysia as 4 .... gift to 5 .... sultan in 6 .... eighteenth century. Biologists from 7 .... Columbia University's Centre for Environmental Research and Conservation compared DNA samples from Borneo elephants with Asian elephants in Sumatra, India and elsewhere. 8 .... findings confirmed their suspicions: Borneo's elephants are genetically different. In fact 9 .... DNA differences are so great between them and their closest relatives (elephants in Peninsular Malaysia) that 10 .... populations may have separated up to 300,000 years ago, say 11 .... scientists. The animals became isolated when 12 .... island became totally cut off from the mainland due to 13 .... rise in sea level. Borneo's elephants are, therefore, 14 .... important, separate population.

3 <u>Underline</u> the most suitable words.

Report on holiday survey

1 *This/That* survey aimed to find out about **2** *people's / the people's* ideal holidays. We used **3** *the interviews / interviews* and **4** *the questionnaires / questionnaires* to collect **5** *our/their* data. **6** *Both/All* of **7** *those/these* methods of data collection were quick and simple to carry out and **8** *neither/none* of them were too demanding of the public. **9** *Our findings / Findings* show that many people like to take their holidays in the summer. **10** *This/The* view was reinforced by the destinations suggested by **11** *the people / people* involved in **12** *a survey / the survey*. **13** *The beach holidays / Beach holidays* were the most popular, particularly in **14** *the Spain / Spain* or **15** *the France / France*. **16** *Most/Both* people in the survey said they looked forward to their holiday. **17** *Each/All* person we interviewed agreed that it was important to have at least one holiday **18** *every/all* year. **19** *The price of the holiday / the holiday's price* was important to most people, with general agreement that value for money was a primary consideration.

---

4 **Fill in the gaps with words from the box.**

~~both~~	each	every	my	neither	none	this	that
that	their	those					

My home town is smaller than London, but there are some similarities. **1** _Each_ of the two cities is famous for its architecture. For example, **2** .... Kuala Lumpur and London have tall, modern buildings, set amongst older historical buildings. Although both cities have rivers running through them, **3** .... city is by the sea, which is a shame, as I think some of the most beautiful cities in the world are by the sea.

4 .... major city in the world has one thing in common – being large and busy – and **5** .... is true of both London and Kuala Lumpur. In fact, some people don't like my city because it is so noisy and busy, but **6** .... is one reason why I love it.

A lot of city markets take place in the day-time, but in **7** .... home city they don't open until it's dark! Malaysians tend to buy all their groceries at the night markets. In London people tend to use supermarkets for **8** .... food shopping.

It is always hot in Kuala Lumpur, but London can get very cold. **9** ....'s probably why you get outdoor restaurants all over Kuala Lumpur all year round whereas in London there are almost **10** .... in the winter. In some restaurants in Kuala Lumpur, you can go to the kitchen and point at the food and say, 'I'll have one of **11** ...., please!' You can't do that in London!

D Test practice

Listening Section 4

Questions 1–2

Choose the correct letter A, B or C.

1 Health club membership in Europe
   A has reached 36 million.
   B has declined in recent years.
   C has followed a similar trend to America.

2 If people today ate the same amount as their parents did
   A they would gain weight.
   B they would have more energy.
   C they would feel healthier.

Questions 3–4

Choose TWO letters A–E.

According to the speaker which TWO factors have contributed to the change in our fitness levels?

A availability of better food
B different working conditions
C labour-saving devices
D changes in healthcare
E diets which do not work

Question 5

Choose the correct letter, A, B or C.

5 Which of the following machines has been available for less than ten years?
   A

   B

   C

Questions 6–10

Which exercise method do the following statements apply to?

    A using an elliptical trainer
    B running on the road
    C using a treadmill

*Write the correct letter **A**, **B**, or **C** next to Questions 6–10 below.*

  6 The impact on the body is more than twice your own body weight.
  7 The impact on the body is almost the same as your own body weight.
  8 It has the same impact on the body as walking does.
  9 It is the best method for losing weight at speeds over 14 kph.
10 It has the highest impact on the joints.

Grammar focus task

Look at the following extracts from the recording. Which words or ideas do the underlined words refer to in the text?

1 Unfortunately, instead of eating less than their parents did, many consume a lot more.

2 On top of this, the change in employment patterns over the past ...

3 And this is where exercise machines come in.

4 That's an amazing number of people

5 As its name implies, the machine delivers an elliptical motion ...

6 In that respect, ellipticals are superior.

7 After that, just keep going and going and going ...

A Context listening

1 You are going to hear a conversation between Chi Wen, a student from Hong Kong who is studying in Australia, and her homestay host Mrs Smith. Which household chores do you think Chi Wen will have to do?

2 ∩ 9 **Listen and write**

A if Mrs Smith will do this	B if Chi Wen will do this	C if both of them will do it

1 cook dinner
2 make breakfast
3 buy food

4 make lunches
5 wash clothes

6 wash sheets
7 clean the house

3 9 ◀◀ **Listen again and fill in the gaps.**

1 I can introduce .... to a friend of ...., Yi Ling.

2 I know ....'s really enjoying .... here in Australia.

3 Now, I have had a lot of students staying with .... over the years and I do have a few rules.

4 First of all, my husband and .... want everyone to feel at home so .... treat everyone like ....'re a member of our own family.

5 And what about other meals? Can I cook for ....?

6 Yes, everyone makes their own breakfast and I always make sure there is plenty of food in the fridge so .... can prepare .... a packed lunch if you like.

7 I expect everyone to wash and iron for ....

8 Can I use .... to make local calls?

4 Put the words you wrote in Exercise 3 into four groups.

I, ...

me, ...

myself, ...

mine, ...

B Grammar

1 Personal and possessive pronouns（人称及物主代词）

Subject personal pronouns:	*I, you, he, she, it, we, they*
Object personal pronouns:	*me, you, him, her, it, us, them*
Possessive pronouns:	*mine, yours, his, hers, ours, theirs*

代词用来取代名词，避免名词的重复：
I can introduce you to my friend, Yi Ling. **She**'s a student from Taiwan. (**not** ~~Yi Ling's a student~~)

主语代词用在动词前：
I only arrived last month.

宾语代词在动词或介词后面：
I have had a lot of students staying **with me** *over the years.*

物主代词用于指代物主限定词和名词：
I don't have a phone here. Can I use **yours**? (= your phone)

⚠ 注意：*Its* 不是物主代词。

2 Reflexive pronouns（反身代词）

Reflexive pronouns:	*myself, yourself, himself, herself, itself, ourselves, yourselves, themselves*

在以下情形使用反身代词：
- 当动词的主语和宾语一致时：
  You *can prepare* **yourself** *a packed lunch if you like.*

- 强调主语或宾语：
  I clean the kitchen and the living areas **myself**. (= I do it, not anybody else)

- 和 *by* 连用，意指 *on my own / on your own*：
  I clean the kitchen and the living areas **by myself**. (= on my own)

- 祈使句中的一些固定搭配常用到 *yourself / yourselves*：
  Help **yourself**.   *Look after* **yourself**. (= be careful)   *Enjoy* **yourselves**.

⚠ 注意下列 *each other / one another* 的用法：
The boys taught **themselves** *English.* (= each boy taught himself English)
The boys taught **each other/one another** *some new words.* (= each boy taught the other boy some new words)

3 Some special situations（一些特殊情况）

It

*It*的用法：

◆ 作为主语用在句首，没有实质意义。这些句子的内容通常是关于天气、时间或距离：

It didn't always rain.   It's five o'clock.   It's 10 km from the sea.

◆ 当实际主语是动词不定式或-*ing*形式时，*it*用在句首，引起句子：

It won't take long to settle in. (= to settle in won't take long)

◆ 指代短语、整个句子或想法：

I only arrived last month and I am still finding it all a bit strange, actually. (= living in a foreign country)

⚠ 注意：表示某事存在或不存在时，使用*there be* +名词短语，而不是*it*：

There's *a good coffee shop near here.* (**not** ~~It is a good coffee shop near here~~.)

You and we

指代广义上的每个人时，可使用：

◆ *you*：

In Australia you often eat sandwiches for lunch. (= people in Australia)

◆ *we* （当我们自身也包括在这个指代群体中时）：

We often eat lunch in a bit of a hurry. (= Australian people in general, and the speaker is Australian)

They

they 的用法：

◆ 可以指专家或权威机构：

They have changed the law recently. (= the government)
They have discovered a new kind of beetle. (= scientists)

◆ 当不清楚或无需指明被指代者性别时：

I asked a student if they liked learning English and they said no!

One/ones

使用 *one* / *ones* 避免可数名词的重复使用：

I do have a few rules. The most important one is that I want everyone to feel at home. (= the most important rule)

C Grammar exercises

1 Fill in the gaps with *it, its, itself, they, their* or *themselves*.

Anatomy of a bat

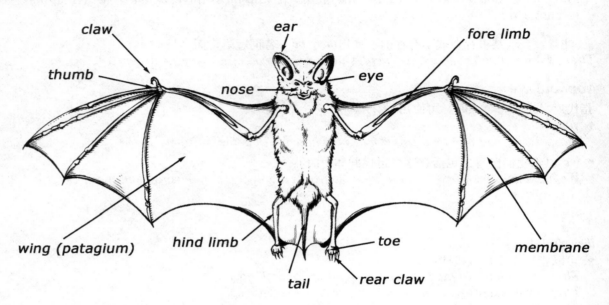

claw ear fore limb
thumb eye
nose
wing (patagium) hind limb toe membrane
tail rear claw

The entire wing of a bat is called the *patagium*. Many species also have a membrane between **1** ......*their*...... hind limbs enclosing the tail. The *patagium* is full of fine blood vessels, muscle fibres and nerves. When it is cold, these bats wrap **2** .... up in **3** .... wings like a coat. In warm weather **4** .... flap **5** .... wings in order to cool **6** .... bodies.

The bat has claws on **7** .... thumbs and sometimes on the toes of **8** .... fore and hind limbs. The rear claws enable **9** .... to hang **10** .... on to a tree branch or ledge.

All bats are active at night or at twilight, so **11** .... eyes are poorly developed. Instead **12** .... use **13** .... nose and ears to orientate **14** ....

2 Find and correct 13 places where nouns could be replaced with the pronouns in the box to make the email sound more natural.

He	He	he	he	he	him	himself	*it*	it	it	mine
They	us	yours								

To: **Liz Jenkins**

From: **Sandy Moore**

Subject: **University life**

Dear Liz

I'm sorry I haven't emailed you for a while. I'm really busy with my studies at the moment. My course is going well and I'm enjoying ~~my course~~ ^{it} a lot. The trouble is that my course takes up all my time. How is your course going?

I hope you will be able to visit me soon. I'd like you to meet my friends. My best friend here is Paul. Paul lives in the flat next to my flat, and I usually eat most of my meals with Paul. At the moment I'm doing most of the cooking though, because Paul had an accident last week. One of the reasons for the accident is connected to some changes at the university recently. The university authorities have decided that students shouldn't be allowed to bring cars up to the campus, so more and more of the students are cycling. Because of this new rule, Paul was riding his bicycle to the university. While he was cycling along a car driver drove into the back of his bike. The car driver didn't stop and check if he was okay. Luckily Paul was not badly hurt and managed to pick up his bike and get to the doctor's surgery. The doctor said his finger was probably broken and strapped his finger up, so he can't hold anything in his right hand at the moment and Paul can't really cook for Paul.

Anyway, he'd like to meet you, so we must arrange a time for you to come here.

Get in touch soon.
Love, Sandy

3 Fill in the gaps with a suitable pronoun or *there*.

Teacher: Do you think that governments spend too much on space exploration nowadays?

Student: Well, I think that **1** ....*there*........ are a lot of different factors to take into consideration. For example some countries want to show the rest of the world that **2** .... are successful and **3** .... can do this with a space exploration program. **4** .... seems that **5** .... is more important for these countries to impress the world than to look after their own people. Sometimes **6** .... is difficult to understand this because every country in the world has **7** .... problems and has poor people that need to be looked after because they can't look after **8** .... So, yes, I do think that these countries should look after people first before **9** .... start trying to send men to the moon! **10** .... are too many other problems here on earth that we need to sort out.

4 Underline the correct words.

There are many reasons why **1** we / they should recycle household waste. The main reason is to avoid using up valuable resources making new things when **2** it is / we are not necessary. However, I do not think the government should make **3** it / the law compulsory for people to recycle their waste.

If the government makes a law that all households must recycle **4** their / its rubbish, **5** the law / it could lead to more problems. For example, how can **6** you / people check that people are recycling everything? **7** It is not practical to do this. / To do this is not practical. In addition, there is the argument that individuals should be allowed to decide for **8** each other / themselves whether to throw something away or to recycle **9** it / something.

I believe the most sensible approach is for the government to put more money into recycling schemes. The most successful are **10** the ones / them where the government gives each household special boxes to put different kinds of waste in, and **11** the government / they provide a regular collection service. **12** They / There are separate boxes for plastic, metal, glass etc. This makes **13** to recycle easier for people / it easier for people to recycle and **14** they / there are therefore less likely to throw things in the rubbish bin.

D Test practice

Academic Writing Task 2

You should spend about 40 minutes on this task.

Write about the following topic.

> *Governments spend millions of dollars each year on their space programmes. Most recently, Mars is the focus of scientists' attention. Some people think this money would be better spent on dealing with problems closer to home.*
>
> *Do you agree or disagree?*

Give reasons for your answer and include any relevant examples from your own knowledge or experience.

You should write at least 250 words.

Grammar focus task

Look at these extracts from a model answer. Match the pronouns (1–5) to the uses (A–E).

... However, some people believe this cannot justify the huge amount of money spent on space research when there is a greater need for **1** it here on earth ...

... For example, the United States and the USSR raced each other to see who could put a man on the moon first. **2** It would have been much easier and cheaper if **3** they had pooled resources and information, and made a joint expedition into space ...

... **4** It is very difficult to argue against these criticisms ...

... In my opinion, **5** we need a balance between how much money is spent on space exploration and how much money is invested into solving problems here on earth. With continued co-operation between nations over space travel more will be achieved for less money. This should leave more money to be spent on problems at home ...

A a subject which doesn't carry a specific meaning

B to refer to *the United States and the USSR*

C to refer to *money*

D to refer to people in general

E to replace an infinitive as a subject

10

Adjectives and adverbs

describing things; adding information about manner, place, time, frequency and intensity

1 You are going to hear a man talking about a recent trip. Look at the following pictures and try to guess which three countries the man visited.

2 🎧 **10** Listen to check if you were right.

3 **10◄◄** Listen again and complete the table below. Write no more than two words for each answer.

Countries visited	Interesting facts
1	◆ many **2** .... and beautiful mosques
3	◆ travelled there by **4** .... ◆ good for **5** .... ◆ bought a beautiful **6** ....
7	◆ visited Gujarati Textile **8** .... ◆ great examples of **9** .... embroidery ◆ lots of wildlife in **10** .... areas ◆ saw incredible **11** .... birds and several poisonous **12** ....

4 Look at Exercise 3 and make a list of all the adjectives.

........interesting........   ....

....

....

....

B Grammar

1 Adjectives（形容词）

形容词修饰名词。

How adjectives are used

形容词可（用在）：

◆ 名词前：
*There are so many **historical buildings***.
*It was well worth the trip, especially if you like **local crafts***.

◆ 下列动词的后面：*be, become, get, seem, appear, look, smell, taste, feel*。
*The mosques in particular **are very beautiful***.
*They always **seem pleased** to see you*.

◆ 在 *find / make / keep* + 宾语的后面：
*Work hard on your research if you want to **make your trip enjoyable** and **rewarding***.
*I **found the insects** rather **frightening***.

◆ 与其他形容词或名词连用来修饰名词：
*a **long**, **tiring** boat ride* (adjective + adjective + noun + noun)

The order of adjectives

当多个形容词一起使用时，将表达观点的形容词置于描述所谈事物的特征或类型的形容词前：
*a **beautiful Turkish** carpet* (*beautiful* = opinion + *Turkish* = type: **not** *a Turkish beautiful carpet*)

经常用名词作为形容词补充有关类型的信息：
*the Gujarati **Textile Museum***

当使用两个以上的形容词来描述事物的特征或类型时，它们通常按照下列顺序排列：
尺寸—> 温度—> 年龄—> 外形—> 颜色—> 民族—> 材料—> 类型
Indian silk embroidery　　　*small mountain villages*
hot black coffee　　　*a beautiful old round table*

当动词或名词后面有两个或更多的形容词时，在最后两个形容词之间用 *and*：
*The people are very **welcoming and friendly** towards visitors*.

两种颜色之间用 *and*：
*vivid **blue and green** feathers*

Adjectives ending in *-ed* and *-ing*

一些与情感相关联的形容词是由动词而来，有两种可能的形式，通常是 *-ed* 或 *-ing*，比如 *tired / tiring*。用 *-ed* 形式来描述我们的感受是怎样的：
*I was **fascinated** to see the extraordinary range of patterns*.
*I was **amazed** at the variety of wonderful animals*.

用 *-ing* 形式来描述那些引发情感的事物或人：
*It's an absolutely **amazing** city to visit*.
*India is a **fascinating** country*.

2 Adverbs（副词）

副词给出有关动词、形容词或其他副词的信息。副词告诉人们某事是如何发生或完成的方式（*how*）、地点（*where*）、时间（*when*）、频率（*how often*）或强度（*how much*）。副词有时可以是单个词或词组。

How adverbs are used

副词通常表示：

◆ 方式：这类副词经常由形容词加-ly构成
careful → carefully happy → happily
这类副词通常出现在动词（和宾语，如果有宾语的话）后面：
*I plan my trips **very carefully**. (**not** I plan very carefully my trips)*

◆ 地点：通常跟在动词后面
*It was the first time I had been **there**.*
*Try to stay **near the old part of the city**.*

◆ 时间：如*today, tomorrow, now, since2003, for three minutes*，这类词可以放在句首或句尾
*I had a very memorable trip **last year**. (**or Last year** I had a very memorable trip.)*

◆ 频率：这类词通常出现在动词前面，但在*be*动词或助动词的后面
*I **often travel** for my job.*
*I **have always enjoyed** my visits there.*
*He's **never** late.*

◆ 强度：这类副词影响形容词或副词的力度

fairly, quite,	*very, extremely,*	*absolutely,*
rather, pretty	*highly, really*	*completely, totally*

weaker   stronger

处在级别较强一端的副词只能与某些形容词连用。这些形容词通常是些能表达极限意思的"极端"形容词（如*terrifying, excellent, exhausted*）。其他一些"非极端"形容词（如*frightened, good, tired*）从不与这些意味强烈的副词搭配。比较：
*There are some **absolutely stunning** examples of Indian silk embroidery. (**not** fairly stunning)*
*The people are **very friendly**. (**not** absolutely friendly)*

*Really*能与大多数形容词连用。

⚠ 不能强化描述类型的形容词或名词。(**not** a very Textile Museum).

The order of adverbs

当两个或更多副词出现在句子结尾时，通常按如下顺序排列：
方式 → 地点 → 时间：
*I'll meet you **outside the station at six o'clock**. (outside the station = place, at six o'clock =* time)

Irregular adverbs

有些方式副词与其形容词形式相同（如*hard*, *fast*, *straight*, *late*, *early*）：
*Work **hard** on your research.* (adverb)
*This is a **hard** exercise.* (adjective)

*Hard*是形容词也是副词，*hardly*是一个副词，意思是"非常少"（*very few*）：
*He **hardly** had time to say hello.* (= he had very little time to say hello)

*Good*是个形容词，*well*是个副词：
*He spoke **very good** English.* (describes *English*)
*He spoke English **very well**.* (describes how he spoke)

但在谈论健康时，*well*也可用作形容词：
*She's not **well** – she's got a cold.*

Grammar extra: Adjectives

有些形容词后面可以跟 *to* + 不定式来增加它们的意思（如*able*, *likely*, *right*, *wrong*, *lucky*）。有些形容词可以表达情感（如*surprised*, *afraid*, *happy*, *delighted*）：
*I'll be **happy to answer** questions.*
*I was **fascinated to see** the extraordinary range of patterns.*

一些形容词后面可以用介词 + *-ing*形式（参照Unit 19）：
*People are **tired of hearing** politicians' promises.* (**not** ~~tired to hear~~)
*I am not very **good at taking** photographs.* (**not** ~~good to take photographs~~)

C Grammar exercises

1 Read the test task and the students' responses. Some of the adjectives they used are underlined. If they are used correctly, put a tick (✓). If they are wrong, write the correct answer.

> **Describe a favourite place.**
> **You should say:**
>   **where it is**
>   **what kind of place it is**
>   **what makes it special**
> **and explain why you like it so much.**

My favourite place is a **1** <u>quiet little</u> wood near my home town in Indonesia. I like it because it is a **2** <u>green peaceful</u> place. It is full of **3** <u>old tall</u> trees and there are lots of **4** <u>wild interesting</u> animals.	**1** .... ✓ .... **2** ..*peaceful green*.. **3** .... **4** ....
I'm going to tell you about my bedroom. I love it because it is full of my things. The walls are painted with **5** <u>blue yellow</u> stripes, and there is a **6** <u>wooden dark</u> floor. There is a **7** <u>lovely old</u> photo of my family by my bed, and all my precious books are on the shelves.	**5** .... **6** .... **7** ....
My favourite place is the town I grew up in. It has **8** <u>an ancient beautiful ruined</u> castle and lots of **9** <u>historical old</u> buildings. The streets are **10** <u>narrow winding</u>, and there are lots of good shops. It is **11** <u>busy noisy</u>, but I like that. I feel good there because I have so many **12** <u>childhood happy</u> memories.	**8** .... **9** .... **10** .... **11** .... **12** ....

2 Write the missing adjectives and adverbs.

..dramatic.. – *dramatically*   ..impressive.. – ....slight.. – ....

..steady.. – ....sharp.. – ....steeply.. – ....

Now use the words to fill in the gaps on the next page. Use one pair of words for each question.

Coffee sales

1 a Sales of coffee showed a ....slight........ increase between 2004 and 2006.

   b Sales of coffee increased ......slightly...... between 2004 and 2006.

Domestic car market

2 a The domestic car market showed an .... growth of 50% for three consecutive years from 2001 to 2003.

   b The domestic car market grew .... by 50% for three consecutive years from 2001 to 2003.

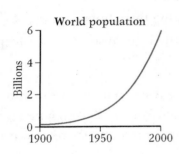

World population

3 a The world population grew .... between 1950 and 2005.

   b The world population experienced a .... growth between 1950 and 2005.

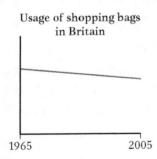

Usage of shopping bags in Britain

4 a The number of British households using their own shopping bags when shopping fell .... between 1965 and 2005.

   b There was a .... fall in the number of British households using their own shopping bags when shopping between 1965 and 2005.

Average house prices

5 a House prices climbed .... during the first half of the year before falling .... in August.

   b There was a .... climb in house prices during the first half of the year before a .... fall in August.

3 Match the beginnings (1–8) and the endings (a–h) of the sentences. Join them by adding a suitable *-ed* or *-ing* adjective formed from one of the verbs in the box. Use each verb once.

| excite frighten interest ~~please~~ relax surprise tire satisfy |

1 I was really   pleased ..c..   a adventure I've ever had. I can't
2 Martin's excellent exam results   wait to go back!
   were very   ....   b as he had hardly had time to
3 The jungle was full of strange   study.
   noises and I felt   ....   c when I opened my present
4 After so much hard work, it was   because it was just what I wanted.
   a very   ....   d after exercise.
5 Paula wasn't   ....   e moment when I finally finished
6 Having a warm bath can be very ....   the project.
7 My trip through the jungle was   f so I had a warm bath.
   the most   ....   g during the whole trip.
8 After walking so far I felt very ....   h in the lecture so she fell asleep.

4 Underline the correct words.

Environmentalists and conservationists tell us that there are ways that each of us can help to **1** *very reduce / greatly reduce* our impact on the planet. We can **2** *work hard / hardly work* to conserve energy and we can invest in equipment to help us create our own power. People **3** *say often / often say* that they want to save the planet, but the only way to do this is to **4** *take immediately action / take action immediately*.

It is **5** *really important / important really* for individuals to **6** *responsibly act / act responsibly* and try to reduce their contribution to greenhouse gases. There are several ways we can do this. For example there are mini wind turbines that you **7** *can install easily / easily can install* on your roof as well as very efficient solar panels that **8** *work good / work well* all year round to provide electricity.

But if this is all too expensive, there are other ways to conserve energy that actually save you money. In cooler weather, simply keep the heat **9** *inside safely / safely inside* by closing doors after you so that the warmth doesn't escape. It is **10** *absolutely essential / very essential* that we all take this seriously and do our best to lead a more sustainable life.

D Test practice

General Training Reading

Questions 1–8

*Look at the information about five museums **A–E** in Seoul, South Korea.*

For which museum are the following statements true?

*Write the correct letter **A–F** next to Questions 1–8.*

NB *You may write any letter more than once.*

1 This museum also functions as an occasional venue for performing arts. ....
2 You can learn about natural history in this museum. ....
3 This museum is the only one of its kind in Korea. ....
4 This is the most high-tech of the museums. ....
5 A historical building once stood where this museum stands today. ....
6 This museum contains something for the very distant future. ....
7 The exhibits in this museum include objects from the distant past. ....
8 You can take classes one day a week at this museum. ....

A Namsangol Traditional Folk Village

Located just north of Namsan Park, this re-creation of a small village depicts the architecture and gardens of the Chosun Dynasty (1393–1910). There are five restored traditional houses from that era. A large pavilion overlooks a beautiful pond and an outdoor theatre hosts dance and drama performances on weekends. There is also a hall displaying traditional handicrafts and a kiosk selling souvenirs. Recently, a time capsule containing 600 items representing the lifestyle of modern-day people of Seoul was buried to celebrate the city's 600th anniversary. In 2394, it will be opened!

B Eunan Museum

This privately-owned museum displays rare specimens of animals, ores, and species of insects collected from around the world. The building comprises six floors, one under ground and five above. Among the fauna on exhibition are shellfish, insects, butterflies and birds. The collection is housed on the lower floors. On the third floor is a library and the fifth floor has a study room and an ocean exhibition hall. One aim of the museum is to bring animal extinction to the attention of the public.

C National Museum of Korea

This is one of the most extensive museums in Seoul, housing art and archaeological relics from Korean prehistory through to the end of the Chosun Dynasty (1910). Throughout the three-floor museum, there are 4,500 artefacts on display in 18 permanent galleries. Audio guides, touch screens, and video rooms all help to bring the ancient world alive here. In addition to regular exhibitions, the museum offers special educational programs such as public lectures, arts and crafts classes, and special tours.

D Seoul Metropolitan Museum of Art

Established in 1988, this museum is located on the former site of Kyonghee-gung palace. There are four floors with six exhibition halls. The collections include more than 170 Korean paintings, Western paintings and prints. Spend a peaceful and relaxing day amidst beautiful works of art. If you are an art enthusiast and would like to learn, the museum offers art courses every Friday.

E Korea Sports Museum

This is the sole museum in Korea dedicated to sports. It displays about 2,500 items tracing back to 1920, when Korea's first sports organization was founded. You can browse through sports memorabilia such as badges, medals, photographs, trophies, and mascots related to national and international sports events. Make sure not to miss the taekwondo-related exhibits.

Questions 9–14

Read the information below and answer Questions 9–14.

Gear Guide — Buying a Backpack

Most walkers will know the value of a good backpack. Choosing one is a different matter, as any trip to an outdoor shop will reveal. To help, gear expert Peter Hawkins examines the ins and outs of a backpack.

A quick glance through my outdoor trade directory reveals 49 companies that sell or make rucksacks. If they all produce ten backpacks then we have a frightening number for the humble beginner to choose
5 from. So before you set foot in an outdoor shop consider what you want your rucksack for.

The first and most vital consideration is your anticipated load. If your walks are short summer evening strolls then a small sack would be fine, but if your walks are day-long and year-round then your sack will need to be bigger. Mine typically contains a flask, packed lunch, waterproofs, clothing I've peeled off during the day, first aid kit and an emergency shelter. In winter I add a sleeping bag and a torch. I need
10 a sack with a reasonable capacity.

My current backpack is a Craghopper AD30 (30 litres) which is just big enough. Admittedly I do often lead walking parties in remote places so perhaps my added responsibilities cause me to carry more. Compare my list with yours to see if you need as much carrying space.

The second consideration is weight. Choose a light sack, but make sure it can take the weight of what
15 you are carrying and it supports the load comfortably on your back.

The next thing to consider is the rucksack's features. Today you can get quite technically advanced backpacks boasting excellent features: advanced fabrics, a variety of side and lid pockets, loops for walking poles, internal frames, adjustable straps, hip belts and clever ventilation systems to keep your back cool.

You also need to look inside. It may seem obvious, but you should choose a backpack that allows you
20 easy access. Some have narrow necks that make removing bulky items difficult. It's also important to choose a backpack that fits the length of your back. Being six feet I need a long, thin rucksack rather than a short, wider one. If I use the latter, I have a hip belt round my stomach!

Last, and probably least, we have the look of the sack to consider. Obviously you can't see it when it's on your back, but why buy something that won't look good on you? After all, there's no shortage of
25 colours or designs to choose from.

Questions 9–14

Do the following statements agree with the opinions of the writer in the Reading passage?

Next to Questions 9–14 write

YES   *if the statement agrees with the opinions of the writer*
NO   *if the statement contradicts the opinions of the writer*
NOT GIVEN *if it is impossible to say what the writer thinks about this*

9 Few companies make backpacks. ....
10 When choosing a backpack, people should think about their needs. ....
11 The Craghopper AD30 is more comfortable than other brands. ....
12 Manufacturers still need to solve the problem of backpacks causing your back to get hot.
   ....
13 A person's physical shape and size is an important consideration when choosing a
   backpack. ....
14 The style of a backpack is less important than other considerations. ....

Grammar focus task

Look at the adverbs taken from the second reading passage and say whether each one
gives information about time, place, manner, intensity or frequency.

a often (*line 11*)   ....

b comfortably (*line 15*)   ....

c today (*line 16*)   ....

d quite (*line 16*)   ....

e inside (*line 19*)   ....

11

Comparing things
comparative and superlative adjectives and adverbs;
other ways of comparing; comparing nouns and quantities

1 You are going to hear a talk comparing the performance of older and younger athletes. Before you listen look at the phrases from the talk. Which ones would you associate with young athletes and which ones would you associate with older athletes?

breaking records   strongest in the world   greatest increases in speed
peak fitness   physical improvement   four minutes quicker each year
Olympics   complete a marathon   set record running times

2 🎧 **11** Listen and check if you were right.

3 **11◀◀** Listen again and say whether these sentences are true or false. Correct the sentences that are false.

1 Older athletes are getting faster and fitter.

2 Runners aged 50+ are speeding up less rapidly than young runners.

3 Women aged 60–68 running the New York marathon run on average two minutes faster each year.

4 Older athletes are less likely to achieve their peak fitness than younger athletes.

5 People grow weaker because they are less active than when they were younger.

4 Underline the language used to compare in Exercise 3.

1 Which sentences contain adjectives?

2 Which sentences contain adverbs?

3 Which word is used as both an adjective and an adverb?

B Grammar

1 Comparing adjectives（形容词的比较级）

形容词	比较级	最高级
单音节形容词：*hard*	形容词+*-er*: *harder*	*the* +形容词+*-est the hardest*
以e结尾的单音节形容词：*nice*	形容词+*-r nicer*	*the* +形容词+*-st*: *the nicest*
以元音+辅音结尾的 单音节形容词：*fat*	形容词+最后的 辅音字母重复+*-er fatter*	*the* +形容词+最后的 辅音字母重复+*-est*: *the fattest*
以y结尾的双音节形容词*happy*	形容词去掉y + *ier*: *happier*	*the* +形容词去掉y + *iest*: *the happiest*
双音节或多音节形容词: *enjoyable*	*more* +形容词: *more enjoyable*	*the most* +形容词：*the most* *enjoyable*
不规则形容词: *good, bad, far*	*better, worse, further/farther*	*the best, the worst,* *the furthest/farthest*

Comparative adjectives

形容词的比较级用于比较两个或更多的事物、人或地方：
*Younger runners will always be **faster** than older runners.*

也可用于比较两个不同时间的同一事物、人或地方：
*I'm much **fitter** than I was last year.*

形容词的比较级后加 than表示进行比较的事物。
当被比较的事物在上下文中已经很清楚时，有时则无需用*than*从句：
*Older athletes are getting **faster and fitter**.* (than in the past)

Superlative adjectives

形容词的最高级用于群体中某事物与该群体中剩余其他事物之间的比较：
*The Olympics is probably **the most exciting** sports event in the sports calendar.*

我们可以通过以下方式修饰最高级：
◆ *one of the* / *some of the* +最高级+复数名词：
   *It's one of the few chances we get to see **some of the best athletes** in the world competing against each other.*
   *Tamsin is **one of the most generous people** I know.*

◆ 序数词：
   *Our team was **the third best** in the competition.*

*the*可以用形容词性的物主代词替换：
***my** best friend*
***his** greatest achievement*

2 Comparing adverbs（副词的比较级）

More / most + 副词用于比较某事进行的状况：

*Runners aged 50 and over are speeding up **more rapidly** than younger people.*

*Women aged 60 to 68 improved **the most markedly**.*

跟形容词形式一样的副词（如 *hard, fast, straight, late, early, quick*）加 *-er/-est*:

*Women aged 60 to 68 run on average four minutes **faster** each year.*

某些副词也存在不规则的变化形式（如 *well, better, best; badly, worse, worst; far, further, furthest; little, less, least*）：

*I did **worse** than I had expected in the exam, so I was disappointed.*

3 Other ways of comparing（其他表比较的方式）

less / the least 表示 *more / the most* 的相反面：

*You might imagine that the Masters Games would be **less** exciting to watch.*

*That was probably **the least** enjoyable meal I've ever had!*

可以用以下方式强调：

◆ 用 *even, far, a great deal, a little, a lot, much* + 比较级：

*Older women showed **much greater** increases in speed than expected.*

◆ 在正式英语中，用 *slightly, considerably, significantly* + 比较级：

*The figures for 2003 were **significantly higher** than those for the year 2000.*

*The number of women in higher education was **only slightly lower** than the number of men.*

⚠ 不能将 *very* 与比较级连用（不能说 ~~the number of women was very lower~~.）

可以用 *as* + 形容词 / 副词 + *as* 来说两件事物相同或类似：

*My car is **as old as** yours.* (= the two cars are the same age)

*Older athletes are **as likely** to achieve their peak fitness **as** younger athletes.* (= they have the same chance of achieving this)

可以用 *just, almost, nearly, half, twice, three times* 等词来增加意思：

*In 2005, our team was **almost as successful as** in 2003.*

*He can run **twice as fast as** the others in his team.*

可以用 *not as* + 形容词 / 副词 + *as* 来说两件事物不同：

*While they may **not be as fast as** their younger counterparts ...*

可以通过重复比较级来表达事物的发生已有一段时日：

*Each year athletes seem to be getting **better and better**.*

*Our atmosphere is gradually becoming **more and more polluted**.*

*It seems **less and less likely** that there will be a general election this year.*

可以用 *the* + 比较级 + *the* + 比较级来表达两件事物同时变化或改变：

*It would seem that **the longer** athletes keep competing **the greater** their chances of setting new records are.*

The sooner the better.

4 Comparing quantities（比较数量）

quantifier	comparative	superlative
a lot / much / many	*more*	*the most*
a few	*fewer* (+ plural countable noun)	*the fewest* (+ plural countable noun)
a little	*less* (+ uncountable noun)	*the least* (+ uncountable noun)

对复数名词或不可数名词，可以用 *more* 或 *most* 来比较数量：
*Today's top sportspeople receive a lot **more money** than in the past.*

可以将 *fewer* 或 *the fewest* 与复数可数名词连用，*less* 或 *the least* 与不可数名词连用：
*25 years ago few 60-year-old men and even **fewer women** would have considered running a marathon.*
*There used to be **less information** available about fitness.*

可以通过下列方式强调：
◆ *a lot / many + more / fewer +* 复数可数名词：
  *Increased sponsorship has given today's athletes **many more opportunities** to succeed.*

◆ *a lot / much + more / less +* 不可数名词：
  *Today's athletes need to do **much more training** than in the past.*

◆ 重复 *more / less / fewer*：
  *So much in our society is about making **more and more money**.*

可以用 (*not*) *as many / much +* 复数 / 不可数名词 (+ *as*) 来说明事物是相同的或存在差异的：
*There aren't **as many people** doing sports at school* (as there used to be).

可以用 *half, twice, three times* 等与 *as many / much…as* 连用来增加更多特定的信息：
*In 2004 China won nearly **twice as many** silver medals **as the US**.*
*The US won more than **three times as many** medals **as Great Britain**.*

Grammar extra: Comparing nouns

可以用 *like, the same* (*as*), *similar to* 等词来表达事物之间如何相似：
*Older athletes can achieve **the same** degree of physical improvement **as** those in their twenties and thirties.*
*He swims **like** a fish.*
*This film is **similar to** this director's last one.*

C Grammar exercises

1 Fill in the gaps with the adjectives in the box in a comparative or superlative form.

| brave | effective | exciting | expensive | ~~fast~~ | happy | good | heavy | small |

1 I travelled through Turkey by train because it was _the fastest_ way to cross the country.
2 Scientists have discovered a tiny bacteria living in the deep ocean. They say it is .... living organism known to man.
3 It is almost impossible to find a parking space in the city centre so it is .... to travel by public transport if you need to go there.
4 Pain killers are much .... now so they reduce pain a lot faster than in the past.
5 I like all kinds of sports, but I think football is .... game to watch because it is so fast-moving.
6 Nick did a bungee-jump, but I was too scared. He's much .... than me.
7 I think people from the north of my country are .... than people from the south. In the south no one ever seems to smile, but it's the opposite in the north.
8 The website listed hotels in a wide price range. I was amazed that the .... ones cost over $500 a night.
9 Weightlifters these days are lifting .... weights than ever before.

2 Fill in the gaps with the words in brackets in a comparative or superlative form.

Teacher: What are **1** _the most obvious_ (obvious) differences you have noticed between your own country and this one?

Student: Oh there are so many! In my country people are **2** _not as interested_ (not/interested) in foreigners as people here, who are much **3** .... (friendly). They are always kind and welcoming. Also, the weather is very different. It's much **4** .... (hot) in my country. It's only autumn but I am feeling cold here already and it's getting **5** .... (cold) every day. I don't like that. Then there's the food. Your food is **6** .... (not/good) ours. Our food is **7** .... (spicy) and **8** .... (delicious). I think it's **9** .... (good) in the world! It is **10** .... (not/expensive) either. I've also noticed that people here eat slightly **11** .... (early) and they eat their meals **12** .... (quickly). And I am beginning to change my own habits too! **13** .... (long) I stay here **14** .... (fast) I seem to be eating.

3 Fill in the gaps in the model answer below. Use one word in each gap.

The charts below show the number and types of books bought by men and women and four different age groups in the UK.

Summarise the information by selecting and reporting the main features, and make comparisons where relevant.

Percentage who buy fiction

Percentage who buy non-fiction

The charts give information about the types of books that British men and women and different age groups buy. The initial impression from the charts is that women tend to buy **1** ....*more*........ books than men overall, although they buy slightly **2** .... non-fiction books. The people that buy the **3** .... books are in the 45+ age group.

Nearly 60% of women buy fiction, which is almost **4** .... as many as the number of men who choose this type of book. Nevertheless, most age groups buy **5** .... fiction books than non-fiction ones showing that non-fiction is generally **6** .... popular than fiction.

The number of people buying fiction increases steadily from ages 16 to 45 with the **7** .... number of books, at just over 40% of the age group, bought by 16- to 24-year-olds and the **8** .... number, at just over 50%, bought by the over 45s.

However, the pattern is different for non-fiction. The number of books bought by 25- to 44-year-olds is **9** .... lower than the number bought by 16- to 24-year-olds and those over 45. Just over 40% of 16- to 24-year-olds buy non-fiction, but this number is not **10** .... high as the number of people aged 45 and over buying non-fiction, at nearly 60%. Only 31% of 35- to 44-year-olds buy non-fiction, and the number of 24- to 34-year-olds is **11** .... lower at 28%.

4 Read the description of the table below. Decide if the <u>underlined</u> comparisons are correct or not. Tick (✓) them if they are right and correct them if they are wrong.

2004 Olympic Games Medal Table					
Rank	Country	Gold	Silver	Bronze	Total
1	United States	35	39	29	103
2	China	32	17	14	63
3	Russia	27	27	38	92
4	Australia	17	16	16	49
5	Japan	16	9	12	37
6	Germany	14	16	18	48
7	France	11	9	13	33
8	Italy	10	11	11	32
9	South Korea	9	12	9	30
10	Great Britain	9	9	12	30

The table shows the number of medals won by the top ten countries in the 2004 Olympic Games. The USA won **1** <u>greatest</u> number of medals overall with a total of 103. They won **2** <u>more silver medals as gold</u> and **3** <u>more medals than</u> any other country in both categories. China had **4** <u>the second high</u> number of medals at 63, but unlike the USA, China won **5** <u>less silver medals than gold medals</u>. While Russia's silver medal total was **6** <u>more good than</u> China's, they did not do **7** <u>well as</u> China in the gold medals, winning just 27. In fact China had a **8** <u>more lower</u> overall medal total than Russia but, as the table is based on the number of gold medals won, they were placed second. Similarly, Germany was **9** <u>significantly successful</u> at winning medals than Japan, with a total of 48 compared to Japan's 37, but because Japan won **10** <u>two more gold medals that</u> Germany they were ranked **11** <u>higher</u>. Great Britain gave **12** <u>the worse</u> performance in this group, winning only nine gold and nine silver medals.

1 <u>the greatest</u>

2 ....

3 ....

4 ....

5 ....

6 ....

7 ....

8 ....

9 ....

10 ....

11 ....

12 ....

D Test practice

Academic Writing Task 1

You should spend about 20 minutes on this task.

> **The chart below shows the average hours worked per day by married men and women in paid employment.**
>
> **Summarise the information by selecting and reporting the main features, and make comparisons where relevant.**

You should write at least 150 words.

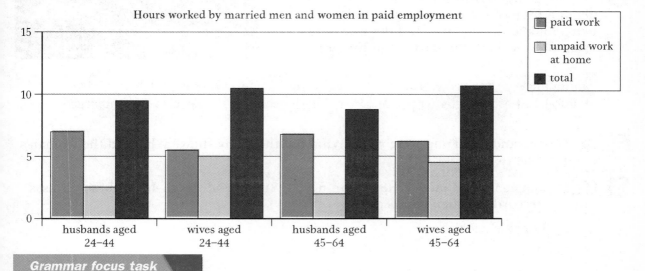

Hours worked by married men and women in paid employment

Grammar focus task

Fill in the gaps in the following sentences using the correct form of the words in brackets and any other words you need.

1 The total number of hours worked by married women with children is .... (*great*) the total number of hours worked by men.

2 Whilst women aged 45 to 64 may work .... (*few*) hours inside the home than younger women, overall they work .... (*great*) number of hours per day due to the extra hours of paid work that they do.

3 Men aged 25 to 44 spend only .... (*slight/more*) time working outside the home than men aged 45 to 64, but this figure is .... (*significant/high*) the number of hours of paid work that women of the same age do.

4 Women in the 25 to 44 age group work almost .... (*many*) hours inside the home as outside, and there is only a slight difference in the 45 to 64 age group.

5 However, men work on average .... (*three/long*) outside the home than inside.

12

The noun phrase
noun + prepositional phrase; noun + participle clause;
noun + *to*-infinitive clause

1 You are going to hear a woman giving a talk about a project she is involved in. Before you listen look at the pictures and the words below. What do you think the purpose of the project is?

abundance	analyze	calculate	car tyres	conservation	debris	diver
habitat	harbour	reef	rope	rubble	seahorses	species	submerged

2 🎧12 Listen and see if you were right. What did the study show? What did the woman's team decide to do?

3 12◀◀ Listen again and match the beginnings (1–8) and endings (a–h) of these phrases. Stop the recording when you need to.

1	this horrible rubbish	a	with bright red bodies
2	the idea	b	of the past
3	the areas	c	of putting rubbish into the harbour
4	other debris	d	with submerged rubbish
5	sea tulips	e	to expand our study
6	a decision	f	lying on the sea floor
7	the rubble	g	cleared of rubbish
8	other possible sites	h	lying at the bottom of the harbour

4 Add the phrases from Exercise 3 to the table below.

noun + preposition	noun + past participle	noun + *-ing*	noun + *to*-infinitive
the idea of putting rubbish into the harbour		this horrible rubbish lying at the bottom of the harbour	

B Grammar

The noun phrase（名词短语）

名词短语是名词为其主要部分的一组词语。有关名词的信息可以放在名词前或名词后。

名词短语中置于名词前的信息通常可以通过以下方式来表达：

◆ 限定词（参见Unit 8）
this horrible rubbish

◆ 形容词和副词（参见Unit 10）
a rich habitat

名词短语中置于名词后的信息通常可以通过下列方式表达：

◆ 介词短语
an abundance of creatures

◆ 过去分词从句
the rubbish contained in the harbour

◆ 现在分词（-ing）从句
the rubbish lying at the bottom of the harbour

◆ to- 不定式从句
a decision to expand

1 Noun + prepositional phrase（名词 + 介词词组）

可以通过使用介词从句在名词后面增加信息。这些短语中的常见介词有 *of, in, for, on, to, with*：

possible sites with submerged rubbish
a rich habitat for an abundance of creatures

Of 是介词短语中最为常见的介词。*Of* 用于数词或量词后：

the number of fish　　*an abundance of creatures* (quantities)
a bottle of water　　*a packet of biscuits* (containers)

也可以用 *of* 来表达归属或占有（参见Unit 8）：

the rubble of the past (**not** ~~the past's rubble~~)
particular areas of the harbour

经常用 *at, in* 和 *on* 来谈论实际位置：

this rubbish lying at the bottom of the harbour
different species living in Sydney Harbour

包含 *with* 的介词短语经常与主要动词为 *have* 的关系从句表达相同的信息。

harbour sites with submerged rubbish (= harbour sites which have submerged rubbish)
sea tulips with bright red bodies (= sea tulips which have bright red bodies)

2 Noun + past participle clause （名词＋过去分词从句）

过去分词从句所给出的信息与带有被动态动词的关系从句（参见Unit 20）相同：
*all of the rubbish **contained in the harbour*** (= rubbish which is contained in the harbour)
*areas **cleared of rubbish*** (= areas which have been cleared of rubbish)
*the data **collected from the sites*** (= the data which is collected from the sites)

在口语和书面英语中，名词＋过去分词从句的使用要比与其等同的关系从句更常见，这是因为前者可以用更少的词汇表达相同的意思。

3 Noun + present participle (-*ing*) clause （名词＋现在分词从句）

现在分词从句所给出的信息与带有主动态动词（经常是现在进行时或过去进行时）的关系从句（参见Unit 20）相同：
*the other debris **lying on the sea floor*** (= the other debris which is lying on the sea floor)

与上同，名词＋现在分词从句的使用要比与其等同的关系从句更为常用。

4 Noun + *to*-infinitive clause （名词＋to-不定式从句）

to-不定式从句用于表达一种目的或意图，通常跟在时间、地点、方式和数量名词后面：
*time **to go***
*the place **to visit***
*a way **to look at it***
*a lot **to look at***

后面跟着 *to*-不定式的名词可与后面也跟着 *to*-不定式的动词（如 *decide* / *decision*; *plan* / *plan*）联系在一起。
*a decision **to expand*** (decide to)
*our plan **to build** a new hospital* (plan to)

C Grammar exercises

1 Fill in the gaps with *of, in, for, on, to* or *with*.

1 My family live in an old, wooden house ...with... shutters.
2 Our main meal .... the day usually includes rice and vegetables.
3 She got the best exam results .... the whole school.
4 At a wedding reception in Britain, all the guests usually get a piece .... the cake.
5 In my country there are special universities .... talented sportsmen and women.
6 You need a large amount .... money if you want to travel around the world.
7 My recent business trip .... Florida was a great success.
8 The house .... the corner is for sale.
9 The weather .... Greece is wonderful compared with here.
10 You should buy a grammar book .... answers, so that you can practise by yourself.

2 Fill in the gaps with the present or past participle of the verbs in brackets.

People commuting to city jobs
from the countryside

%

1985   1995   2005

1 The information ....given......... (*give*) in the graph shows that more and more people .... (*work*) in towns and cities prefer to live in the countryside and commute to work. The number of people .... (*move*) out of towns and cities increased significantly between 1985 and 2005.

2 Our awareness of food quality has changed recently with more people .... (*buy*) organic food and eggs and meat .... (*produce*) from animals that live in natural, comfortable conditions. Since 1980 the quantity of food .... (*grow*) organically in the UK has risen steadily.

☐ Revenue
☐ Costs
☐ Profit

Company A   Company B

3 The graph gives information .... (*concern*) sales and profits of two manufacturing companies. Company A sells pencils .... (*make*) in the UK, whereas Company B sells pencils .... (*manufacture*) overseas. Company B has lower costs .... (*result*) in a higher annual profit.

3 Join the two sentences to make one sentence using a noun phrase. Add prepositions where necessary.

1 I live in Malaysia. I live in the capital city.

I live in the .... *capital city of* .... Malaysia.

2 Many people buy their own home. The number is increasing.

The number of .... increasing.

3 A proposal was made by the education department. It was rejected by the government.

The proposal .... the government.

4 We have computer software. The software's purpose is to predict future earthquakes.

We have computer software .... earthquakes.

5 A new dictionary is about to be published. The dictionary contains more words than ever before.

A new dictionary .... to be published.

6 My favourite novel is a story. The story is based on the author's own experience.

My favourite novel .... own experience.

4 Use noun phrases to replace the underlined sentences.

> **Describe a holiday you have had that was successful.**
> **You should say:**
>   **when the holiday took place**
>   **who you went with**
>   **why it was successful.**

with my friends

I recently had a wonderful holiday in Crete ∧. **1** I went with my friends. When we arrived we saw a bus. **2** The bus was waiting to take us to our hotel. The hotel was nice with good views. **3** The views were of the sea. The location was also very good. **4** There was lots to do nearby. There are lots of Minoan sites. **5** You can visit them. It's a lovely island.

6 It has beautiful beaches. We spent our time sightseeing, lying on the beach and walking. Actually, it was the walking that I liked best. We did one amazing walk. **7** It was through the Samarian Gorge. It took all day, but was well worth it. We saw a snake. **8** The snake was curled up on a rock. And lots of lizards and birds. We got really hot and were very tired when we arrived at the beach at the end of the long walk. It was great to see the sea. **9** It was sparkling in the sun. We ran into the water to cool down. It was the best holiday ever.

D Test practice

Academic Reading

You should spend about 20 minutes on **Questions 1–12** *which are based on the Reading Passage below.*

Practical intelligence lends a hand

Dr Rajendra Persaud explains how practical intelligence is linked to success.

This year, record numbers of high school students obtained top grades in their final exams, yet employers complain that young people still lack the basic skills to succeed at work. The only explanation offered is that exams must be getting easier. But the real answer could lie in a study just published by Professor Robert Sternberg, an eminent psychologist at Yale University in the USA and the world's leading expert on intelligence. His research reveals the existence of a totally new variety: practical intelligence.

Professor Sternberg's astonishing finding is that practical intelligence, which predicts success in real life, has an inverse relationship with academic intelligence. In other words, the more practically intelligent you are, the less likely you are to succeed at school or university. Similarly, the more paper qualifications you hold and the higher your grades, the less able you are to cope with problems of everyday life and the lower your score in practical intelligence.

Many people who are clearly successful in their place of work do badly in standard IQ (academic intelligence) tests. Entrepreneurs and those who have built large businesses from scratch are frequently discovered to be high school or college drop-outs. IQ as a concept is more than 100 years old. It was supposed to explain why some people excelled at a wide variety of intellectual tasks. But

IQ ran into trouble when it became apparent that some high scorers failed to achieve in real life what was predicted by their tests.

Emotional intelligence (EQ), which emerged a decade ago, was supposed to explain this deficit. It suggested that to succeed in real life, people needed both emotional as well as intellectual skills. EQ includes the abilities to motivate yourself and persist in the face of frustrations; to control impulses and delay gratification; to regulate moods and keep distress from swamping the ability to think; and to understand and empathize with others. While social or emotional intelligence was a useful concept in explaining many of the real-world deficiencies of super intelligent people, it did not go any further than the IQ test in measuring success in real life. Again, some of the most successful people in the business world were obviously lacking in social charm.

Not all the real-life difficulties we face are solvable with just good social skills – and good social acumen in one situation may not translate to another. The crucial problem with academic and emotional intelligence scores is that they are both poor predictors of success in real life. For example, research has shown that IQ tests predict only between 4% and 25% of success in life, such as job performance.

Professor Sternberg's group at Yale began from a very different position to traditional researchers into intelligence. Instead of asking what intelligence was and investigating whether it predicted success in life, Professor Sternberg asked what distinguished people who were thriving from those that were not. Instead of measuring this form of intelligence with mathematical or verbal tests, practical intelligence is scored by answers to real-life dilemmas such as: 'If you were travelling by car and got stranded on a motorway during a blizzard, what would you do?' An important contrast between these questions is that in academic tests there is usually only one answer, whereas in practical intelligence tests – as in real life – there are several different solutions to the problem.

The Yale group found that most of the really useful knowledge which successful people have acquired is gained during everyday activities – but typically without conscious awareness. Although successful people's behaviour reflects the fact that they have this knowledge, high achievers are often unable to articulate or define what they know. This partly explains why practical intelligence has been so difficult to identify.

Professor Sternberg found that the best way to reach practical intelligence is to ask successful people to relate examples of crucial incidents at work where they solved problems demonstrating skills they had learnt while doing their jobs. It would appear that one of the best ways of improving your practical intelligence is to observe master practitioners at work and, in particular, to focus on the skills they have acquired while doing the job. Oddly enough, this is the basis of traditional apprentice training. Historically, the junior doctor learnt by observing the consultant surgeon at work and the junior lawyer by assisting the senior barrister.

Another area where practical intelligence appears to resolve a previously unexplained paradox is that performance in academic tests usually declines after formal education ends. Yet most older adults contend that their ability to solve practical problems increases over the years. The key implication for organizations and companies is that practical intelligence may not be detectable by conventional auditing and performance measuring procedures. Training new or less capable employees to become more practically intelligent will involve learning from the genuinely practically intelligent rather than from training manuals or courses.

Perhaps the biggest challenge is in recruitment, as these new studies strongly suggest that paper qualifications are unlikely to be helpful in predicting who will be best at solving your company's problems. Professor Sternberg's research suggests that we should start looking at companies in a completely different way – and see them as places where a huge number of problems are being solved all the time but where it may take new eyes to see the practical intelligence in action.

Questions 1–5

*Choose the correct answer, **A, B, C** or **D**.*

1 Professor Sternberg's study showed that
  A qualifications are a good indicator of success at work.
  B education can help people cope with real-life problems.
  C intelligent people do not always achieve well at school.
  D high grades can indicate a lack of practical intelligence.

2 What is the 'deficit' referred to in the fourth paragraph?
  A People with high IQ scores could not score well in EQ tests.
  B EQ tests were unable to predict success at work.
  C High IQ scores did not always lead to personal success.
  D People with high EQ scores could not cope with real life.

3 Professor Sternberg's research differed from previous studies because
  A he used verbal testing instead of mathematics.
  B he began by establishing a definition of intelligence.
  C he analyzed whether intelligence could predict success in real life.
  D he wanted to find out what was different about successful people.

4 Part of the reason why practical intelligence had not been identified
before Professor Sternberg's study is that
  A the behaviour of successful people had never been studied.
  B successful people are too busy with their everyday lives.
  C successful people cannot put their knowledge into words.
  D successful people are unaware of their own abilities.

5 In order to increase the practical intelligence of employees, companies need to
  A adopt an apprentice-style system.
  B organise special courses.
  C devise better training manuals.
  D carry out an audit on all employees.

Questions 6–12

Classify the following characteristics as belonging to

    A academic intelligence (IQ) tests
    B emotional intelligence (EQ) tests
    C practical intelligence tests

*Write the correct letter **A**, **B** or **C**, next to Questions 6–12 below.*

  6 measures skills which are likely to improve with age
  7 assesses people's social skills
  8 measures the ability to deal with real-life difficulties
  9 the oldest of the three tests
10 high scorers learn from their actions
11 high scorers are more likely to stay calm in difficult situations
12 questions have more than one possible answer

Grammar focus task

Look at the first paragraph of the text and find one example of each of the following types of noun phrase:

1 noun + prepositional phrase

2 noun + past participle clause

3 noun + *to*-infinitive

A Context listening

1 You are going to hear two doctors discussing a patient. Before you listen look at the newspaper headline and guess how it relates to the patient.

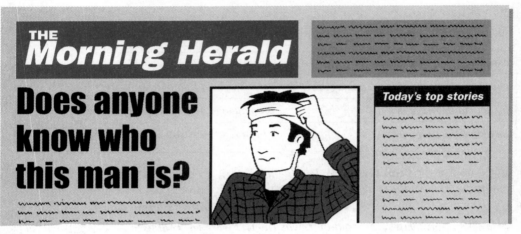

THE Morning Herald

Does anyone know who this man is?

Today's top stories

2 🎧 11 Listen and check if you were right.

3 11◀◀ Listen again and say whether the sentences below are true or false. Correct the sentences that are false.

1 The patient could remember all his personal details.

2 The patient definitely came from Yorkshire.

3 The patient could speak French and Italian.

4 Joe thinks that the patient might have been running away from something.

5 Joe thinks that the patient was definitely unmarried.

6 The patient has been unable to make contact with anyone he knows.

7 Deborah thinks that the patient can't have hit his head.

8 Deborah thinks that the patient will never recover his memory.

4 <u>Underline</u> these words in the questions and answers in Exercise 3.

could	couldn't	might	be able to	must	can't	will

1 Which words refer to ability?

2 Which words refer to certainty or impossibility?

3 Which words refer to possibility?

B Grammar

情态动词（*can*, *could*, *may*, *might*, *must*, *will*, *would*, *shall*, *should*, *ought to*, *need*）是给出有关能力、可能性或必要性的助动词。

情态动词后面跟不带*to*的不定式，情态动词形式不改变：
*He **could** **speak** French and Italian.* (**not** ~~He coulds speak~~)
***Could** you **speak** French before you lived there?* (**not** ~~Did you could speak~~)

1 Ability（能力）

可以用下列动词来谈能力：

Present	*can, can't, be able to, manage to*	*I **can't** swim.*
Past	*could, couldn't, be able to, manage to*	*They weren't able to **find out** his name.*
Perfect	*be able to, manage to*	*Have **you** managed to **finish the report** yet?*
Future	*be able to, manage to*	*I won't be able to **meet you** later.*

谈论现在和过去的能力时，*can / could* 比 *be able to* 更常用：
***Can** you remember much about it?* (= Are you able to remember?)
*He **could** speak French and Italian, but he couldn't remember his name.*

谈论过去某特定场合的能力时，用 *couldn't, was (n't), / were (n't) able to*，而不能用 *could*：
*The police **were able to** find out that he could speak French and Italian.* (**not** ~~The police could find out~~)
*He **couldn't** remember who he was.*

有时用 *manage to* 来表达某事很难达成：
*I've finally **managed to** give up smoking after all these years!*

Be able to 或 *manage to* 可用于完成时或将来时形式：
*Apparently he's **been able to** find his family.*
*Within a year he'll probably **be able to** remember quite a lot.* (**not** ~~Within a year he can probably remember quite a lot.~~)

2 Other uses of *can*（can 的其他用法）

可以用 *can* 来表示 *sometimes*（有时）：
*People **can do** funny things when they've experienced something terrible.* (= people sometimes do funny things)

也可以用 *can* 来提出要求和给予许可：
***Can I** borrow the car this afternoon?*
***You can** borrow it, but I need it later this evening.*

3 Possibility（可能性）

当有证据、信息或信念证明某事可能是真的（假的）的时候，使用 *must*, *might*, *could*, *couldn't* 和 *can'*。情态动词的选择取决于支持我们看法的证据的力度。

very likely	*must*
possible	*might, may, could, may not, might not*
very unlikely	*can't, couldn't*

Could, *may* 和 *might* 表达相同的可能性：
*He **may/might/could** remember some things already.*

Couldn't 和 *can't* 表达的可能性相同。常用于谈论过去：
*The police realised he **couldn't** be Canadian.* (= it was very unlikely that he was Canadian)

⚠ *may not* 和 *might not* 表达的可能性不同于 *couldn't*：
*The supermarket **may/might not** be open today because it's a Bank Holiday.* (**not** ~~the supermarket couldn't be open~~)

Present

用 *may (not)*, *might (not)*, *could (n't)*, *must*, *can't* + 不带 *to* 的不定式来谈论当前的可能性：
*He **may remember** some things already.* (= it is possible he remembers some things now)
*It **can't be** very easy living with someone who doesn't remember any of the past.* (= it is very unlikely that it is easy)

用 *may (not)*, *might (not)*, *could (n't)*, *must*, *can't* + *be* + *-ing* 来谈论说话间可能正在发生或进展中的事物：
*They **must be having** a difficult time adjusting to it all.*
*The phone is engaged. She **might be talking** to her sister on the phone.*

Past

用 *may (not)*, *might (not)*, *could (n't)*, *must*, *can't* + *have* + 过去分词来谈论过去的可能性：
*In the attack he **must have hit** his head.* (= there is strong evidence that he hit his head)
*He **could have had** a wife and children.* (this is a possible situation)
*He **can't have been** married.* (= there is strong evidence that he wasn't married)

用 *may (not)*, *might (not)*, *could (n't)*, *must*, *can't* + *have been* + *-ing* 来谈论过去可能正在发生或进展中的事物：
*He **might have been trying** to run away from his past.*

Future

用 *may (not)*, *might (not)* 和 *could (not)* + 不带 *to* 的不定式来谈论未来的可能性或不确定性：
*He **could make** a total recovery one day.*

用 *may (not)*, *might (not)*, *could (not)*, *must*, *can't* + *be* + *-ing* 来谈论在未来某一时间点可能发生的事情：
*I **might be meeting** John later.*

4 Expressing possibility and opinions in written texts
（在书面文本中表达可能性和观点）

情态动词在书面文本中非常重要，这是因为它们"软化"信息并帮助说明作者所表现的仅是个人观点而非已确认的事实。May（can 也一样）在用于表示"有时"的时候很常见：

比较下列这些句子及教师评语：

Student's work	Teacher's comment
People are unkind about their colleagues but it is simply because they are feeling insecure at work.	How do you know this?
People can be unkind about their colleagues but it may simply be because they are feeling insecure at work.	Good sentence.
Banning cars with high fuel consumption is a good idea, as it will result in less pollution.	This is a very strong opinion.
Banning cars with high fuel consumption may be a good idea, as it could result in a less pollution.	Good sentence. You are making your opinion 'softer'.

5 Alternatives to modals （情态动词的替代）

副词 *certainly*, *probably*, *possibly*, *perhaps* 和 *maybe* 等也可以用于表达与情态动词类似的观点：
*He had **probably** been attacked and robbed.* (= he must have been attacked)

可以用 *it* + *be* + *certain* / *likely* / *probable* / *possible* / *impossible* 来表达能力、概率和可能性：
*It is **possible** to program your computer to translate texts automatically.* (= you can program your computer)
*It is **possible** that the train will be late.* (= the train might be late)

C Grammar exercises

1 Underline the most suitable words. Sometimes both options are possible.

1 He's a concert pianist and he _can_ / _manages to_ play all Beethoven's sonatas.

2 When I lived in a small town I _was able to_ / _could_ walk almost everywhere, but now I live in the capital city I need a car.

3 They worked all night and _could_ / _managed to_ finish the report just in time.

4 The protestors _didn't manage to_ / _couldn't_ persuade the president to change the law.

5 Next year she _can_ / _will be able to_ join the club, but she's not old enough yet.

6 In my country it _can_ / _is able to_ get very cold in the winter.

7 I was nearly late as the bus didn't come, but luckily I _could_ / _managed to_ get a taxi.

8 I hope that I _will be able to_ / _will manage to_ do some sightseeing when I'm in New York next week on business, but I've got a busy schedule.

9 She didn't get good enough grades to go to her first choice of university but she _could_ / _was able to_ get a place at another one.

2 Tick (✓) the sentence, a or b, which best matches the sentence on the right.

1a He might be British.	He has a British passport.
b He must be British. ✓	
2a Our teacher can't be off sick.	I just saw him in the corridor talking
b Our teacher may not be off sick.	to a student.
3a It can be cold in Delhi in December.	I advise you to take some warm
b It must be cold in Delhi in December.	clothes just in case.
4a John can't have been working late last night.	He wasn't home when I called at
b John might have been working late last night.	seven.
5a He can't be a millionaire.	He has shares in the most successful
b He must be a millionaire.	company of all time.
6a I may come to the lecture this afternoon.	It depends if I finish my essay
b I must come to the lecture this afternoon.	before then.
7a The exam may have been very difficult.	Not many people passed it.
b The exam must have been very difficult.	
8a John couldn't know how to get here.	We will have to give him directions.
b John might not know how to get here.	

111

3 Replace the <u>underlined</u> phrases with a suitable past modal phrase.

The mummy of Djedmaatesankh, a young woman from the ninth century BC, lies behind a glass display in the Royal Ontario Museum. 2,800 years ago she lived in Thebes with her husband on the east bank of the river Nile. They were well-off, although as a double-income couple without children 1 <u>it is likely they were</u> rather unusual. Djedmaatesankh was a musician at the great Temple of Amun-Re at nearby Karnak, where her husband was a temple doorkeeper. 2 <u>It is possible that their jobs at the temple provided</u> the couple with a small wage and other benefits to supplement their main income from a piece of fertile Nile land on which 3 <u>it is possible that they grew</u> crops of barley, sesame, or dates.

We can only guess at what Djedmaatesankh's life would have been like, and try to imagine what her problems were. 4 <u>It is possible she was</u> anxious about her inability to have children and certainly, as she approached her thirties, 5 <u>it is highly likely that she worried</u> about her health.

Looking upon a face from so long ago, a face not unlike that of any other young woman in Egypt today, ties us more personally to history. In a way that 6 <u>was impossible for her to imagine</u>, Djedmaatesankh has achieved a degree of fame in our 21st century, appearing in dozens of newspapers and magazines.

1 *they must have been*

2 ....

3 ....

4 ....

5 ....

6 ....

4 Read the following essay. Find seven places where you can add *may*, *can* or *can't* to soften the verbs.

'Children can be adversely affected by the influence of television.'
To what extent do you agree with this statement? Give reasons for your answer.

Almost every family has a television these days, and many children watch a whole range of programmes every day. Some people believe that television ~~is~~ ∧ harmful to children, saying   *can be*
that it influences behaviour in a negative way.   ....

There are a lot of programmes on television that are not educational and that contain
violence and bad language. However, watching violence on television encourages violent   ....
behaviour in children. This is true in cases of children who have already exhibited violent   ....
tendencies, but it isn't true of all children, otherwise we would have an epidemic of child   ....
crime. It is also argued that bad language on television encourages the same in children.   ....

Nevertheless, overall I believe that restricting children's television viewing to mainly
educational programmes shown at a time of day when there is no violence or bad
language will overcome any risks of television being a bad influence.   ....

D Test practice

Listening Section 4
Questions 1–10

Complete the summary below.

Write **NO MORE THAN TWO WORDS** *for each answer.*

The history of soap

In ancient times soap was used to clean **1** .... Soap was not seen as a means of personal hygiene until **2** .... times. Ancient people had little technology but many **3** .... so were probably able to discover soap by chance. Soap was probably only used in **4** .... societies. There is no evidence that tribespeople at the time of the British **5** .... used soap.

The history of soap has mostly been discovered from **6** .... The earliest known use of soap in 2500 BC was to wash **7** .... The Egyptians made soap by mixing salts with oil taken from **8** .... The Romans saw washing themselves as a social activity. They removed dirt using steam and a **9** .... When Pompeii was excavated, they discovered a **10** .... for making soap.

Grammar focus task

Listen to the first part of the recording again and fill in the gaps with a modal and the verb in brackets in the correct form.

1 While you .... (*find*) some information on the origins of soap, it is not a substance which has excited a great deal of study so far.

2 We can only assume that other activities .... (*provide*) the basis from which this key concept arose.

3 So, how is it that these primitive people from over two thousand years ago .... (*discover*) soap?

4 I carried out some experiments using basic techniques to try to find out what people without any chemical knowledge .... (*observe*).

5 I was able to demonstrate that they would indeed .... (*make*) a soap that is not dissimilar to the one we know today.

Decide whether the modals are used to show ability or possibility in these sentences.

14 Modals 2

obligation and necessity; suggestions and advice; adverbs

A Context listening

1 You are going to hear a man asking a colleague for advice about living in Hong Kong. Before you listen, look at the pictures and guess which of these topics they talk about.

accommodation   clothes   food   language lessons

social life   transport   weather   work permits

2 🎧 14 Listen and check if you were right.

3 14◀◀ Now listen again and fill in the gaps in the colleague's advice.

1 You .... a few days to recover from jet lag.

2 You .... the underground system as much as possible.

3 You .... some Cantonese to travel on the public light buses.

4 You .... loose change on the ferries and the buses.

5 You .... to speak Cantonese in some market stalls.

6 You .... a work permit before you go.

7 You .... too casually for work.

8 You .... any guide books in England.

9 You .... lots of passport photos with you.

4 Complete the table below with words from Exercise 3.

strong obligation or necessity	advice or suggestions	no obligation or necessity
need to		

B Grammar

当必要做某事时，需使用有关义务和必要性的表达方式。这种需要可以是内在的（讲话者感觉到做某事是必要的）或外在的（规则或形势使做某事成为必要）。

1 Obligation and necessity （义务和必要性）

动词 *must (mustn't), have to, have got to* 和 *need to* 可以用来表达义务和必要性：
*You'll **need to** allow a bit of extra time to get over jet lag.*
*You **have to** get a work permit before you go.*
*You **mustn't** dress too casually for work.*

Must 是个情态动词，其形式没有变化：
*He **must** try a bit harder.* (**not** ~~he musts~~)

当这一"义务"来自讲话者的时候，需用 *must*：
*You **must** invite me to visit you.* (the speaker wants this)

当存在一种制度性的规则或法律时，*have to* 或 *need to* 比 *must* 更常用；
*You **have to** get a work permit before you go.* (this is a rule)

Have to 在口语中比 *must* 更常用，但在书面语中二者皆可。*Have got to* 在英语口语中的使用比书面写作中更常见：
*I'**ve got to** find somewhere to live quite quickly.*

Must 常用于标示牌、告示和印刷信息中：
*All employees **must** hold a valid work permit.*

谈论现在时的义务和必要性，可以用 *must (n't), have to, have got to* 或 *need to*。*Have to* 或 *need to* 可以用过去时和将来时：
*You **will have to learn** some Cantonese.* (**not** ~~You will must learn~~)
*He **had to get up** really early to catch the ferry to work.* (**not** ~~He must got up early~~)

⚠ *Must* 和 *ought to* 通常不用于疑问句中：
*What sort of things **do you need to** know?* (**not** ~~What sort of things must you / ought you to know?~~)

2 No obligation （无义务）

使用 *not have to, not need to* 和 *needn't* 来表达没有义务或必要做某事：
*You **needn't** buy lots of guide books before you go.* (= it is not necessary to buy guide books before you go)

⚠ *mustn't* 与 *don't have to, don't need to, needn't* 的意思并不相同：
*You **don't have to** wait for ages.* (= it is not necessary to wait)
*You **mustn't** wait here.* (= it is not allowed to wait here)

谈论过去无义务，可以用 *needn't have* + 过去分词，*didn't need to* 或 *didn't have to*：
We **didn't have to** worry about work permits when I was there.
I **needn't have bothered** to get a work permit. (= it wasn't necessary)

Didn't need to 和 *needn't have* 的意思有区别：
John picked me up from the station so I **didn't need to get** a taxi home. (= it wasn't necessary so I didn't get a taxi)
I **needn't have got** a taxi because John's flat wasn't far from the station. (= I got a taxi but it wasn't necessary)

谈到将来的时候，可以用 *not have to* 或 *not need to*：
I hope I **won't have to** work late tonight.
He's **not going to need to** come to the meeting after all.

3 Suggestions and advice （意见与建议）

可以用情态动词 *should (n't)* 和 *ought (not) to* 来提出意见或建议：
You **should** try and use it whenever you can. (= I think it is a good idea)
You **ought to** take lots of passport photos with you.
You **shouldn't** dress casually for work.

可以用 *must* 来给出强烈的建议：
You **must** phone me when you get there.

4 Adverbs （副词）

Also, *always*, *never*, *sometimes*, *just* 和 *only* 等副词出现在情态动词后：
You **should always** carry plenty of loose change.
You **must never** do that again.

可以在动词前加 *really* 来做特别强调：
You **really have to** see it to believe it.

5 Formal written English （正式书面英语）

表达义务、必要性和意见的动词在提出观点的正式的写作和学术创作中很普遍：
Governments **should** take advice from the experts before making new laws.
Companies **need to** consider cultural differences when engaging in business with overseas organisations.

C Grammar exercises

1 **Underline** the correct words. Sometimes both options are possible.

1 In my office you *have to* / *don't have to* wear a suit but lots of people do.

2 These pills *must not* / *don't have to* be taken if you are under twelve years old.

3 I *must* / *have to* leave now because I have a meeting.

4 I *didn't need to go* / *needn't have gone* to the station to pick her up because she decided to get the bus, so I finished my essay instead.

5 Notice to all conference participants: Please note that you *must* / *have got to* register before entering the conference hall.

6 You *mustn't* / *don't have to* smoke inside but you can smoke outside.

7 When I was at university I *must* / *had to* write my assignments by hand because there weren't any computers then.

8 British dog-owners *have to* / *must* have passports for their dogs when they travel abroad.

9 Next year I *'ll have to* / *'ll must* get a job to pay back all the money I've borrowed from the bank for my university fees.

10 The interview went really well so I *didn't need to worry* / *needn't have worried* about it so much beforehand.

2 **Fill in the gaps below with the correct form of** (*not*) *have to*, *must*, (*not*) *need* **or** *should*.

1 A: I'm going to Florence next week so I ....*'ll have*........... to buy a guidebook.

   B: Ah, well, you're in luck. You .... buy a book because I've got a small guide to Florence I can lend you.

2 A: What's Mike doing these days?

   B: He's studying really hard. He .... pass his exams in order to get the promotion his company have promised him.

3 A: .... (*you*) wear a uniform at work?

   B: Yes, and I find it rather strange because I've never worn one before. When I was at school we .... wear a uniform although the girls .... wear skirts and not trousers.

4 A: The rules for university fees have just changed. I was really lucky because I .... pay for my education, but unfortunately my brother .... pay when he goes to university next year.

   B: Yes, I know. My sister will be affected too.

5 A: The bread's in the oven. Can you remind me to get it out in 20 minutes? I .... forget like last time when I burnt the loaf.

B: I'm sorry. I'm afraid I .... go now, so I won't be able to remind you. Can't you set a timer?

A: Oh, ... (*you/really*) go? I'd hoped you'd stay to lunch and have some of my bread!

6 A: I've just joined the tennis club. They've got all sorts of rules, you know.

B: Really? Like what?

A: Well, you .... wear white clothes on the courts, of course. But the really silly rule is that you .... turn your mobile off as soon as you arrive at the club. I don't want to do that – what if I'm needed at work or something?

B: Perhaps they don't know you're a doctor. You .... tell them.

3 **Read the extract from an Academic Writing Task 2. Decide if the <u>underlined</u> phrases are correct or not. Tick (✓) them if they are right and correct them if they are wrong.**

Pollution is causing enormous problems all over the world these days. Governments **1** <u>need to act</u> quickly to stop this problem before it is too late.

The first thing I believe we **2** <u>absolutely should do</u> is reduce the amount we use our cars. Our governments **3** <u>must to encourage</u> us to use public transport. In my country, public transport is not very reliable, so the first thing that governments **4** <u>have to do</u> is to ensure that buses and trains are a viable alternative to the car. They **5** <u>also should reduce</u> the costs to the public of travelling on public transport.

However, it is not only the government that **6** <u>needs to make</u> an effort. All of us **7** <u>should make</u> some effort to reduce pollution. First of all we **8** <u>ought try</u> to walk or cycle if we can, rather than using our cars. In the past people **9** <u>must walk</u> or cycle because they did not have cars. It is a shame that we have become so dependent on cars now. Secondly, we **10** <u>should trying</u> to share car use with our friends and colleagues.

All of us **11** <u>will must make</u> some changes to our lives if we want to reduce pollution. Fortunately, we **12** <u>mustn't make</u> big changes to make big improvements in the situation.

1 ....✓.............	5	9 ....
2 *absolutely must do*	6	10 ....
3	7	11 ....
4	8	12 ....

4 Fill in the gaps with the correct form of (*not*) *have to*, *ought to* or *must*(*n't*) and the verbs in brackets.

Teacher: Do you think it's a good thing for young people to travel to different countries before settling down to a job?

Student: Yes, I think it's a really exciting and interesting thing to do.

Teacher: What 1 <u>do you have to think</u> (*you/think*) about if you're going to go travelling?

Student: Well, you 2 .... (*consider*) lots of things first. For example, you 3 .... (*have*) enough money in the first place, so you 4 .... (*work*) a bit first to save some money. Then another important thing to consider is who to go with. You 5 .... (*travel*) with a friend, but it is probably safer and less lonely if you do. Also, you 6 .... (*learn*) a bit about the countries before you go. It's a good idea to research cultural issues, so that you don't offend people by your behaviour. If you go to Nepal, for example, you 7 .... (*shout*) or raise your voice in public, and you 8 .... (*always/walk*) around a Buddhist temple in a clockwise direction. You 9 .... (*find out*) these things before you go.

Teacher: What things 10 .... (*you/arrange*) before you travel?

Student: Well, to visit some countries you 11 .... (*have*) a visa, so you 12 .... (*organise*) that before you go.

D Test practice

General Training Reading Section 2
Questions 1–13

Read the passage below and answer Questions 1–6.

School rules

A Pupils are required to be in their classrooms by 8.30 a.m. each morning for registration. Pupils coming late will be punished accordingly. Pupils may not leave the school grounds during the normal working day without permission. During study periods and recreation students in the sixth form may leave the school grounds provided that parents have given written authorization at the beginning of the year.

B Students must come to school in proper attire. If this basic rule is not observed, the school reserves the right to refuse entry to any student.

C The school strongly disapproves of pupils taking paid employment. It should certainly never interfere with school activities, and will not be accepted as an excuse for missing any school commitment.

D In the case of a pupil being absent from school, please telephone on the first day in all instances. Messages can be left on the answering machine before 7.30 a.m. or you can send an email to the school address to reach us by 8.30 a.m. at the latest.

E Except in the case of illness, students are expected to be present for the entire school year. Routine medical and dental appointments should be arranged so as not to conflict with school commitments, as should family travel.

F The school regards the completion of careful and regular work at home as an indispensable part of the curriculum. Every pupil has a study plan outlining his/her evening obligations day by day and parents are asked to ensure that their child has a suitable place and time in which to do the work prescribed. If a pupil appears to be doing too little work, parents should contact the form teacher at once.

G Homework can be excused only after the receipt and approval by the teacher concerned of a letter from a parent setting out the reasons. Social engagements are not acceptable as an excuse. It is essential that pupils endeavour to catch up on any missed work as soon as possible.

H During the holidays the school and its grounds are out-of-bounds for all pupils, unless accompanied by a teacher. Pupils visiting the school's sports hall or any of the school's grounds or taking part in a school visit of any kind, whether in term or in the holidays, are subject to school rules.

I No pupil may drive a car or motorbike within the school grounds without permission from the headmaster. Permission to come by bicycle should be obtained from the form teacher. Bikes must be walked onto the school grounds. Cycle helmets must be worn and lights used after dark. Rollerblades, roller skates and skateboards are not permitted within the school grounds at any time.

J Bicycles must not be chained to the school railings. Any bicycles brought onto school grounds should be clearly labelled with the owner's name and must be left locked in the bicycle sheds provided.

K Parents are strongly advised to put name tags on their children's belongings. The school cannot be held responsible for any loss or theft of students' property. Students must keep track of their belongings and not leave them lying around unattended.

Questions 1–6

*The reading passage has eleven rules labelled **A–K**.*

Which rule contains the following information?

*Write the correct letter **A–K** next to Questions 1–6 below.*

***NB** You may use any letter more than once.*

1 information about what to do if your child cannot attend school
2 the person to contact about how much homework your child should be doing
3 advice about how students can keep their bicycles secure
4 the school's opinion about schoolchildren working to earn money
5 details of what parents should do if their child cannot complete their homework
6 rules about visiting the school property outside of school time

Questions 7–13

Read the passage below and answer Questions 7–13.

School of Independent Study

The University's Independent Study online and correspondence courses offer you the flexibility to reach your educational goals without giving up your life. The study materials you use in your course have been developed by the university faculty so the material you cover is the same as in the courses offered on campus. The only difference is that you can study and take tests when it's convenient for you!

Tuition and fees

The Independent Study tuition fee is $115 per course. Students may take as many courses as they want. There is a shipping and handling fee of $30 for each course. All Independent Study students must purchase a Study Guide at a cost of $30. The university also charges a connectivity fee of $12 per course. Students enrolling for the first time will be charged a $9 per course Academic Excellence fee; for returning students this fee is just $3 per course. A $15 Academic Records fee is charged once each term, regardless of the number of courses taken. This fee entitles a student to free replacement copies of end-of-course documentation for life. Tuition and fees for out-of-state students are the same as those of local residents.

Time limits

A course can be finished in a minimum of two weeks per module and must be finished in a maximum of four weeks. For example, if your course has three modules you must remain in it for a minimum of six weeks and a maximum of twelve weeks. If you need to meet a deadline, you should take these minimum and maximum periods into account. These periods are calculated from the date you receive your first lesson from the Independent Study office. Modules cannot always be completed in the minimum amount of time. You need to make sure that you know whether your instructors are on vacation at any stage during your enrolment, as this could affect the return of assignments, exams and final grades. Your enrolment is valid for nine months, which begins on the day we post your enrolment application.

Questions 7–13

Look at the following statements.

Next to Questions 7–13 write

TRUE	*if the statement agrees with the information*
FALSE	*if the statement contradicts the information*
NOT GIVEN	*if there is no information on this*

7 The course content offered through the School of Independent Study is different to the other courses the university offers.

8 Students will receive all course materials by post.

9 The Study Guide is optional for Independent Study students.

10 Students will need to pay for extra copies if they lose their final certificate.

11 Students are able to complete each module in less than two weeks.

12 Students may take four weeks to complete a module if necessary.

13 Some modules take longer than two weeks to complete.

Grammar focus task

This is an extract from the second text. Without looking back, fill in the gaps with the correct modal verb or *need to*.

A course can be finished in a minimum of two weeks per module and **1** .... be finished in a maximum of four weeks. For example, if your course has three modules you **2** .... remain in it for a minimum of six weeks and a maximum of twelve weeks. If you **3** .... meet a deadline, you **4** .... take these minimum and maximum periods into account. These periods are calculated from the date you receive your first lesson from the Independent Study office. Modules cannot always be completed in the minimum amount of time. You **5** .... make sure that you know whether your instructors are on vacation at any stage during your enrolment, as this could affect the return of assignments, exams and final grades.

Are the verbs used to show obligation, necessity or advice?

Reported speech
tense changes; time references;
reporting questions; reporting verbs

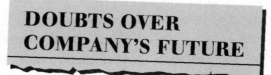

A | Context listening

1 You are going to hear an interview with Christopher West, the Managing Director of a company called Angleside. Before you listen, look at the newspaper headlines below. Which of the topics in the box do you think Mr West mentions?

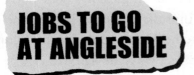

JOBS TO GO AT ANGLESIDE

DOUBTS OVER COMPANY'S FUTURE

> voluntary redundancy   early retirement   low profits   good business sense
> a promising future   poor relationship between management and workers

2 ⏵15a Listen to the first part of the recording and check if you were right.

3 15a◄ Listen to the first part again and fill in the gaps.

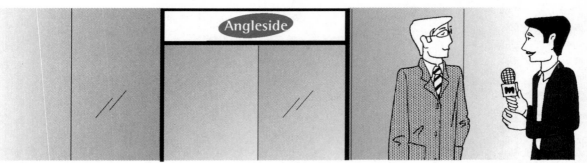

Mr West:	However, we **1** .... voluntary redundancy and early retirement and **2** .... to cover most of the jobs this way.
Interviewer:	And what has led to this situation? **3** .... a result of Angleside's poor performance over the past five years?
Mr West:	No, the company **4** .... badly. This **5** .... nothing to do with the figures. It just makes good business sense.
Interviewer:	So **6** .... that your figures **7** .... the basis for this decision to cut jobs?
Mr West:	Absolutely. We **8** .... the way we operate our business two years ago.

4 Here is the journalist's radio report. Fill in the gaps with the verbs in the box.
∩15b Then listen to the second part of the recording to check your answers.

| announced | asked | assured | claimed | denied | hoped | promised | said |

At local company Angleside, up to 150 employees will lose their jobs. Christopher West, the Managing Director, **1** .... they would be offering voluntary redundancy and early retirement and **2** .... to cover the job losses in this way. I **3** .... Mr West if these cuts were a result of Angleside's poor performance over the past five years but he **4** .... that the company had not been doing well and **5** .... that the job losses have nothing to do with the figures. West **6** .... that they decided to make changes two years ago. He **7** .... me that the company would continue to operate in the future and **8** .... to do his best for the employees.

5 What are the main differences between the texts in Exercise 3 and Exercise 4?

B Grammar

可以用转述语在书面或演讲中转述某人已经讲过的内容。

1 Tense changes（时态变化）

当转述某人已经讲过的内容的时候，有时会改变主要动词的时态：需要将时态"往前"推回一个时态：

Original tense of main verb		Tense in reported speech
present simple *I **live** in Italy.*	→	**past simple** *She said she **lived** in Italy.*
present continuous *I'm **living** in Italy.*	→	**past continuous** *She said she **was living** in Italy.*
past simple *I **lived** in Italy.*	→	**past perfect** *She said she **had lived** in Italy.*
past continuous *I **was living** in Italy.*	→	**past perfect continuous** *She said she **had been living** in Italy.*
present perfect *I've **lived** in Italy.*	→	**past perfect** *She said she **had lived** in Italy.*
past perfect *I'd **lived** in Italy.*	→	**past perfect** *She said she'**d lived** in Italy.*
be going to *I'm **going to live** in Italy.*	→	***was/were going to*** *She said she **was going to live** in Italy.*
will *I'll **live** in Italy.*	→	***would*** *She said she **would live** in Italy.*
may / might *I **may/might live** in Italy next year.*	→	***might*** *She said she **might live** in Italy next year.*
can *I **can live** in Italy.*	→	***could*** *She said she **could live** in Italy.*
must *I **must live** in Italy.*	→	***had to*** *She said she **had to live** in Italy.*

但是，我们经常不选择改变时态。这可能是因为：

◆ 所转述的内容至今为止依然正确：
'This **has** nothing to do with the figures.'
→ *He said that the job losses **have** nothing to do with the figures.* (at the time of reporting this fact is still true)

◆ 原来时态是一般过去时或过去完成时：
'We **decided** to change the way we operate our business two years ago.'
→ *West claimed that they **decided** to make changes two years ago.*

2 Reporting verbs（转述动词）

当转述某人所说的内容时，不可能使用与原始语句完全相同的词语。可以从很多转述词语中选择一些以帮助我们用较少的词汇传达大体意思。以下是一些常见的转述动词：

reporting verb (+ *that*)
agree, admit, announce, argue, believe, claim, complain, deny, explain, insist, promise, propose, reply, request, say, state, suggest, think, warn: *The director **claimed** (**that**) they decided to make the changes two years ago.*

reporting verb + someone + *that*
assure, inform, persuade, remind, tell: *He **assured the interviewer that** the company would continue to operate in the future.*

reporting verb + *to*-infinitive
agree, ask, claim, offer, promise, propose, refuse: *He **promised to do** his best for the employees.*

reporting verb + someone + *to*-infinitive
advise, ask, encourage, invite, persuade, remind, tell, urge, warn: *They **urged the employees to stay** calm.*

reporting verb + preposition + *-ing* / noun
*argue about, complain about: He **complained about the terrible food**.* *apologise for: The company **apologised for** causing redundancies.* *insist on: The manager **insisted on** seeing the staff.* *complain to: He **complained to the manager**.*

reporting verb + someone + preposition + *-ing* / noun
*accuse of: They **accused the company of** planning badly.* *advise about, remind about: They **reminded her about the meeting**.* *advise on, congratulate on: He **advised me on the deal**.* *blame for, thank for: They **thanked her for** coming.*

reporting verb + *-ing* / noun
accept, admit, deny, suggest: *The director **denied** having financial problems.* *The employees **accepted the offer** of early redundancy.*

reporting verb + someone (+ noun)
offer, promise, refuse: *He **offered her** a job.*

⚠ 有些动词不止有一种用法（如 *admit*，*claim*，*offer*，*persuade*）：
*West **claimed that they decided** to make the changes two years ago.*
*West **claimed to have decided** to make the changes two years ago.*

3 Time references etc. （时间参照等）

如果在不同于原来时间的另一时间转述原话，有时还需要对另外一些词语或短语进行变换景

today → that day   tomorrow → the following day / the next day
yesterday → the day before   next week → the following week
now → then / straight away   this → that
here → there

*He said he would see me **tomorrow**.* (reported on the same day)
*He said he would see me **the next day**.* (reported at a later date)

有时候，上下文背景要求变化代词：
*'**I like you**.'* → ***He** said **he** liked **her**.*
*'**I like you**.'* → ***I** said **I** liked **her**.*

4 Reporting questions （转述问题）

当我们转述问题时，用陈述句词序：
*I asked Mr West **how he was going to** deal with the problem.* (**not** ~~I asked Mr West how was he going to deal with the problem.~~)

转述有疑问词 (*who*, *what*, *where*, *why*, *when*, *how*) 的问句来保留疑问 :
*'**What** has led to this situation?'*
→ *The interviewer asked **what** had led to this situation.*

可以用 *if* 或 *whether* 转述 *yes* / *no* 疑问句：
'Are these cuts a result of Angleside's poor performance over the past five years?'
→ *I asked **if/whether** these cuts were the result of Angleside's poor performance over the past five years.*

⚠ 转述疑问句不能用问号。

Grammar extra: Other ways of reporting

也可以用其他表达方式来转述话语，如 *according to*（在口语、书面语中都很常见 ，
apparently, *supposedly*, *seemingly*（口语中更常见）
According to the radio programme, they are cutting 150 jobs.

C Grammar exercises

1 Here is a conversation between Tanya and her teacher.

When are you taking the IELTS test? Have you registered yet?

Yes. I'm doing it next Saturday.

Do you feel prepared for it?

Well, your classes have been really helpful, so I think so.

You've made excellent progress.

Thank you. I'm feeling very nervous though.

Oh, try not to worry. You've worked very hard.

Yes, I have. I think I'll be alright once I'm doing the test.

A week later, Tanya tells her friend about the conversation. Fill in the gaps.

To: Clara

From: Tanya

Subject: IELTS test on Saturday!

Hi Clara

I was talking to my teacher about my IELTS test last week. She asked
1 _me when I was taking_ the test. I said 2 .... Saturday. She asked
3 .... prepared for it. I replied 4 .... really helpful. She
told 5 .... excellent progress. I said 6 .... very nervous.
She told 7 .... worry and said 8 .... very hard. I said
9 .... alright once I 10 .... the test.

2 Underline the correct verb in each sentence.

1 Some people *argue/remind* that banning cars from city centres would reduce pollution.

2 The organisation campaigns against pollution and for the environment and they *insist/urge* people to start walking and cycling more.

3 My boyfriend is always forgetting things so it was a good thing I *reminded/suggested* him to bring his passport when we went on holiday.

4 I was very unhappy with the service so I *complained/insisted* to the manager and he gave me a discount on my meal.

5 I needed to talk to my boss so I *reminded/suggested* a meeting and we arranged one for later that day.

6 The students felt very strongly about the issue and *refused/insisted* on seeing the vice-chancellor to discuss it.

7 I asked him really nicely but he still *refused/denied* to help me.

8 The tennis player regretted his actions and *blamed/apologised* for his behaviour afterwards.

9 Jane was having difficulties sleeping and the doctor *advised/suggested* her to take some rest from her heavy work schedule.

10 The armed robbers *warned/announced* the bank staff not to move or they might use their guns.

3 Correct the mistakes in these sentences.

1 I met Annie and ~~she said me~~ she was getting married. *she told me / she said*

2 The education minister encouraged students take out a loan to cover their fees. ....

3 At the interview he asked did I want to start the job tomorrow! ....

4 The speaker urged people that they should vote for him. ....

5 We agreed making our presentation to the group first. ....

6 My tutor promised mark the first draft of my dissertation immediately. ....

7 Jacques invited us going to his house for dinner on Friday. ....

8 During the Speaking module the examiner asked me what were my hobbies. ....

9 The customers complained the quality of the food. ....

10 When the college announced about the changes, everyone was worried. ....

11 I wanted to pay for myself but my boyfriend insisted to pay. ....

12 The university sent me an email asking me when would I be arriving. ....

4 Report each of the sentences below using a verb from the box. Remember that you do not need to report the original words exactly.

| agree | apologise | ask | ask | deny | encourage | persuaded | ~~promise~~ |
| refuse | suggest | | | | | | |

1 'We are going to lower taxes and reduce unemployment!'
The government promised to lower taxes and reduce unemployment.

2 'I really think you should apply for the job. You'd have a good chance of getting it.'
She ....

3 'No, I won't help you. Do it yourself!'
He ....

4 'Oh, okay, I'll go to the meeting.'
She ....

5 'I didn't cause the accident. It wasn't me.'
He ....

6 'We are very sorry that we lost your application form.'
They ....

7 'Why aren't there many poisonous snakes in Britain?'
He ....

8 'Are you going to the lecture tomorrow?'
She ....

9 'Why don't you have a day off? You could do with a rest.'
She ....

10 'Please come to the theatre with me, Dan. I really think you'll enjoy it.'
'Oh, alright then, Claire.'
Claire ....

D Test practice

Listening Section 3

Questions 1–3

Complete the sentences. Write **NO MORE THAN THREE WORDS AND/OR A NUMBER** *for each answer.*

1 Solar towers create energy from moving ....
2 The first ever recorded use of this type of energy was in the ....
3 The location of the first solar tower was ....

Questions 4–8

Complete the flowchart. Write **NO MORE THAN TWO WORDS** *for each answer.*

Solar tower flowchart

Towers are built using extra strong **4** ....
At the bottom they have a sunlight collector made of
5 .... spread over a large area of ground.

↓

The sunlight collector warms the air beneath it and
operates in a similar way to a **6** ....

↓

The air **7** .... through the tower causing
the turbines to turn.

↓

The turbines create **8** .... megawatts of
electricity.

Questions 9–10

Circle **TWO** *letters A–E.*

What are **TWO** *disadvantages of solar towers?*

    A they are too expensive to run
    B heat escapes from the solar collector
    C they require a great deal of land
    D they cannot produce electricity at night
    E they need to be able to withstand high winds

Look at the extract from the recording and the summary of the discussion below. Complete the summary using reporting verbs from this unit. Do not use *say*.

Luke: But what about at night when there is no sun?

Millie: Well, they've managed to find a way to store the electricity produced during the day so it's no problem at night or even on cloudy days.

Tanya: So, there are no drawbacks then?

Millie: I didn't say that. One problem they do have is that a lot of the energy in the sunlight is lost in the form of heat from the collector, and then, of the remaining heat, a large proportion escapes from the top of the tower. But they're still worth the investment because, as I said, sunlight is free!

Luke 1 .... what happened at night when there is no sun. Millie 2 .... that they had managed to find a way to store electricity produced during the day. She 3 .... having said that there were no drawbacks and 4 .... that one problem was that a lot of the solar energy is lost from the collector. However, she 5 .... that they were still worth the investment because sunlight is free.

A Context listening

1 Freya is doing a course. What job do you think she wants to do?

2 🎧16 Listen and answer these questions.

1 What course is she doing?

2 What does she enjoy most?

3 What fear has she overcome?

3 Complete these sentences from the recording by using the verbs in brackets. 16◀◀ Listen again and check your answers.

1 I decided .... (*do*) an animal management course.

2 I chose .... (*study*) at Fairfield College because it's got a good range of animals and everyone's really friendly.

3 The course is only three days a week, so I've already started .... (*work*) part-time at a pet shop.

4 I prefer .... (*take*) time so I can get to know them.

5 I don't even mind .... (*clean*) them out.

6 They've let us .... (*treat*) some minor problems, like removing splinters from paws.

7 They make us .... (*handle*) all kinds of animals including spiders and snakes.

8 I remember .... (*feel*) really scared.

9 As long as you remember .... (*do*) it the way you've been taught, it's fine.

10 Before, if I heard him .... (*bark*), I just told him .... (*be*) quiet.

11 I'd really like .... (*work*) in either a zoo or a safari park.

4 All the verbs you have written in Exercise 3 follow other verbs. Which verbs are followed by:

1 (object +) *to*-infinitive ....

2 (object +) *-ing* ....

3 object + infinitive without *to* ....

Which verb is followed by two different patterns?

B Grammar

同时使用两个动词时，第二个动词的形式取决于第一个动词。第二个动词可以是 *to-* 不定式、不加 *to* 的不定式或者 *-ing*。

⚠ 注意：很多动词后面可能跟 *that* 从句，例如：*recommend*，*suggest*，*tell*（参见 Unit 15）。

1 Verb + *to*-infinitive（动词＋to- 不定式）

一些动词后面直接跟 to- 不定式，不需要宾语：

> agree aim appear arrange attempt be able be likely claim decide deserve
> fail hope learn manage offer plan promise refuse seem tend try

*Was animal care something you always **hoped to do**?*
*I **decided to do** an animal management course during my last year at school.*

一些动词后面经常会跟宾语＋to- 不定式：

> advise allow encourage force get persuade remind teach tell warn

*This course **has taught me to respect** all animals and overcome my fears.* (**not** ~~This course has taught to respect all animals~~)
*I just **told him to be** quiet.*

当 get 有 *persuade* 或 *make* 的意义时，后面跟宾语＋to- 不定式：
*If you want to **get your teachers to notice** your work you should make sure you hand it in on time.*

一些动词后面跟 to- 不定式时，宾语可有可无：

> ask choose dare expect help intend need prefer prepare want

*I didn't **want to touch** the snakes.*
*They **wanted us to touch** the snakes.*

2 Verb (+ preposition) + *-ing*（动词（＋介词）＋-ing 形式）

一些动词后可直接跟动词的 *-ing* 形式：

> avoid approve of can't help can't stand carry on consider deny don't mind
> enjoy feel like finish give up imagine include insist on involve keep mention
> mind practise put off recommend resist suggest think of/about

*I **prefer** deal**ing** with the customers but I **don't mind** clean**ing** out the animals and feed**ing** them.*
*We've **practised** handl**ing** animals.*

当动词后跟除 to 以外的介词时，其后的动词通常是 *-ing* 形式：
*I **was thinking about** doing another course.*

3 Verb + *to*-infinitive or *-ing*（动词＋to- 不定式或 -ing 形式）

一些动词后面可跟 to- 不定式，也可跟动词的 *-ing* 形式，这两种形式在意思上差别很小。

| attempt | begin | bother | continue | hate | like | love | prefer | start |

I've started working at a pet shop. (= I've started to work at a pet shop.)
I like feeding the animals. (= I like to feed the animals.)

⚠ 注意：*would like ／ would love ／ would prefer* 后跟 *to-* 不定式。
*I'd really **like to work** in either a zoo or a safari park.*
*I'd **prefer to stop** studying for a while.*

而一些动词后面加 *to-* 不定式，或者加 *-ing* 时，两种形式在意义上有所区别：

| forget | go on | need | remember | stop | try |

verb	+ *to*-infinitive	+ *-ing*
go on	◆ one action follows another: *After university she **went on to get** a job as a vet.* (= she finished university and then she got a job as a vet)	◆ an action is repeated or continued: *She **went on** talking even though the film had started.* (= she continued talking)
remember	◆ you remember before you do the action: *As long as you **remember to do** what you've been told, it's fine.* (= 1 remember 2 do what you've been told)	◆ you remember after doing the action: *I **remember** feeling really scared.* (= 1 I felt scared 2 I remembered that feeling)
forget	◆ the action did not happen: *I **forgot to post** my application form.* (= I didn't post it)	◆ the action happened: *I'll never **forget** meeting you that cold winter's day.* (= we did meet) This form is usually in the negative.
stop	◆ there are two actions and the first stops so that the second can begin: *I **stopped to ask** the way.* (= I stopped and then I asked)	◆ there is one action which stops: *I'm going to **stop** studying for a while.*
try	◆ make an effort to do something. You may not always be successful: *I **try to find out** why he's barking.*	◆ experiment with doing something: *She **tried** adding a bit more sugar but it still tasted horrible.*
need	◆ the subject of the sentence will do the action: *I **need to mend** my jeans.* (= I will mend them)	◆ there is a passive meaning: *My jeans **need** mending.* (= we don't know who will mend them)

4 Verb + object + infinitive without *to* (动词＋宾语＋不带to的不定式)

| feel | hear | help | let | make | notice | see | watch |

Make 和 *let* 后面经常跟宾语＋不带 *to* 的不定式：
They **made us handle** all kinds of animals including spiders and snakes.
They **let us take** it slowly.

⚠ 注意：当 *make* 用于被动时态时，需要跟 *to-* 不定式：
I **was made to handle** all kinds of animals including spiders and snakes.

Help 后面的不定式可加 *to*，也可以不加：
The course **helped me understand** my own dog better. (= The course helped me to understand my own dog better.)

5 Negatives (否定)
如果想否定第二个动词时，使用 *not*：
I chose **not** to study at this college.
I enjoy **not** working late.

C Grammar exercises

1 **Fill in the gaps with the correct form of the verbs in brackets.**

Tutor: So have you managed **1** .…to finish.. (*finish*) the assignment, Kumiko?

Kumiko: Well, I've nearly finished but I forgot **2** ……………… (*add*) a bibliography, so I'd
                   like **3** ……………… (*have*) an extension, if that's possible?

Tutor: How long will you need **4** ……………… (*do*) it?

Kumiko: I aim **5** ……………… (*finish*) it today, but maybe two days would be the best thing.

Tutor: Yes, that's fine. Have you begun **6** ……………… (*work*) on your dissertation yet?

Kumiko: Yes, I started **7** ……………… (*write*) my questionnaire a couple of weeks ago, but I
                   stopped **8** ……………… (*complete*) this assignment. I'm planning **9** ……………… (*get*)
                   the questionnaire ready by the end of the week, and I'm hoping **10** ………………
                   (*show*) it to you for your comments before I use it. Could we meet next week?

Tutor: Yes, of course. I'm afraid I can't find my diary though. I remember **11** ………………
                   (*put*) it in my briefcase this morning, but it doesn't seem **12** ……………… (*be*)
                   there. Why don't you email me with a suitable time?

Kumiko: Yes, okay.

Tutor: So, I'll see you in the seminar tomorrow. Don't forget **13** ……………… (*email*) me!

Kumiko: Thank you, I'll try **14** ……………… (*remember*).

2 Underline **the correct form of the verbs.**

1 Mario remembered *to give* / *giving* his assignment to his tutor because he had spoken
     to her about its length, but she insisted that she had never received it.

2 If you can't find the information at the library, try *to look* / *looking* on the Internet.

3 She studied medicine at university and went on *to become* / *becoming* a surgeon.

4 Look at Mum's car! It definitely needs *to clean* / *cleaning*!

5 I'll never forget *to fall* / *falling* off that swing when I was a child.

6 I was really nervous about the interview, and although I tried *not to worry* / *not
     worrying*, I was awake most of the night.

7 The new government needs *to take* / *taking* notice of the opinions of the people.

8 It seems that the new system of sending out reminders has worked, because this year
     90% of members remembered *to renew* / *renewing* their membership in time.

9 Economists predict that house prices will go on *to rise* / *rising* for at least another year.

10 We weren't able to see the concert because Tamsin forgot *to bring* / *bringing* the tickets.

16

3 Decide if the <u>underlined</u> sections are correct or not. Tick (✓) them if they are right and correct them if they are wrong.

Teacher: What impact do you feel a good learning experience at school can have on people in terms of future learning?	
Student: Oh, well, obviously, having a good experience as a student will **1** <u>allow you feel</u> positive about learning in general. If you've had supportive teachers at school who **2** <u>encouraged you to work</u> hard, you are more likely **3** <u>to go on to be</u> conscientious in your university studies.	**1** *allow you to feel* **2** ....✓ **3** ....
Teacher: Can you give me an example?	
Student: Well, with my art classes, my teacher was so supportive that I **4** <u>tried very hard pleasing</u> her. However, I have had other teachers who **5** <u>have made me to feel</u> useless, and that **6** <u>made me wanting</u> to give up.	**4** .... **5** .... **6** ....
Teacher: How can teachers ensure that their students have a positive learning experience?	
Student: I think teachers **7** <u>need to be</u> interested in their students. If they aren't interested, their students **8** <u>will stop to make</u> an effort. Also, if students **9** <u>enjoy being</u> in class, they are more likely to learn. Students **10** <u>don't mind to work</u> hard if they like what they are doing. So teachers should **11** <u>try to make</u> their classes stimulating.	**7** .... **8** .... **9** .... **10** .... **11** ....
Teacher: Do you think that the curriculum in schools allows teachers to be creative and make their lessons interesting?	
Student: Yes, in my country teachers must follow a curriculum, but the government **12** <u>doesn't force them teach</u> in a certain way. That means that teachers can **13** <u>decide to teach</u> the topic however they like. So, teachers can still be creative and **14** <u>let their students deciding</u> how they learn.	**12** .... **13** .... **14** ....

138

4 Fill in the gaps in the letter using both of the verbs in brackets.

Dear Sir,

I am writing to complain about the service I received in your hotel at the weekend. I arrived at your hotel at lunchtime on Friday and your receptionist 1 _told me to take_ (tell/me/take) a seat while she dealt with some other customers. I 2 _____ (not feel like/wait) after a long journey but I sat down anyway. However, after your receptionist 3 _____ (finish/talk) to the other customers she walked away and left no one behind the desk. After about ten minutes, I rang the bell, but still no one came. I 4 _____ (try/find) someone else to help me, and when I 5 _____ (fail/do) this I went behind the desk and called through the door. The receptionist was sitting in the back room at the computer. When she 6 _____ (see/me/stand) in the doorway, she apologized and said she 7 _____ (need/send) an urgent email and 8 _____ (carry on/look) at her screen.

If this had been the only poor service I received during my stay, I would not 9 _____ (bother/write) this letter. However, later that evening, in the dining room, I had another bad experience. Your menu only had one vegetarian dish, so I ordered this. Imagine my horror when I 10 _____ (start/eat) and discovered meat in the dish. I 11 _____ (consider/leave) immediately, but instead I explained the situation to the waiter. I 12 _____ (expect/him/get) me another vegetarian meal, but instead he simply shrugged his shoulders, removed the plate and walked away.

I 13 _____ (hope/receive) a full apology from you for this poor service and some recompense for the unpleasant time I experienced whilst staying in your hotel. I 14 _____ (advise/you/give) your staff some customer care training in the immediate future.

Yours faithfully,
Geraint Rees

Academic Reading

*You should spend about 20 minutes on **Questions 1–13** which are based on the Reading Passage below.*

How consumers decide

Professor John Maule from the University of Leeds describes new research into the way that consumers choose a product.

Understanding consumers

Consumers are creatures of habit: they buy the same products time and time again, and such is their familiarity with big brands, and the colours and logos that represent them, that they can register a brand they like with barely any conscious thought process. The packaging of consumer products is therefore a crucial vehicle for delivering the brand and the product into our shopping baskets.

Having said this, understanding how consumers make decisions, and the crucial role of packaging in this process, has been a neglected area of research so far. This is surprising given that organisations invest huge amounts of money in developing packaging that they believe is effective – especially at the retail level. Our Centre for Decision Research at Leeds University's Business School, in collaboration with Faraday Packaging, is now undertaking work in this area. It has already led to some important findings that challenge the ways in which organisations think about consumer choice.

The research has focused on two fundamental types of thinking. On the one hand, there's 'heuristic processing', which involves very shallow thought and is based on very simple rules: 1) buy what you recognize, 2) choose what

you did last time, or 3) choose what a trusted source suggests. This requires comparatively little effort, and involves looking at – and thinking about – only a small amount of the product information and packaging. One can do this with little or no conscious thought.

On the other hand, 'systematic processing' involves much deeper levels of thought. When people choose goods in this way, they engage in quite detailed analytical thinking – taking account of the product information, including its price, its perceived quality and so on. This form of thinking, which is both analytical and conscious, involves much more mental effort.

The role of packaging is likely to be very different for each of these types of decision making. Under heuristic processing, for example, consumers may simply need to be able to distinguish the pack from those of competitors since they are choosing on the basis of what they usually do. Under these circumstances, the simple perceptual features of the pack may be critical – so that we can quickly discriminate what we choose from the other products on offer. Under systematic processing, however, product-related information may be more important, so the pack has to provide this in an easily identifiable form.

Comparing competition

Consumers will want to be able to compare the product with its competitors, so that they can determine which option is better for them. A crucial role of packaging in this situation is to communicate the characteristics of the product, highlighting its advantages over possible competitors.

So, when are people likely to use a particular type of thinking? First, we know that people are cognitive misers; in other words they are economical with their thinking because it requires some effort from them. Essentially, people only engage in effort-demanding systematic processing when the situation justifies it, for example when they are not tired or distracted and when the purchase is important to them.

Second, people have an upper limit to the amount of information they can absorb. If we present too much, therefore, they will become confused. This, in turn, is likely to lead them to disengage and choose something else.

Third, people often lack the knowledge or experience needed, so will not be able to deal with things they do not already understand, such as the ingredients of food products, for example.

And fourth, people vary in the extent to which they enjoy thinking. Our research has differentiated between people with a high need for thinking – who routinely engage in analytical thinking – and those low in the need for cognition, who prefer to use very simple forms of thinking.

Effectiveness varies

This work has an important impact on packaging in that what makes packaging effective is likely to vary according to the type of processing strategy that consumers use when choosing between products. You need to understand how consumers are selecting your products if you are to develop packaging that is relevant. Furthermore, testing the effectiveness of your packaging can be ineffective if the methods you are employing concern one form of thinking (e.g. a focus group involving analytical thinking) but your consumers are purchasing in the other mode (i.e. the heuristic, shallow form of thinking).

For the packaging industry it is important that retailers identify their key goals. Sustaining a consumer's commitment to a product may involve packaging that is distinctive at the heuristic level (if the consumers can recognize the product they will buy it) but without encouraging consumers to engage in systematic processing (prompting deeper level thinking that would include making comparisons with other products).

Conversely, getting consumers to change brands may involve developing packaging that includes information that does stimulate systematic processing and thus encourages consumers to challenge their usual choice of product. Our work is investigating these issues, and the implications they have for developing effective packaging.

Questions 1–6

Do the following statements agree with the information given in the Reading Passage?

Next to Questions 1–6 write

TRUE   *if the statement agrees with the information*
FALSE   *if the statement contradicts the information*
NOT GIVEN *if there is no information on this*

1 Little research has been done on the link between packaging and consumers choosing a product.
2 A person who buys what another person recommends is using heuristic thinking.
3 Heuristic processing requires more energy than systematic processing.
4 The concept of heuristic processing was thought up by Dr Maule's team.
5 A consumer who considers how much a product costs is using systematic processing.
6 For heuristic processing, packaging must be similar to other products.

Questions 7–8

*Choose the correct answer **A, B, C** or **D**.*

7 When trying to determine how effective packaging is, testing can be made 'ineffective' if
  A you rely upon a very narrow focus group.
  B your consumers use only heuristic thinking.
  C the chosen consumers use only shallow thinking.
  D your tests do not match the consumers' thinking type.

8 If a retailer wants consumers to change brands their packaging needs to be
  A informative.
  B distinctive.
  C familiar.
  D colourful.

Questions 9–13

Complete the summary below.

*Write **NO MORE THAN TWO WORDS** for each answer.*

Write your answers next to Questions 9–13 below.

Comparing competition

For consumers who want to compare products it is important that your packaging stresses the **9** .... of your product.

We know that people only use systematic processing if the **10** .... makes it necessary or desirable. We also know that too much **11** .... could make consumers choose another product. Furthermore, consumers may not fully understand details such as the **12** .... of a product. While some people like using systematic processing, others like to think in a **13** .... way.

Grammar focus task

Look at these sentences from the text. Without looking back, fill in the gaps using the correct form of the verbs in brackets.

1 This is surprising given that organisations invest huge amounts of money in .... (*develop*) packaging that they believe is effective.

2 This requires comparatively little effort, and involves .... (*look at*) – and .... (*think about*) – only a small amount of the product information and packaging.

3 Under heuristic processing, for example, consumers may simply need .... (*be able to*) distinguish the pack from those of competitors.

4 Consumers will want .... (*be able to*) compare the product with its competitors.

5 The role of packaging is likely .... (*be*) very different.

6 People vary in the extent to which they enjoy .... (*think*).

7 Prompting deeper level thinking that would include .... (*make*) comparisons with other products.

8 Conversely, getting consumers .... (*change*) brands may involve .... (*develop*) packaging that does stimulate systematic processing and thus encourages consumers .... (*challenge*) their usual choice of product.

143

Likelihood based on conditions 1
zero, first and second conditionals;
other ways to introduce a condition

A Context listening

1 Simon Brown has just inherited $10,000 from his grandfather and is talking to his father about what to do with it. Look at these pictures. What would you do with the money?

2 🎧**17** Listen to the recording. Which of the things in the pictures do Simon and his father talk about? Do you agree with Simon or his father?

3 Match the first and second halves of these sentences from the recording. **17◀◀** Listen again and check your answers.

1 Unless you invest it properly, ...

2 If I invest it, ...

3 If I went travelling, ...

4 If you were to spend a year travelling around the world, ...

5 If you own a car, ...

6 It would be great ...

7 You won't lose any money ...

8 As long as you get a second-hand one, ...

a you'd probably need an awful lot more money than this!

b if I could drive to work instead of travelling on the bus.

c you won't earn much interest.

d provided that you think of it as a long-term investment.

e you should still be able to invest some money as well.

f I'd lose a year of study.

g you also have to pay for insurance and road tax every year.

h I won't be able to access the money quickly.

4 Look at the sentences in Exercise 3 above. Which words or phrases have a similar meaning to *if*? Do any of the sentences talk about events in the past?

B Grammar

条件句所谈的是一个条件（通常是由 *if* 引入）和一个可能的结果或后果。*If* 从句可置于结果从句前或后。*If* 从句在前的时候，在两个从句中间用逗号隔开。*If* 从句和结果从句可以是肯定的或否定的。

if + present tense, + present tense present tense + *if* + present tense	*If you **heat** water to 100℃, it **boils**.* *Water **boils** if you **heat** it to 100℃.*

1 Zero conditional（零条件句）

我们用零条件句来表示某事是普遍的真理或事实(*if* 与 *every time* 有着类似的意义)：
*If you **own** a car, you also **have** to pay for insurance and registration every year.*

如果所谈事情不再属实，就用过去时：
*When I was a child, **if I helped** my mother, she **gave** me extra pocket money.*

if + present tense, + will/won't (*might/could/going to*) + verb will/won't (*might/could/going to*) + verb + *if* + present tense	*If I **invest** my money, it **will grow**.* *My money **will grow** if I **invest** it.*

2 First conditional（第一条件句）

可以用第一条件句来谈论某事在将来会有一种可能的结果：
*If you **leave** your money in the bank, you **won't earn** any interest and it **may lose** value over time.*

可以用*might，could* 或*may* 代替*will*来表示可能性不是很大的事情：
*If I **invest** it, I **might lose** it all.*

或用 *can* 来表达*sometimes*（有时）之意：
*If you **travel** at rush hour, the trains **can be** very crowded.* (this sometimes happens)

if + past tense, would(n't) (*might/could*) + verb would(n't) (*might/could*) + verb + *if* + past tense	*If I **invested** my money, it **would grow**.* *My money **would grow** if I **invested** it.*

3 Second conditional（第二条件句）

用第二条件句来谈论现在或未来的想象的、不可能的或不太可能的情况。过去时态并不是指过去时间：
*If I **went** travelling, I **wouldn't have** any money left over.*

⚠ 对于动词*be*，可以用 *was* 或*were* 与*I / he / she / it* 连用。
*That's what I would do if I **were/was** you.*

可以用*was / were* +*to*-不定式来指未来不太可能发生的动作：
*If you **were to spend** a year travelling around the world, you'd probably need an awful lot more money than this!*

145

4 Other words to introduce a condition（引出条件的其他词语）

可以用 *when*, *provided that*, *in case*, *so / as long as* 和 *unless* 等其他词语来替代零条件句、第一条件句和第二条件句中的 *if*：

when; as soon as

可以用 *when* 和 *as soon as* 替代 *if* 来表达某事比较可能：

*I'll give you a lift into town **if** I finish my work in time.* (= I am not sure if I will be able to give you a lift)
*I'll give you a lift into town **when/as soon as** I finish this work.* (= I will give you a lift)

unless

可以用 *unless* 来表达一个否定条件，其意义与 *if...not* 类似：

*You won't earn much interest **unless** you invest it properly.* (= if you don't invest it properly)

provided/providing that; so/as long as

当表示强调时上述短语可以替代 *if*。*Provided / providing* 在书面语中比在口语更为常见：

*You won't lose any money **provided that** you think of it as a long-term investment.* (= if you think)
***As long as** you get a second-hand car, you should still be able to invest some money.* (= if you get)

in case

用 *in case* 来表达预防。比较：

*You should keep this reference number **in case** there are any problems.* (= keep the reference number because there might be problems later)
*You should quote this reference number **if** there are any problems.* (= quote this reference number at the time of any problems)

⚠ *in case* 通常不用作句子的开头。

C   Grammar exercises

1   Match the beginnings (1–8) and the endings (a–h) of these sentences.

1 If I win the competition, ..c..

2 If you boil milk, ...

3 What will you do ....

4 What happens to the engine ....

5 If I get all my work done in time, ...

6 I might buy a new laptop computer ....

7 If you agree to enrol in the diploma course, ...

8 If you put the sofa there, ...

a we'll give you the job.

b if you don't get accepted at Macquarie University?

ⓒ I'll take you somewhere nice to celebrate.

d if you put diesel fuel into a petrol-driven car?

e it forms a skin on the top.

f I'll be home by six o'clock tonight.

g you won't be able to open the cupboard.

h if my boss allows me to work from home sometimes.

2   Fill in the gaps in the extracts below using the verbs in brackets in the correct form.

1 My parents ...would love... (love) it if I .... (become) a doctor but I'm not sure I'd be able to face all those years of study. Also if I .... (be) a doctor, I .... (hate) all those hours you have to work.

2 These days I use the Internet more and more to do my shopping. If I .... (not/have) my computer, I .... (not/know) what to do. I buy clothes, books and DVDs online as well as holidays. If you .... (not/find) what you want in the shops, you .... (find) it on the Internet. I'm going to Barcelona in a few weeks and I'm going to buy my ticket on the Internet because it .... (save) me about £50 if I .... (do) it that way.

3 This production of Shakespeare's play .... (surprise) you, unless you .... (be used to) seeing all the characters being played by just two people!

4 Eggs are best kept at a cool room temperature, so I don't keep my eggs in the fridge. If I .... (keep) them in the fridge I .... (take) them out half an hour before cooking. However, not everyone has somewhere cool to keep eggs. If you .... (not/have) a cool place to store them in your home, you .... (have to) use the fridge, but just remember to take them out in time.

3 Decide if the <u>underlined</u> verbs are correct or not. Tick (✓) them if they are right and correct them if they are wrong.

Teacher: Is it better to have one special friend or lots of good ones?	
Student: I think that if you have lots of friends, you **1** <u>will be lucky</u>. However, I feel that everyone should have someone special. If you **2** <u>won't have</u> a special friend, you won't have someone to talk to at difficult times in your life.	**1** ...*are lucky*... **2** ....
Teacher: When do people make most friends?	
Student: Well, everyone makes friends when they are at school. If you **3** <u>are</u> in an environment where everyone is your own age, you **4** <u>would probably</u> make friends.	**3** .... **4** ....
Teacher: Do you think that friends need to be similar ages?	
Student: Well, generally friends from school are similar ages. But when you **5** <u>started</u> work, for example, you meet people of different ages. If you get on well with someone and you **6** <u>will have</u> a lot in common, then age **7** <u>won't be</u> important.	**5** .... **6** .... **7** ....
Teacher: Do people need to have things in common to be friends?	
Student: Well, yes. If you **8** <u>like</u> the same things, you will probably get on well. But having said that, I have a very good friend who is completely different from me. She loves sport and I hate it. If you asked me why we were friends, I **9** <u>am not able</u> to say! Maybe it's just chance – if you are in a certain place at a certain time you **10** <u>become</u> friends, but if you **11** <u>will meet</u> the same person at a different time in a different place it **12** <u>didn't</u> happen.	**8** .... **9** .... **10** .... **11** .... **12** ....
Teacher: What different roles do friends play in people's lives?	
Student: Well, your friends are the people you choose to be with. And if you **13** <u>will need</u> help, you often turn to your friends. It works the other way too. When your friends need you, you **14** <u>will help</u> them.	**13** .... **14** ....

4 Underline the correct words.

1 I'll put my umbrella in my bag *in case* / *provided that* it rains later.

2 *Unless* / *As long as* you pay me in advance, I'll buy the tickets for you.

3 I'm going to get fat *if* / *unless* I stop eating so much chocolate.

4 You must follow the instructions accurately *in case* / *unless* you want to risk damaging the machine.

5 When I travel on planes I always put my toothbrush in my hand luggage *in case* / *if* my suitcase gets lost.

6 Ice skating is fun *as long as* / *when* you are willing to fall over a lot!

7 Dear Mr Brown, I am writing to inform you that your library books are overdue. *Provided that* / *When* you return them immediately, you will not be fined.

8 I've just signed the contract for the job in Indonesia, starting in April. *When* / *If* I move there, I'll have to sell my car.

9 I wouldn't stay out in the sun too long *as long as* / *if* I were you.

10 I don't really like going to parties *unless* / *as long as* I know most people there.

D Test practice

D Test practice

Academic Reading

*You should spend about 20 minutes on **Questions 1–13** which are based on the Reading Passage below.*

Endangered chocolate

A The cacao tree, once native to the equatorial American forest, has some exotic traits for a plant. Slender and shrubby, the cacao has adapted to life close to the leaf-littered forest floor. Its large leaves droop down, away from the sun. Cacao doesn't flower, as most plants do, at the tips of its outer and uppermost branches. Instead, its sweet white buds hang from the trunk and along a few fat branches which form where leaves drop off. These tiny flowers transform into pulp-filled pods almost the size of rugby balls. The low-hanging pods contain the bitter-tasting, magical seeds.

B Somehow, more than 2,000 years ago, ancient humans in Mesoamerica discovered the secret of these beans. If you scoop them from the pod with their pulp, let them ferment and dry in the sun, then roast them over a gentle fire, something extraordinary happens: they become chocolatey. And if you then grind and press the beans, which are half cocoa butter or more, you will obtain a rich, crumbly, chestnut brown paste – chocolate at its most pure and simple.

C The Maya and Aztecs revered this chocolate, which they frothed up with water and spices to make bracing concoctions. It was edible treasure, offered up to their gods, used as money and hoarded like gold. Long after Spanish explorers introduced the beverage to Europe in the sixteenth century, chocolate retained an aura of aristocratic luxury. In 1753, the Swedish botanist Carolus Linnaeus gave the cacao tree genus the name *Theobroma*, which means 'food of the gods'.

D In the last 200 years the bean has been thoroughly democratized – transformed from an elite drink into ubiquitous candy bars, cocoa powders and confections. Today chocolate is becoming more popular worldwide, with new markets opening up in Eastern Europe and Asia. This is both good news and bad because, although farmers are producing record numbers of cacao bean, this is not enough, some researchers worry, to keep pace with global demand. Cacao is also facing some alarming problems.

E Philippe Petithuguenin, head of the cacao program at the Centre for International Cooperation in Development-Oriented Agricultural Research (CIRAD) in France, recently addressed a seminar in the Dominican Republic. He displayed a map of the world revealing a narrow band within 18° north and south of the equator, where cacao grows. In the four centuries since the Spanish first happened upon cacao, it has been planted all around this hot humid tropical belt – from South America and the Caribbean to West Africa, east Asia, and New Guinea and Vanuatu in the Pacific.

F Today 70% of all chocolate beans come from West Africa and Central Africa. In many parts, growers practise so-called pioneer farming. They strip patches of forest of all but the tallest canopy trees and then they put in cacao, using temporary plantings of banana to shade the cacao while it's young. With luck, groves like this may produce annual yields of 50 to 60 pods per tree for 25 to 30 years. But eventually pests, pathogens and soil exhaustion take their toll and yields diminish. Then the growers move on and clear a new forest patch – unless farmers of other crops get there first. 'You cannot keep cutting tropical forest, because the forest itself is endangered,' said Petithuguenin. 'World demand for chocolate increases by 3% a year on average. With a lack of land for new plantings in tropical forests, how do you meet that?'

G Many farmers have a more imminent worry: outrunning disease. Cacao, especially when grown in plantations, is at the mercy of many afflictions, mostly rotting diseases caused by various species of fungi, which cover the pods in fungus or kill the trees. These fungi and other diseases spoil more than a quarter of the world's yearly harvest and can devastate entire cacao-growing regions.

H One such disease, witches broom, devastated the cacao plantations in the Bahia region of Brazil. Brazil was the third largest producer of cacao beans but in the 1980s the yields fell by 75%. According to Petithuguenin, 'if a truly devastating disease like witches broom reached West Africa (the world's largest producer), it could be catastrophic.' If another producer had the misfortune to falter now, the ripples would be felt the world over. In the United States, for example, imported cacao is the linchpin of an $8.6 billion domestic chocolate industry that in turn supports the nation's dairy and nut industries; 20% of all dairy products in the US go into confectionery.

I Today research is being carried out to try to address this problem by establishing disease resistant plants. However, even the best plants are useless if there isn't anywhere to grow them. Typically, farmers who grow cacao get a pittance for their beans compared with the profits reaped by the rest of the chocolate business. Most are at the mercy of local middlemen who buy the beans then sell them for a much higher price to the chocolate manufacturers. If the situation is to improve for farmers, these people need to be removed from the process. But the economics of cacao is rapidly changing because of the diminishing supply of beans. Some companies have realised that they need to work more closely with the farmers to ensure that sustainable farming practices are used. They need to replant areas and create a buffer for the forest, to have ground cover, shrubs and small trees as well as the canopy trees. Then the soil will be more robust and more productive. They also need to empower the farmers by guaranteeing them a higher price for their beans so that they will be encouraged to grow cacao and can maintain their way of life.

Questions 1–3

*Choose the correct letter, **A, B, C** or **D**.*

Write your answers next to Questions 1–3 below.

1 The flowers of the cacao plant appear

    A at the end of its top branches.
    B along all of its branches.
    C mainly on its trunk.
    D close to its leaves.

2 In Africa, banana trees are planted with the cacao plants in order to

    A replace the largest trees.
    B protect the new plants.
    C provide an extra crop.
    D help improve soil quality.

3 In paragraph H, what is the writer referring to when he says 'the ripples would be felt the world over'?

    A the impact a collapse in chocolate production could have on other industries
    B the possibility of disease spreading to other crops
    C the effects of the economy on world chocolate growers
    D the link between Brazilian growers and African growers

Questions 4–9

*The Reading Passage has nine paragraphs labelled **A–I**.*

Which paragraph contains the following information?

*Write the correct letter **A–I** next to Questions 4–9 below.*

4 a list of the cacao growing areas
5 an example of how disease has affected one cacao growing region
6 details of an ancient chocolate drink
7 a brief summary of how the chocolate industry has changed in modern times
8 the typical lifespan and crop size of a cacao plantation
9 a reference to the scientific identification of the cacao plant

Questions 10–13

Complete the notes below.

Write **NO MORE THAN TWO WORDS** from the passage for each answer.

Write your answers in spaces 10–13 below.

Ways of dealing with the cacao plant's problems

- Need to find plants which are not affected by **10** ....
- Chocolate producers need to work directly with farmers instead of **11** ....
- Need to encourage farmers to use **12** .... methods to grow cacao plants
- Make sure farmers receive some of the **13** .... made by the chocolate industry

---

Grammar focus task

Without looking back at the exam task, fill in the gaps with the verbs from the box in the correct tense.

become	dry	grind	happen	let	obtain	press	roast	scoop

Somehow, more than 2,000 years ago, ancient humans in Mesoamerica, discovered the secret of these beans. If you **1** .... them from the pod with their pulp, **2** .... them ferment and **3** .... in the sun, then **4** .... them over a gentle fire, something extraordinary **5** .... They **6** .... chocolatey. And if you then **7** .... and **8** .... the beans, which are half cocoa butter or more, you **9** .... a rich, crumbly, chestnut brown paste – chocolate at its most pure and simple.

18

Likelihood based on conditions 2
third conditional; mixed conditionals;
wishes and regrets; *should(n't) have*

A Context listening

1 You are going to hear Simon Brown talking to his friend, Anna, about his car. Look at the pictures below. Why do you think he regrets buying it?

2 🎧 **18** Listen and decide if the following statements are true or false.

1 Simon bought a second-hand car.
2 The price of petrol nearly doubled last month.
3 Simon has saved very little money from his job.
4 Simon took his father's advice about the car.
5 Simon has a lot of money.

3 **18◀◀** Listen again and complete these sentences.

1 If I .... a second-hand car, I .... to take out this big bank loan.
2 It probably .... so bad if the price of petrol .... last month.
3 If I .... a bit before buying the car, I .... to save quite a bit by now.
4 If only I .... to him, none of this ....
5 If I .... his advice, I .... a small fortune now.

4 Look at your answers to Exercise 4 and answer these questions.

1 Which tense is used in the *if* clause in sentences 1, 2, 4 and 5? ....
   Does it refer to present or past time? ....

2 Which sentences refer to a past situation in the result clause? ....
   Which structure is used? ....

3 Which sentences refer to a present situation in the result clause? ....
   Which structure is used? ....

B Grammar

1 Third conditional（第三条件句）

if + past perfect, *would(n't) have* + past participle	*If you'd asked me, I'd have done it.*
would(n't) have + past participle + *if* + past perfect	*I'd have done it if you'd asked me.*

第三条件句描述的是过去的假设情形。我们用第三条件句来设想过去并没有发生的事情的结果：
If I'd bought a second-hand car, I wouldn't have taken out this big bank loan. (= he bought a new car so he did take out a bank loan)

可以用*might*或*could*替代*would*来表达某件事的确定性较小：
If I'd saved more money, I might have gone on that college trip last week.

2 Mixed conditionals（混合条件句）

if + past perfect, *would(n't)* + verb	*If I'd saved more, I'd be rich.*
if + past simple, *would(n't) have* + past participle	*If I was sensible, I'd have saved more.*
if + past perfect, *would(n't) be* + ing	*If I hadn't saved, I wouldn't be going on holiday.*
if + past continuous, *would(n't)* + verb	*If I was going on holiday soon, I'd be happy.*
if + past simple, *would(n't) be* + ing	*If I didn't have savings, I wouldn't be going on holiday.*

当*if*从句中的时间与结果从句中的时间并不一致时，使用复合条件句。

我们可以复合（混合）过去时间和现在时间来设想：

◆ 假设的过去情况或行为的现在结果

　　　　过去情况　　　　　　　　　　　　现在结果
If I'd taken his advice, I'd own a small fortune now instead of a big debt! (= I didn't take his advice so now I don't own a small fortune)
It wouldn't be so bad if the price of petrol hadn't almost doubled last month.

◆ 假设的现在情况的过去结果

　　　　现在情况　　　　　　　　　　　　过去结果
If you got on better with him, you might have listened to his suggestions. (= you don't get on with your father so you didn't listen to his suggestions)
If he had more qualifications, he would have got the job.

我们可以复合（混合）过去时间和未来时间来设想：

◆ 假设的过去情况或行为的未来结果

　　　　过去情况　　　　　　　　未来结果
If I hadn't broken my wrist, I'd be playing tennis later. (= I did break my wrist so I am not playing tennis later)
If I'd bothered to get tickets, I'd be going to the concert tonight. (= I didn't bother to get tickets so I am not going to the concert)

我们可以复合（混合）未来时间和现在时间来设想：

◆ 假设的未来情况或行为的现在结果

          未来情况   现在结果

*If I **wasn't meeting** my manager later, **I'd be** at the conference now.* (= I am meeting my manager later, so I'm not at the conference now)

◆ 假设的现在情况的未来结果

          现在情况   未来结果

*If I **was** at home in America, **I'd be seeing** my mother tomorrow because it's her birthday.* (= I am not at home in America, so I won't be seeing my mother tomorrow)

3　Wishes and regrets（希望和遗憾）

可以使用 *wish* + 过去动词来谈论与我们的意愿相反的情况：
*I wish I **could** help you.* (= I can't help you and I am sorry about that)
*I wish my father **wasn't** always right!* (= he is always right and I find that annoying)

用 *wish* + *something / someone* + *would* + 不带 *to* 的不定式来表达我们想某事发生或某人改变其行为。这个用法不与状态动词连用：
*I wish they **would stop** talking so loudly!* (= they are talking loudly and I want them to stop)
*I wish this holiday **would go on** forever.*

用 *wish* + 过去完成时来谈论令我们遗憾的过去的情况：
*I wish **I'd thought** about the other costs before I bought it.* (= I didn't think about the other costs and I regret it now)

可以用 *never* 来强调：
*I wish I'd **never** bought the car.* (= I did buy it and I really regret it now)

⚠ 可以用 *if only* 替代 *wish* 来表达相同的意思。前者更正式些：
If only I had listened to my father!

4　Should(n't) have

可以用 *should (n't) have* + 过去分词表示过去发生的或未曾发生的是一个错误或糟糕的事情：
*I **should have listened** to him.* (= but I didn't)

可以用 *never* 来强调：
*I **should never have bought** it!* (= I did buy it and now I regret it)

Grammar extra: *If it wasn't for ...*

可以使用 *if it wasn't / weren't for* + 名词短语来说某情形取决于另外一种情形、人或事：
If it wasn't/weren't for the car, I'd have no money worries now. (the car is the reason for my worries)

可用 *if it hadn't been for* 来谈论过去的情况：
If it hadn't been for your advice, I would have made the wrong decision.

C Grammar exercises

1 Fill in the gaps with the correct form of the verbs in brackets.

Tutor: Tell me what you intend to write in your evaluation of your research.

Student: Well, firstly, if I _'d had_ (**1** *have*) a larger number of questionnaires returned, I _____ (**2** *get*) more useful data.

Tutor: Is there anything you could have done to improve that?

Student: Well, I suppose I _____ (**3** *receive*) more completed questionnaires if I _____ (**4** *make*) the questions easier to answer, for example, 'yes/no' questions.

Tutor: Yes, I think you are right. People are too busy to answer complicated questions. Any other things you might change?

Student: Yes. I think I _____ (**5** *be*) more successful with my interviews as well if I _____ (**6** *plan*) the questions more thoroughly beforehand, although I'm not sure about that. If I _____ (**7** *prepare*) the questions in more detail, it _____ (**8** *restrict*) the interviewees too much. Oh, and another thing: if I _____ (**9** *start*) collecting data sooner, it _____ (**10** *not/be*) such a rush in the end.

Tutor: Good. I must admit that if you _____ (**11** *not/leave*) it all so late, I _____ (**12** *be able to*) support you more. If you _____ (**13** *come*) to see me before you sent out your questionnaires, I _____ (**14** *help*) you. It is a shame that your data was so disappointing because your research questions were very interesting.

2 Read about two scientific discoveries that were made due to chance and complete the sentences.

> Alexander Fleming's most famous discovery happened entirely by accident. One day he was cleaning the culture dishes in his lab when he saw mould growing on one of the plates. There weren't any germs growing around the mould, so Fleming decided to grow more of it for experiments. He discovered that the mould acted against bacterial infections. However, Fleming's initial publication about his discovery was largely ignored by the medical community so he abandoned his research in 1932. It wasn't until 1935, when the researchers Florey and Chain saw Fleming's research papers, that the drug, penicillin, was developed.

1 If Fleming hadn't been cleaning the culture dishes, he *wouldn't have seen mould* growing on one of the plates.

2 Fleming wouldn't have grown more of the mould if there .... growing around it.

3 If his initial publication hadn't been received so poorly by the medical community, he .... in 1932.

4 Penicillin might not have been developed if Florey and Chain ....

Harold Ridley, an ophthalmologist, developed a revolutionary way of helping people with poor eyesight as a result of cataracts[1]. During World War II, Ridley worked with RAF pilots with eye injuries. He noticed that their eyes did not become infected when they had eye injuries caused by bits of Perspex from the windows of their planes. As a result of this observation he decided to implant plastic lenses in the eyes of people with cataracts. Surgeons had earlier tried replacing the lens in the eye with a glass one, but the operations always failed because the body rejected the glass lens. Ridley's operations with plastic lenses were successful. However, the medical community opposed Ridley's discoveries and it took many years for the technique to be accepted. Today over 200 million people have their sight because of Harold Ridley.

[1] Cataracts are regions of dead cells within the lens of the eye, and can cause blindness.

5 If Harold Ridley .... pilots during World War II, he wouldn't have noticed the effects of Perspex splinters on their eyes.

6 If the pilots' eye injuries had become infected from bits of Perspex, he .... to implant plastic lenses in cataract patients' eyes.

7 If earlier surgeons had used plastic lenses, the operations ....

8 It wouldn't have taken so many years for the technique to become widely available if the medical community .... Ridley's discoveries.

3 Find and correct the mistakes in the sentences below.

1 If I hadn't ~~ate~~ *eaten* so much I wouldn't have a stomach ache now.

2 What would you done if you'd failed the exam?

3 I am starting university next autumn if I hadn't had such bad exam results.

4 If the government would have kept their promise, taxes wouldn't have gone up last year.

5 I would have finished my essay on time if I didn't have the accident.

6 If I was getting married next weekend, I was very excited by now.

7 If the economic conditions had been better when I bought this house, I might make a fortune by now.

8 Life today will be very different if Thomas Edison hadn't invented the electric light.

9 If you were more considerate, you didn't make so much noise last night.

10 If I didn't go to university, I wouldn't be doing this job now.

4 Fill in the gaps using *wish* or *should* and the words in brackets in the correct form.

1 You _shouldn't have left_ (*not/leave*) school so young. You'd have a better job now.

2 I really .... (*you/ask*) me before borrowing the car yesterday. I needed to use it.

3 I'm not enjoying my degree course at all. I .... (*I/not/choose*) physics. I .... (*choose*) maths instead because I used to love it at school.

4 I .... (*I/study*) languages at school because now I travel regularly for work to Berlin and Paris.

5 That man is really annoying me. I .... (*he/stop*) whistling.

6 We're lost again. We always get lost when you have the map. You .... (*let*) me have the map from the start!

7 I .... (*I/have*) more time to work on this assignment. I'm worried I won't finish it by the deadline.

8 I .... (*it/stop*) raining. I want to go for a walk.

9 I have terrible problems with my knees. I .... (*I/not/do*) so much running when I was younger.

10 You .... (*not/tell*) Paula about the party – it was meant to be a surprise.

Academic Reading

*You should spend about 20 minutes on **Questions 1–13** which are based on the Reading Passage below.*

The Giant Panda

For more than 100 years, scientists have argued over exactly what a panda is. Now, finally, with the help of DNA testing, the panda has been admitted to the *ursidae* (bear) family, and the spectacled bear of South America has been confirmed as its closest living relative.

In 1869, French Jesuit missionary Pere David first described the giant panda to western science. With just a pelt and reported sighting to go on, he classified it as a bear. However, the following year, zoologist Alphonse Milne Edwards dissected the first specimen and concluded that it had more in common with the red panda, a member of the raccoon family. For more than a century, scientists quarrelled over whether the giant panda belonged to the bear family, the raccoon family or a separate family of its own.

They had good reason to be confused. The giant panda shares many physical characteristics with the red panda. Both have evolved to feed on bamboo, grasping and eating it in the same way, with similar teeth, skulls and forepaws. They also both have a distinctive cry which they use to communicate with others in their group.

In the mid-1980s there were several studies involving DNA comparisons between the species. The first investigations linked the giant panda with bears, but in 1991 further tests contradicted these findings and placed it in the raccoon family with the red panda. By the year 2000, approximately twelve studies had been completed, and all except two placed the panda in the bear family. The data from these two studies was reanalysed by other researchers, who finally concluded that the giant panda was indeed a bear.

Today, there are eight species of bear. Along with dogs, their closest relatives, cats, raccoons and weasels, they belong to the order *Carnivora*, a group of meat-eating predators that evolved some 57 million years ago. The ancestors of modern bears split from this group about 34 million years ago, and today the panda is our oldest living bear, followed by the spectacled bear. Both are survivors of an ancient lineage dating back 18 million years. The rest – the brown, black, polar, Asiatic black, sloth and sun bears – are relatively modern, dating back four to five million years.

Researchers have found that the spectacled bear and the panda have several physical features in common. The spectacled bear's muzzle is comparatively short and it has blunt molar teeth and large jaw muscles, which are good for grinding fibrous vegetation – vegetation such as bamboo. Indeed, scientists in Venezuela have found that bamboo makes up 70% of the diet of some spectacled bear populations. For most spectacled bears, however, the bromeliad, a tropical plant with fleshy leaves, is their main food source. Most species of bromeliad grow in trees, and spectacled bears therefore have to be adept tree climbers because they spend their lives foraging for these plants, as well as fruits, in the cloud forest of the Andes.

The giant panda's diet is famously dull, with bamboo representing 99% of its intake. This is rather strange given that its physiology is typical of a carnivore and it has no special adaptation for digesting cellulose, the main constituent of plant cell walls. A panda manages to digest only about 17% of the bamboo it eats (a deer living on grass achieves 80% efficiency). It typically feeds for 14 hours a day, consuming 20 kg or more of bamboo. Unable to store fat effectively, it continues eating in the bitterly cold winter, at a time when many other bears hibernate.

With such a specialised diet, the giant panda has evolved a sixth digit, a prehensile elongated wrist bone called the radial sesamoid. They use this 'false thumb' to roll bamboo leaves into fat, cigar-shaped wads which they then sever using their powerful jaws. They feed mainly on the ground but are capable of climbing trees as well. The spectacled bear is a more frequent climber and will even climb spiky cacti plants to reach fruit at the top. They also construct tree nests to act as a bed as well as a platform to feed from fruit-laden branches.

Very occasionally, the giant panda supplements its diet with meat which it scavenges. Spectacled bears eat carrion, too, and some have been known to kill small calves. Spectacled bears are highly adaptable and are found in a wide range of habitats including rainforest, dry forest and coastal scrub desert. In contrast, the giant pandas live at an altitude of between 1,200 and 3,500 metres in mountain forests that are characterised by dense strands of bamboo.

There have been many theories as to why the panda has such a distinctive coat, but the most convincing argument is that of George Schaller, one of the first western scientists to study wild pandas. He believes the contrasting coat may help prevent close encounters with other pandas. 'In pandas, a stare is a threat,' Schaller says. 'The eye patches enlarge the panda's small, dark eyes tenfold, making the stare more powerful. A staring panda will hold its head low, so presenting the eye patches. To show lack of aggressive intent, a panda will avert its head, cover its eye patches with its paws or hide its face.' Interestingly, the spectacled bear is the only other bear with comparably obvious markings around the eye.

Questions 1–8

Classify the following characteristics as belonging to

    A the giant panda
    B the spectacled bear
    C both the giant panda and the spectacled bear

Write the correct letter **A**, **B** or **C** next to Questions 1–8 below.

1 an extra thumb on each paw
2 a tendency to sleep in trees
3 their species originated 18 million years ago
4 the ability to adjust to different environments
5 the use of noises to socialise with each other
6 the ability to climb trees
7 the eating of meat
8 a similarity to a type of raccoon

Questions 9–13

Complete the sentences with words taken from the passage.

Use **NO MORE THAN TWO WORDS** for each answer.

Write your answers in spaces 9–13 below.

 9 The panda's digestive system is that of a ....
10 The giant panda must eat constantly because it can only .... a small amount of bamboo.
11 In winter, giant pandas cannot .... because of their feeding habits.
12 Spectacled bears build .... to help reach their food.
13 Giant pandas may use their .... to threaten other pandas.

Look at the following extracts from the passage. Complete the sentences below using verbs in brackets in the correct form.

For more than 100 years, scientists have argued over exactly what a panda is. Now, finally, with the help of DNA testing, the panda has been admitted to the *ursidae* (bear) family.

1 If scientists .... (*have*) DNA testing 100 years ago, they .... (*be able to*) discover what a panda was.

However, the following year, zoologist Alphonse Milne Edwards dissected the first specimen and concluded that it had more in common with the red panda, a member of the raccoon family.

2 If Alphonse Edwards .... (*not/dissect*) a giant panda, scientists .... (*not/think*) the giant panda was a raccoon.

They had good reason to be confused. The giant panda shares many physical characteristics with the red panda; both have evolved to feed on bamboo, grasping and eating it in the same way, with similar teeth, skulls and forepaws.

3 If the giant panda .... (*not/resemble*) a red panda, there .... (*not/be*) so many arguments among scientists.

In the mid-1980s there were several studies involving DNA comparisons between the species. The first investigations linked the giant panda with bears, but in 1991, further tests contradicted these findings and placed it in the raccoon family with the red panda.

4 If the 1991 DNA tests .... (*not/contradict*) the earlier findings, then the argument .... (*be*) resolved earlier.

19 Prepositions

prepositions after verbs, adjectives and nouns;
prepositional phrases

A Context listening

1 A student is being interviewed for a teacher training course. Which of the following do you think she says she's worried about?

finding accommodation   transport
lots of hard work   finding maths difficult
controlling the class   having the right clothes
pupils being rude to her   being unprepared to teach

2 🎧 **19a** Listen and see if you were right.

3 **19a** ◄◄ Listen again and complete the interviewer's notes below.

Notes

Reasons for applying for this course:
- has always been **1** .... teaching
- wants to gain a teaching qualification

Reasons for choosing our college specifically:
- can **2** .... accommodation **3** .... her brother
- was **4** .... the description of the course in the prospectus
- is keen on **5** .... teaching before doing it

Expectations of the course:
- a friend **6** .... her **7** .... the hard work

Concerns about the course:
- feels she is not very **8** .... maths
- has no **9** .... teaching
- **10** .... not being able to control the class
- unsure what to do if pupils **11** .... her

4 Look at your answers to Exercise 3. Find at least one example of each of the following:

1 verb + *about*   ....
2 adjective + *about*   ....
3 adjective + *at*   ....
4 verb + *at*   ....

5 adjective + *in*   ....
6 noun + *of*   ....
7 verb + *with*   ....
8 adjective + *by*   ....

B Grammar

从句中介词的选择经常取决于介词前面的形容词、动词或名词。

1 Verb + preposition（动词＋介词）

Verb	Preposition
care, complain, hear, know, learn, say something, talk, think, warn, wonder, worry, write	*about*
aim, fire, laugh, look, point, shout, yell	*at*
choose, decide, differentiate, distinguish	*between*
aim, apologise, apply, forgive, hope, long, prepare, search, wait, watch, wish	*for*
learn, prevent, stop	*from*
assure, convince	*of*
concentrate, count, depend, insist, rely	*on*
apologise, explain, present, speak, talk, write	*to*
be, deal, go out, play, stay	*with*

⚠️ *marry* 不与介词连词：
She married him last year. (**not** ~~She married with him~~)

当想指出主题时，说或想的动词（如 *complain, know, learn, say something, talk, think, warn, somebody, wonder, write*）后面常用 *about*：
*That way you can **learn about** teaching before being asked to do it.*

⚠️ 一些其他的说或想的动词（如 *discuss, debate, consider, mention*）后面不需要用介词：
*We need to **discuss** the problem.* (**not** ~~discuss about~~)

有些说的动词（如 *apologise, explain, present, speak, talk, write*）后面常跟 *to* ＋人来表明讲话所针对的人：
*Have you **talked to anyone** who has done this course?*

用 *at* ＋人／物放在某些动词（如 *aim, fire, laugh, look, point, shout, yell*）后面来表明动词的焦点是哪个人或物：
*If they **shout at me** in class, I'm not sure what I'll do.*

在动词后常用 *for* 来表明我们想要引入某事的欲望：
*I'm **aiming for a good mark** in my next assignment.*

⚠️ 如果 *aim, hope* 和 *long* 后面跟的是动词，要在它们后面用 *to*：
*I'm **hoping to** get a better mark than last year.*

2 Adjective + preposition（形容词＋介词）

Adjective	Preposition
anxious, annoyed, concerned, depressed, excited, upset, worried	*about*
amazed, annoyed, astonished, awful, bad, clever, excited, good, skilled, surprised, terrible, useless	*at*
amazed, annoyed, astonished, concerned, disturbed, excited, impressed, inspired, shocked, surprised	*by*
bad, concerned, good, responsible	*for*
disappointed, interested	*in*
frightened, scared, terrified	*of*
aware, clever, cruel, generous, good, kind, mean, nasty, nice, polite, rude, selfish, true, typical, unkind	*of*
cruel, good, kind, mean, nasty, nice, polite, rude, unkind	*to*
annoyed, bored, concerned, disappointed, fed up, impressed, obsessed, pleased, satisfied, wrong	*with*

谈论能力的形容词（如 *awful, bad, clever, good, skilled, terrible, useless*）后面常跟 *at*：
*I'm not very **good at** maths.*

有些描述害怕的形容词（如 *frightened, scared, terrified*）后面跟 *of*：
*There are some aspects of the course that I am a bit **scared of**.*
*Most people are **frightened of** being in front of a class for the first time.*

在以 *it*, *that* 或 *this* 开头的句子中描述行为的形容词常跟 *of*：
*Would you like a cup of tea of coffee?   That's very **kind of** you.*

描述指向其他人行为的形容词（如 *cruel, good, kind, mean, nasty, nice, polite, rude, unkind*）后面经常跟 *to*：
*I'm worried about the pupils being **rude to** me.*

3 Noun + preposition（名词＋介词）

Noun	Preposition
anything, information, nothing, something	*about*
excuse, explanation, ideas, in return, need, reasons, reputation, responsibility	*for*
change, decrease, drop, experience, fall, increase, rise	*in*
experience, knowledge, understanding	*of*
effect, impact, influence	*on*
in association, experience	*with*

4 Prepositional phrases（介词词组）: *by, in, at, on, of*

以下情形用*by*：

◆ 来谈论处于被动语句中的人
   *But you will be taught how to deal with those things **by the tutors** on the course.*

◆ 来解释事情是如何做的
   *You can remove any dirty marks **by wiping** it with a wet cloth.*

◆ 来谈论交通和交流，如 *by plane*，*by email*
   *We'll be in touch **by email** soon if that's okay.*

◆ 来谈论机会，如 *by chance, by accident, by mistake*
   *I saw the advertisement for the job **by chance** and decided to apply for it.*

下列表达中，用*in*：*in love, in pain, in private, in touch, in debt, in danger, in a rush, in fashion, in luck, in the end*。
*Don't forget to keep **in touch** while you're away!*

下列表达中，用*at*。

◆ *at first, at large, at peace*:
   ***At first** I was impressed by the reputation of the university but I also like the course you offer.*

◆ *at work, at home, at school, at the airport, at university*:
   *I've just finished my first degree **at Stamford University**.*

我们用*on*来说你为什么会在某地，如 *on holiday*，*on business*，*on duty*。

用*of*与表达数量的词连用，如*all*，*any*，*both*，*either*，*neither*。

Grammar extra: Prepositions

在介词后面，也可以用名词、代词或-*ing*：
*I was really impressed **with the description** of the course in your prospectus.*
*If they shout **at me** in class, I'm not sure what I'll do.*
*Well, I've always been interested **in teaching**.*

否定句中，*not* 放在介词与-*ing*之间：
*I'm worried **about not** being able to control a class.*

C Grammar exercises

1 Choose the correct word (A, B or C) to complete each sentence.

1 I still haven't forgiven her .... her behaviour in front of my boss.

   Ⓐ for   B of   C from

2 I'm going to .... to your parents about your exam results.

   A talk   B discuss   C ask

3 I'm scared .... making a fool of myself when I give the presentation.

   A for   B to   C of

4 I'm very .... in you. You've made a real mess of things.

   A concerned   B astonished   C disappointed

5 The new drug prevents the bacteria .... growing.

   A to   B from   C in

6 There are many things .... with our society today.

   A bad   B wrong   C disturbing

7 It was very generous .... you to offer to help me.

   A of   B about   C for

8 The president first became .... in politics as a student.

   A aware   B involved   C enthusiastic

2 In nine of these sentences there is a wrong preposition. <u>Underline</u> each mistake and write the correction.

1 There has been a rise in the number of people buying their own homes. .....✓.....

2 It is not difficult to distinguish amongst the emotional response to this crime and the law's response. ....

3 There is no need about a new school in this area. ....

4 We want the government to promise to make a change in the law. ....

5 I hate the way she always laughs to people. ....

6 I've decided to apply to that job in the newspaper. ....

7 Professor Ho has a good knowledge about his subject. ....

8 I'm afraid I broke this glass in accident. ....

9 My husband's staying at my cousin while he is on business in America. ....

10 I gave him one of my paintings in return for his help when I moved house. ....

11 Why do governments always insist in doing things that are unpopular? ....

12 When I was in school I did much more sport than I do these days. ....

3 Fill in the gaps in the conversation with a word from the box and a preposition.

~~anxious~~	bad	choose	depend	effect	obsessed	rely	true	worried

Teacher: Do you think that money can solve all problems?

Student: No, not really. Of course, I would be **1** ....*anxious*.... ..*about*.. money if I didn't have very much, but I believe that too much money can be **2** .... you.

Teacher: So you think it is possible to have too much money?

Student: Well, there are lots of stories in the media about people who have won lots of money in the lottery and realised that they are not happier as a result. I think that large amounts of money can have a negative **3** .... people.

Teacher: Do you think that people **4** .... modern technology like computers too much and that people are **5** .... having the latest high tech equipment?

Student: Well, yes, in some countries. But this isn't **6** .... many people in the world who are only **7** .... their next meal. In rich countries people always want a new gadget to make life easier but I'm not sure these machines do actually do that. When we go shopping we have to **8** .... hundreds of different brands of the same thing, and when these things go wrong we don't know what to do. I would prefer it if life were simpler and we didn't **9** .... expensive technologies so much.

4 Fill in the gaps in the letter with a preposition.

FIVE STAR HOTELS

★ ★ ★ ★ ★

Dear Mr Rees,

Thank you for your letter of 21 June. I was very disturbed 1 ....by.... your account of what happened in our hotel last week, and I am writing to apologise 2 .... this. I can understand that you were shocked 3 .... the way the employee spoke to you. There can be no excuse 4 .... such behaviour and I fully understand why you felt the need to complain 5 .... the situation. I can provide no explanation 6 .... the way the receptionist behaved.

Our hotel group has a reputation 7 .... being good 8 .... looking after our customers, and I am very sorry that your experience 9 .... our service did not confirm this. I intend to deal 10 .... the staff member appropriately and I will ensure that she does not repeat this behaviour 11 .... sending her on a retraining course next week. I would like to assure you that the behaviour you encountered is not typical 12 .... our staff.

As the manager, I am responsible 13 .... all of our employees so please accept my apologies again and this voucher worth £50 to spend in any 14 .... our hotels.

Yours sincerely,

Clive Martin
Hotel Manager

D Test practice

Listening Section 2

Questions 1 and 2

Choose the correct letter A, B or C.

1 How far away is the nearest big town to Greenville?
  A 10 kilometres
  B 25 kilometres
  C 500 kilometres

2 Which service came to the town recently?
  A fire service
  B medical service
  C weather station

Questions 3–10

Complete the notes below.

*Write **NO MORE THAN THREE WORDS AND/OR A NUMBER** for each answer.*

Volunteer storm spotters

Duties:
- Need to **3** .... the weather station as soon as the storm has passed
- Fill in a **4** ....
- Attach extracts from **5** ....

What to report:
- Hail which measures **6** .... across or larger
- Wind damage e.g. **7** .... that have been brought down
- Flooding caused by heavy rainfall

How do I become a volunteer?
- There will be a **8** .... day next month
- Contact local **9** .... if you want to attend
- Important to sign up before 31st **10** ....

These are some extracts from the recording. Without listening to the text again, fill in the gaps with the correct prepositions.

1 Today we're going to be talking .... what we as a community can do to help each other in severe weather.

2 The National Weather Bureau can provide a lot of helpful information and even warn us .... severe storms.

3 You don't have to be particularly skilled .... anything.

4 They'd also like to hear .... very heavy rainfall.

5 What should you do if you care .... our community and you want to help?

6 This will only take up a day so don't worry too much .... it.

7 You'll need to talk .... the police.

A Context listening

1 You are going to hear part of a radio programme about making sure your home is safe when you are away. Before you listen, look at the picture. What do you think the radio programme will mention?

2 🎧 **20** Listen and see if you were right.

3 **20◄◄** Listen again and complete the advice below using no more than three words from the recording.

How to protect your home

Outdoors

- If you live in an area 1 .... a lot of tall trees, cut off overhanging or dead branches.
- Put away objects 2 .... damaging missiles.

Indoors

- If you are away for a long time then find someone 3 .... on your home for you.
- Install lights 4 .... a timer so that it looks as though you are home.
- Find someone 5 .... your mail regularly.

---

4 Look at your answers and <u>underline</u> all of the relative pronouns (*where, which, who, that*).

Which relative pronoun refers to a place? ....

Which relative pronouns are used to refer to people? ....

Which relative pronouns are used to refer to things? ....

B Grammar

关系从句给出有关名词（名词短语）的信息。关系从句通过关系代词（如*who*，*which*）与名词（或名词短语）联系在一起。关系代词可以是句子的主语，也可以是句子的宾语；在该从句中，不会再使用另一个代词来指这个名词：

*Why not install lights **which** have a timer?* (**not** ~~Why not install lights which they have a timer?~~)

⚠ 有时会用分词从句来替换关系从句（参见Unit 12）：

the man sitting beside me (= the man who is sitting beside me)
the food kept in the fridge (= the food which is kept in the fridge)

1 Relative pronouns（关系代词）

我们用

◆ *who*来指人：
*Please welcome **Mike Bowers**, **who** is going to talk to us about how to look after your home.*

◆ *which*来指物：
*These are dangerous if you live in **a flat which** is in a large high-rise building.*

◆ *that*来指人或物：
*Find **someone that** can check on your home while you're away.*
*Store away any **objects that** could become damaging missiles.*

在英语口语中，*that*常替代 *who*，*which*，并且更常见。
⚠ *That*不能用于非限定性关系从句中（如下）。

◆ *where*来指地方：
*This is your home, **the place where** you keep your most treasured possessions.*

◆ *when*来指时间：
*Programme them to come on at **times when** you would normally be home.*

◆ *whose*来表达所有：
*You're **a person whose job** involves a lot of travel.*
*He lives in **an old house**, **whose roof** needs repairing.*

◆ *why*在*the reason*或*reasons*后面：
*There are often very good **reasons why** one house is burgled and another is not.*

2 Defining relative clauses（限定性关系从句）

限定性关系从句在名词后面给出更清楚的限定名词的信息：
*Find someone **who can collect your mail for you**.*
*Store away any objects **that could become damaging missiles** if it gets windy.* (the relative clause identifies the type of objects)

没有这些关系从句，所指的人、地点或物都是不清楚的：
Store away any objects if it gets windy. (we do not know which objects)

当关系代词指的是限定性关系从句中的宾语时，可以省略。比较：

*Maybe there's a neighbour (**that**) you can ask.* (*neighbour* is the object of the verb)
*In the evening, a house **that**'s very dark can really stand out.* (*house* is the subject of the verb: **not** ~~a house is very dark can really stand out~~)

3 Non-defining relative clauses （非限定性关系从句）

非限定性关系从句给出有关事物的额外的、非根本性的信息。比较：

I applied to the university, which is located in the centre of the city. (there is only one university, so its location is extra information: non-defining)
I applied to the university which is located in the centre of the city. (there is another university which is not in the centre of the city: defining)

非限定性关系从句在书面英语中比在口语中更为常用。

非限定性关系从句

◆ 不使用关系代词 *that*；
  *The burglars got in through the kitchen window, **which** the owners had forgotten to shut.*
  (**not** ~~the kitchen window, that the owners~~)

◆ 关系从句可以用逗号将其与主要从句分割开来。可能有两个逗号或一个逗号，这取决于连词从句是出现在句子中间还是末尾：
  *A letterbox can become full of uncollected letters, **which is a great help to a burglar**.*
  *Mr Smith, **who was my primary school teacher**, got married last week.*

◆ 不能省略关系代词：
  *My new house, **which** I have just redecorated, is much larger than my old house.* (**not** ~~My new house, I have just redecorated~~)

◆ 关系代词可以指单独一个名词短语或整个从句：
  *My neighbour, **who** lives upstairs, often looks after my flat.* (*who* refers to my neighbour)
  *Some people seem to think it's just a matter of locking all the doors, **which** is fine as long as there are no nasty storms while you are away.* (*which* refers to the whole of the first phrase)

比较限定性关系从句与非限定性关系从句的关键性差异：

限定性关系从句	非限定性关系从句
◆ 限定你正在谈论的事物	◆ 给出附加的非本质信息
◆ *that* 可以替换 *who* 或 *which*	◆ 不能用 *that*
◆ 如果关系代词指的是宾语的话，可以省略	◆ 关系代词不可省略
◆ 无逗号	◆ 必须有逗号

4 Prepositions（介词）

当介词用于关系从句的时候，在口语中他们通常出现在从句的结尾：

*You may have a neighbour that you can rely **on**.* (informal)

在正式文体中，介词可以置于关系代词 *which* 或 *whom* 前：

*I was unsuccessful in obtaining a place at any of the universities **to which** I applied.*

*My boss, **for whom** I have worked for over 30 years, has decided to retire.*

Grammar extra: Common collocations with relative pronouns

我们经常用 *the one* 来限定关系从句：

*He's **the one who** suggested I became a teacher.*

*My father is **the one that** taught me to play the piano.*

*That house is **the one where** I grew up.*

Where 可用在 *the situation*, *the stage* 或 *the point* 等表达式后面：

*We were in **a situation where** there were no easy solutions.*

*I'm almost at **the stage where** I'm ready to quit my job and go into business for myself.*

*I've reached **the point where** I feel I should just give up.*

C Grammar exercises

1 Match the beginnings (1–10) and endings (a–j) of these sentences, and join them by adding a relative pronoun. In which two sentences can the relative pronoun be left out?

1 The college has many students ...who... ..d..

2 My cousin Phillip is a solicitor; he was the one ....

3 I went to a school ....

4 I visited the theatre ....

5 Why don't you call again at a time ....

6 Mrs Jackson is the kind of teacher ....

7 Faraday was the man ....

8 Is there any reason ....

9 What was the name of that company ....

10 That's the woman ....

a Mozart performed many of his operas.

b flat I rent.

c every student wants to have.

d are classed as 'mature' because they are over 21.

e advised me to study law.

f I'm not as busy.

g invented the first electric motor.

h factory burned down yesterday?

i didn't have very good sports facilities.

j manufacturers like to keep demand above supply?

2 Rewrite the sentences below as single sentences using non-defining relative clauses.

1 My father lives in a small house full of ornaments. This makes it really difficult to clean.
   My father lives in a small house full of ornaments, which makes it really difficult to clean.

2 Some students take a year out before university. This allows them to work or travel.
   Some students ....

3 The Guggenheim Museum is in Bilbao. It only displays contemporary art.
   The Guggenheim Museum, ...

4 My English teacher is leaving. His lectures are very interesting.
   My English teacher, ...

5 The lecture was about current economic policy. It was not very easy to understand.
   The lecture ....

6 In 1951 my parents arrived in New York. They stayed there for the rest of their lives.
   My parents arrived in New York ....

7 I gave my assignment to the faculty secretary. She was not very friendly.
   I gave my assignment ....

3 There is a mistake with relative clauses in each of the email extracts below. Find the mistakes and correct them.

1
> I wonder if you can help me. I want to get in touch with the woman which we met at the meeting last week. Do you know the one I mean?

........~~which~~ who........

2
> I'm sending this email to ask for more information about the language courses which I saw them advertised in *The Daily Star* yesterday.

....

3
> How are you getting on with your new job? I'm finding my new job exhausting, that is not surprising considering I have to travel so much.

....

4
> I really enjoyed the lecture which you gave it on Wednesday, and am thinking about doing my assignment on the same topic.

....

5
> You left your notebook at my house. Do you need it? It's the one which in you have written your lecture notes.

....

6
> I'm just emailing you to find out if you want to go to the cinema on Thursday. I've got today's newspaper which has a list of films. If you're free, let me know.

....

7
> Can you pick up some shopping on your way home? I want some of those bread rolls what we had last week. Will you be able to stop at the shop?

....

8
> You are clearly a person who life is full and busy and that is why we think you would like our *Ladies Personal Organiser*. For just £15.99 you ...

....

4 Read the description of how chocolate is made. Add the relative clauses (a–i) to the text in the gaps and write in the appropriate relative pronoun *where*, *which* or *that*.

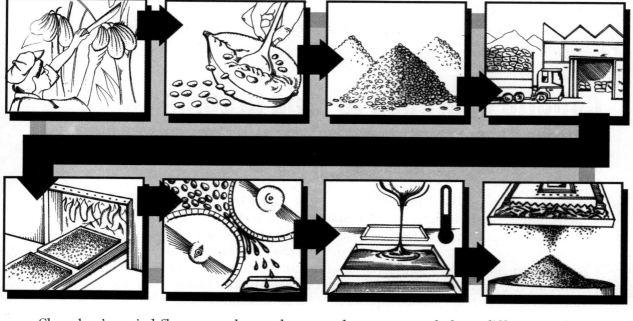

Chocolate's varied flavours, colours, shapes and textures result from different recipe traditions **1** ....g...... . The essential ingredient in all chocolate is cocoa, which is made from the cream-coloured beans **2** .... The cacao tree, **3** .... , produces a fruit about the size of a small pineapple, **4** ....

After harvesting, the cocoa beans are removed from the pods and piled in heaps **5** .... The dried beans are then transported to factories **6** .... The shells are then removed and the beans are ground into chocolate liquor – a thick brown liquid **7** .... This liquor contains a high percentage of fat (cocoa butter), **8** .... The solid block of cocoa that remains is then made into a powder **9** .... , or is mixed back with some of the cocoa butter, sugar and other flavour such as vanilla to make the different kinds of chocolate.

a .... is removed by using presses

b .... they are sorted and roasted

c .... are left for several days to dry

d .... can be used to make a hot chocolate drink

e .... grows in equatorial regions such as South America, Africa and Indonesia

f .... forms a solid at about room temperature

g ....which.... have evolved in different parts of the world

h inside .... are the tree's seeds

i .... grow in pods on the cacao tree

Academic Reading

*You should spend about 20 minutes on **Questions 1–12** which are based on the Reading Passage below.*

Robotic approach to crop breeding

Jennifer Manyweathers takes a look at a robot that is being used to identify drought-tolerant crop varieties

A The Australian sunflower industry is the major source of polyunsaturated fatty acids found in margarines and spreads. Recognised as the type of fatty acid most able to protect against heart disease, it is in everybody's best interest that Australia has a competitive and healthy sunflower industry, but in Australia there is a constant struggle with the harsh climate. However, thanks to one special robot, farmers may be able to win the battle against drought.

B Dr Chris Lambrides, a research fellow at the University of Queensland, is nearing the end of a project that aims to develop more drought-tolerant sunflowers by selecting flowers that use water more efficiently. He's done this with the help of a robot developed by the Australian National University's Research School of Biological Sciences.

C Plants undergo photosynthesis to produce energy in the form of sugar. This involves allowing carbon dioxide to enter the leaves through pores called stomata. Transpiration is the mechanism by which plants lose water through their leaves. This system is thought to facilitate the passage of minerals through the plant and is vital for healthy plants.

D However, in conditions of drought, the plants that can use the available water efficiently and lose less to the environment will be more likely to thrive and, in a commercial sense become more profitable. These plants are classified as having a high transpiration efficiency. When plants transpire, the leaves become cooler due to evaporation. Therefore, by measuring the temperature of the leaves, scientists can determine how much water is being lost through transpiration.

E   When the project first began, the researchers used hand-held infrared thermometers to measure the temperature difference between leaves of different varieties of sunflowers in an experimental plot. Wind can affect leaf temperature, and the research team discovered that its initial approach did not cater for changes in wind speed, which could not be controlled as an experimental variable. The team therefore needed a technique to measure temperature continuously that would allow it to examine the effects of other variables such as humidity. They needed a robot.

F   They designed a robot with two infrared thermometers set at 180° to each other. The robot runs on an oblong track around the experimental plot and the thermometers operate on each side of the track. In order to minimize any variables from the two thermometers, they are rotated 180° at the beginning of each run and the results are averaged. The infrared thermometers can be rotated on an angle to examine different parts of the foliage.

G   The robot is also able to detect light intensity. It has a garage on the track, where it waits until the light intensity is high enough to give useful results. If the skies darken due to rain, heavy cloud cover or sunset, the robot makes its way back to the garage to wait.

H   The main difficulty faced by the research group was to find an agronomist who could grow the perfect crop of sunflowers. The sunflower canopy had to be complete, with no visible soil, so that the thermometers would only measure the temperature of the plants and not the surrounding environment. Eight varieties of sunflower were examined. The data collected by the robot has been used by the research team to determine which variety has the highest transpiration efficiency.

I   This is not the first time such methods have been used to determine drought-resistance in plants. The team and their robot have already made a major breakthrough in the Australian wheat industry with Drysdale Wheat, which signalled the arrival of a new technique for selecting drought-resistant species.

Questions 1–4

Complete the sentences with words taken from the passage.

*Use **NO MORE THAN TWO WORDS** for each answer.*

Write your answers next to Questions 1–4.

1 In terms of our health, sunflowers are important in defending humans against

....

2 The research team wanted to find a sunflower that could cope well in .... conditions.

3 The name of the process which is believed to help keep plants in good condition is

....

4 The research team had to rethink their initial approach when they realised they needed to measure the impact of external conditions such as .... and ....

Questions 5–12

*The reading passage has nine paragraphs labelled **A–I**.*

Which paragraph contains the following information?

*Write the correct letter **A–I** next to Questions 5–12.*

5 the precise growing conditions required to allow the experiment to work

6 a description of the how the robot operates

7 an explanation of two important processes used by plants

8 a reference to a previous study using a different crop

9 details of what the robot does when conditions are poor

10 the name of the group responsible for making the robot

11 the number of different types of sunflower tested

12 the purpose of taking the temperature of the plants

Look at these extracts from the text. For each extract answer the following questions.

1 Do they contain defining or non-defining relative clauses?
2 Which words or ideas do the relative pronouns refer to?
3 Does the relative pronoun act as the subject or the object of the verb?

1 Dr Chris Lambrides, a research fellow at the University of Queensland, is nearing the end of a project that aims to develop more drought-tolerant sunflowers by selecting flowers that use water more efficiently.

2 ... the research team discovered that its initial approach did not cater for changes in wind speed, which could not be controlled as an experimental variable.

3 It has a garage on the track, where it waits until the light intensity is high enough to give useful results.

4 The main difficulty faced by the research group was to find an agronomist who could grow the perfect crop of sunflowers.

5 The team and their robot have already made a major breakthrough in the Australian wheat industry with Drysdale Wheat, which signalled the arrival of a new technique for selecting drought-resistant species.

21 Ways of organising texts
subject choice; introductory *it*; ellipsis;
organising information; *it-* and *what-*clauses

A Context listening

1 You are going to listen to a student interviewing a woman for a survey on shopping habits. Look at these questions. How would you answer them?

> Do you live alone?

> Do you always shop at the same place?

> **Super Market**

> How many times a week do you do the shopping?

> Do you always shop on the same day?

2 ⌂ 21 Listen and compare your answers with the woman in the interview.

3 21◄ Listen again and fill in the gaps. <u>Underline</u> the subject of each verb.

1 'No, ... with my family – my husband and three children.'

2 'And how many times a week .... the food shopping?'

3 'Oh, ... it on my own. If .... with the others, ...
too many things in the trolley and .... me a fortune!'

4 '........................... the food shopping on Thursdays because .... Monday to
Wednesday and .... fewer people in the supermarket on Thursday than on
Friday.'

5 'Well, ... it once but .... it.'
'And .... you why not?'
'Well, what I like is being able to see the products and walking around the shop and
maybe buying things that aren't on my shopping list, you know. .... do
that on your computer, can you?'

4 Now read part of the student's written report. What is the difference between the kinds
of words that are used as subjects in the spoken text in Exercise 3 and the <u>underlined</u>
words that are used as subjects in the written report?

Nowadays <u>people</u> appear to do their shopping on a weekly basis at large supermarkets. <u>These
supermarkets</u> seem to have largely replaced the smaller, individual shops. <u>Most people</u> tend to go to the
same store on the same day of the week and, according to my survey results, it is still the women who
do most of the shopping. In general, <u>the people who were interviewed</u> were not positive about online
shopping. However, it is important to note that <u>the respondents</u> were interviewed at the supermarket
and were not a random sample of the general public.

B Grammar

Ways of organising texts（组织文章的方式）

1 The subject（主语）
我们根据上下文来选择不同种类的词作主语。

在非正式场合（如对话中），主语经常是 *I*，*you*，*we* 等人称代词：
*'First **I** need to ask about your household. Do **you** live alone?'*
*'No, **I** live with my family.'*

在正式背景（如学术写作）中的主语经常是名词或名词短语，这样使消息听上去更像是事实而非人为：
Most people tend to go to the same store on the same day of the week each time.

The introductory *it*
当代词并不指任何一个名词（如*it is important*，*it is clear*，*it is possible*，*it is difficult*，*it is likely*，*it seems*，*it appears*）时，经常可以用以*it*开头的表达。当句子主语是不定式，*-ing*或*that*从句时，可以用引导词*it*。这种结构在书面语中比在口语中更常见：
***It is important to note** that these respondents were interviewed at the supermarket.* (**not** ~~To note that these respondents were interviewed at the supermarket is important.~~)
***It is clear that** women do most of the shopping.* (**not** ~~That women do most of the shopping is clear.~~)

2 Ellipsis: leaving words out（省略）
可以省略动词的主语以避免重复。任何其他重复的词语如助动词或其他动词也是一样：
The respondents were interviewed at the supermarket and (they) were not a random sample of the general public.
The students were researching and (they were) planning their seminar presentations.

3 Organising information in a text（组织文章信息）
在正式写作中，我们经常用前面已经提到的信息来做从句或句子的开头，将新的信息放在从句或句子的末尾。为了用一种有组织的并且合乎逻辑的方式展开文章，可以用从句末尾的信息作为下一句的开头。这种Z字型模式在学术写作中非常常见，用以开始并发展新的观念。

新信息
*People appear to do their shopping on a weekly basis at **large supermarkets**.*

***These supermarkets** seem to have largely replaced **the smaller, individual shops**.*
前面提过的信息　　　　　　　　　　　　新信息

第一句中的新信息在第二句中就成为已知信息了。

4 Adding emphasis or contrast in a text（在文章中加入强调和对比）

可以用 *it*-从句和 *what*-从句来强调或突出直接跟在它们后面的信息。

It-clauses

> it +be +主要强调的内容+关系从句   *It is still **the women who** do most of the shopping.*

比较下列句子：
The women still do most of the household shopping at local supermarkets. (no emphasis)
*It is still **the women who** do most of the household shopping at local supermarkets.* (emphasizes the women)

⚠ We cannot say: ~~They are still the women who do most of the shopping.~~

What-clauses

> what + 次要强调的内容 + be + 主要强调的内容   *What I like is being able to see the products.*

比较下列句子：
I like seeing the products.
What I like is seeing the products. (highlights being able to see products in contrast with online shopping where you can't see products)
正常情况下*what*-从句后面用单数动词。

5 Repeating ideas in a text（在文中重点观念）

可以在文中使用近义词来连接观念。这些近义词可以是：

◆ 代词：
   Most people tend to go to the same store on the same day of the week each time, and *they* spend between £100 and £200 a week on their household shopping. (they = most people)

◆ 同义词或改说：
   These *supermarkets* seem to have largely replaced the smaller, individual shops. Most people tend to go to the same store on the same day of the week each time. (supermarket = store)

（更多避免重复的信息，可参照Unit 9。）

C Grammar exercises

1 Rewrite sentences 1–8 using *it-* or *what*-clauses to emphasize the underlined words.

1 I find <u>writing essays</u> really difficult.
   What <u>I find really difficult is writing essays.</u>

2 The government needs <u>a lot more loyal supporters</u>.
   What ....

3 We don't want words. We want <u>action</u>.
   We don't want words. What ....

4 I really like reading novels. I don't enjoy <u>watching TV</u>.
   I really like reading novels. What ....

5 In my country <u>the bride</u> is the most important person at a wedding.
   In my country it ....

6 Governments should be dealing with <u>the causes of poverty</u>, not the results of it.
   It ....

7 I first decided to study medicine <u>when I was ill in hospital as a child</u>.
   It ....

8 When you are seriously ill <u>your family</u> suffer the most.
   When you are seriously ill it ....

2 Look at the sentences from the first paragraph of an essay answering this question.
   'The camera has changed the way we look at the world and the way that we celebrate special occasions.' To what extent do you agree with this statement?

The beginnings of the sentences are mixed up, but the endings are in the correct order. Match the beginnings (a–g) to the endings (1–7).

a Unfortunately, <u>this</u> can often interfere   ..d..   1 has brought many changes to our lives.

b However, it is also true that the   ....   2 the way we see and experience the world.
   photographs record the event   ....   3 and use <u>it</u> to create photographic
                                                     records of their experiences.
c But has the photograph become

(d) The invention of the camera   ....   4 more important than the event or
                                                     experience it is recording?
e On important occasions such as weddings,

f One of <u>these</u> is   ....   5 cameras often have a primary role.

g Most adults in this country have a camera   ....   6 with the enjoyment of the occasion.
   these days   ....   7 so that in can be remembered in the future.

Look at the <u>underlined</u> words. What do they refer back to?

3 Fill in the gaps with a subject from the box.

A one kilowatt solar panel	a solar roof
~~Global energy consumption~~	Many countries
Solar panels, solar water heaters and wind generators	the government
These renewable energy systems	they
This rise	

The Future of Energy

A look at the challenge of providing the world with energy without damaging the environment.

1 _Global energy consumption_ is predicted to rise nearly sixty per cent in the next twenty years. 2 .... is due to factors such as population growth, urbanization, and economic and industrial expansion.

3 .... have set themselves renewable energy targets, hoping to be able to generate a proportion of the electricity by such renewable means as wind or solar power. On a cloudy day in Britain 4 .... can generate enough electricity for the household to play 140 hours of TV and make 35 cups of tea. 5 .... saves up to a ton of CO_2 emissions each year. 6 .... all help to provide alternative sources of energy for private homes and 7 .... are no longer prohibitively expensive. 8 .... can make savings for householders in the long run, and in Britain 9 .... is providing financial help with the cost of installing them.

4 Read the test task and the model answer. A teacher has <u>underlined</u> the problem areas and written comments. Write the corrections below.

Many health problems in adults such as obesity and heart disease can be linked to poor diet. Research shows that it is important to encourage healthy eating patterns at an early age in order to avoid ill-health as an adult.

What action can be taken to encourage children to eat more healthily?

1 <u>To educate our children about healthy eating and physical exercise is important</u>. Children need to learn what to eat and **2** <u>children need to experience</u> eating a wider variety of foods.	**1** grammar problem **2** avoid repetition
Packed lunches which are produced by the same person every day tend to contain the same food items every day too and also **3** <u>these foods tend not</u> to be the healthy option. Very often the contents of children's lunch boxes are crisps, sweets and biscuits.	**3** avoid repetition
In order to prevent the problems associated with poor diet, such as obesity and heart disease in adulthood, parents need to encourage their children to eat a greater variety of healthier foods. **4** <u>The lack of experience of eating different kinds of foods often</u> leads to poor diet in adults. Experiencing a wider variety of foods can lead to a more rounded and nutritious diet and **5** <u>experiencing a wider variety of foods can therefore lead</u> to better health.	**4** add emphasis **5** avoid repetition
6 <u>To provide support and help to parents is important</u>. One way to do this is to implement a system whereby all children get the same food. **7** <u>No child would feel ashamed or embarrassed by the contents of their lunch boxes with this system</u>. Although difficult to achieve, this would control the foods that all children ate, thereby ensuring a healthy diet. **8** <u>Eating a healthy diet</u> as a child undoubtedly has a huge influence on how healthy we are as adults.	**6** grammar problem **7** try starting with 'This system ...' **8** avoid repetition

1 .....It is important to educate our children about healthy eating and physical exercise.....

2 ....

3 ....

4 ....

5 ....

6 ....

7 ....

8 ....

D Test practice

Academic Writing Task 2

You should spend about 40 minutes on this task.

Write about the following topic:

> *Children today play very violent games. This must be the reason for the increase in violence and crime in most major cities of the world.*
>
> *What are your opinions on this?*

Give reasons for your answer and include any relevant examples from your own knowledge or experience.

Write at least 250 words.

Grammar focus task

Put the sentences of the first paragraph of this model answer in the correct order. What is the new information in each sentence?

.... These games have become more violent over the past few years.

.... Some are concerned that playing violent games might encourage them to become aggressive in real life.

1
.... Nowadays most children regularly play games on a computer or on their television.

.... What we need to establish is whether or not this is actually true.

.... In fact, many parents worry about this and the effect these games are having on their children.

A   Context listening

1 You are going to hear a student representative talking to new students and answering their questions. Before you listen, match the words (1–8) with the definitions (a–h).

1 union
2 president
3 process (*verb*)
4 represent
5 run (*verb*)
6 election
7 committee
8 facilities

a deal with / handle documentation etc.
b speak for
c buildings, equipment or services
d leader
e working group or board
f organised group or association
g organise/manage
h an organised vote

2 🎧 22 Listen and answer the following questions.

1 What do new students need to do to get a library card?

....

2 What is the students' union?

....

3 What is the students' union responsible for?

....

3 22◀◀ Listen again and fill in the gaps.

Questions

1 '............................. applications quite quickly?'

2 'So, ... the student's union?'

3 'And how .... the executive committee?'

Answers

'Oh, yes. All applications ....
on the spot so they'll be able to issue you a card straight away.'

'No, the union .... by students, seven students to be precise.'

'Well, the executive committee ....
by the students through an election process.'

4 Look at the objects of the verbs in the questions in Exercise 3. What happens to them in the answers?

B Grammar

1 The passive: form （被动态：形式）

主动态表达的是某物正在做什么。被动态表达的是什么事发生在某物上面。动词的被动态可由 *be*+过去分词构成。

Tense	Passive form: *be* + past participle (+ *by* + agent)
present simple	→ *The union **is run** by 7 executive officers.*
present continuous	→ *The union **is being run** by 7 executive officers.*
past simple	→ *The union **was run** by 7 executive officers.*
past continuous	→ *The union **was being run** by 7 executive officers.*
present perfect	→ *The union **has been run** by 7 executive officers.*
past perfect	→ *The union **had been run** by 7 executive officers.*
going to	→ *The union **is going to be run** by 7 executive officers.*
will	→ *The union **will be run** by 7 executive officers.*
Other forms	
infinitive	→ *The union **is to be run** by 7 executive officers.*
-ing form	→ *The university insists on the union **being run** by 7 executive officers.*
used to	→ *The university **used to be run** by 7 executive officers.*
modals	→ *The university **should be run** by 7 executive officers.*
need to / have to	→ *The university **needs to/has to be run** by 7 executive officers.*
need + -ing	→ *The university **needs running** by 7 executive officers.*

⚠ 不及物动词不能用被动态（后面不能跟宾语的动词）连用。
he arrived (**not** *he was arrived*)

2 The passive: use （被动态：用法）

在以下情形用被动态
- 当宾语比主语更重要，施动者或很明显、不重要或不为人知：
  ***All applications are processed** on the spot.* (it is obvious that it is the library staff who process the cards)
- 在正式写作中使其较少出现人格化：
  ***You are advised** to return the application form within three days.* (impersonal)

  主动态更加直接和人格化：
  ***I advise you** to return the application form within three days.*

- 当描述一个过程时：
  *The union **is run** by seven executive officers who **are elected** by students.*

  ⚠ 自然（或生物）过程一般不能使用被动态；上述情况下，人并没有涉及在里面（如，碳循环）：
  *Plants **take up** carbon dioxide from the air as part of photosynthesis.*

注意：如果我们想在下一句中重复前面从句或句子的结尾，该怎么做呢。这时，也许需要用被动态：

Does the university run the union?

No, the union is run by seven executive officers

who are elected by students each year.

The executive officers are held accountable by the union council.

The council is also elected by the student population.

这种模式是典型的学术性写作。

3 Reporting with passive verbs

转述动词和表达想法或感受的动词，可以用

◆ *It* + 被动态动词 + *that* (e.g. *agree, announce, argue, believe, claim, decide, disclose, expect, feel, hope, know, predict, recognize, report, say, suggest, think, understand*):
It was felt that the facilities were in need of renovation.

◆ 主语 + 被动态动词 + *to*-不定式 (e.g. *ask, believe, consider, estimate, expect, feel, know, mean, report, say, see, suppose, think, understand*):
Our sports facilities are said to be among the best in the country. (= people say our sports facilities are among the best in the country)
This building is believed to be the oldest in the town.

4 Have something done

要表达某人给我们提供了有偿服务，可以用 *have* + 宾语 + 过去分词：
You'll need to have your photo taken. (= someone else will take your photograph)

在非正式英语中，也可以使用 *get* + 过去分词形式：
I got my photo taken yesterday.

5 Need + -ing

有时候可以用 *need* + *-ing* 来替代被动态，意思是说有必要做某事而不必说出将由谁来做：
Some facilities need improving around the campus. (= it is necessary to improve some facilities)

C Grammar exercises

1 Read the test task. Fill in the gaps in the model answer with the verbs in the box in the passive.

The flowchart below shows how banana chips are made.
Summarise the information by selecting and reporting the main features and make comparisons where relevant.

| add | distribute | fry | leave | ~~make~~ | peel | put | remove | rinse | sell | slice | soak |

The flowchart shows how banana chips **1** .....*are made*..... . First, the bananas **2** ....

by a special machine and then they **3** .... in water. Next the clean bananas

4 .... into a chipping machine where they **5** .... into thin chips. After this

they **6** .... Once they are dry, the banana chips **7** .... in hot oil in large

deep fat fryers. The cooked banana chips **8** .... from the fryers using a special sieve

which allows all of the oil to drain off. The banana chips **9** .... (then) to cool. When they

have reached the right temperature, spices **10** .... for extra taste. Finally the banana

chips are packaged ready to **11** .... around the world and **12** ....

2 There are 12 mistakes with active or passive verbs in this conversation. Find and correct the mistakes.

Teacher: People <u>are said</u> that the increase in travel will lead to a loss of different cultures around the world. Do you agree?

Student: Well, yes, I suppose that is a possibility. I'm sure the way of life of many people around the world has changed by contact with tourists. But the change might have been happened anyway, I suppose.

Teacher: Yes, maybe. So, do you think we should try to stop the disappearance of native cultures?

Student: Oh, yes. I think it will be very sad if we lose different cultures. They enrich our world, don't they? But it is also argued that many people from poor countries have given opportunities that they wouldn't have had if there wasn't any tourism. Their cultures may have changed, but they have been benefited from improvements in education and health as well as their standard of living.

Teacher: So do you think that improvements like this inevitably bring about a loss of culture, as some people have been suggested?

Student: I suppose I do think that, yes. As we are continued to be provided with better and better education and we have more and more contact with the world outside our own countries, we are being become more and more the same!

Teacher: Can you give some examples of what you mean?

Student: Well, in my country we now have American restaurants and we watch American movies on TV. American culture feels to be too dominant by many people in my country. And English words have been come into my language too.

Teacher: Oh, that's interesting. And do you think that there will one day be only one language in the world?

Student: Well, the way we live has affected in a big way by things like the Internet, email and cheap travel. All countries are using English for these things, and so we all know a little bit of English already. But I am not sure it will use by all countries instead of their own language. That seems unlikely to me.

Teacher: You've made some very interesting points. Thank you.

1 ....say....... 4 .... 7 .... 10 ....

2 .... 5 .... 8 .... 11 ....

3 .... 6 .... 9 .... 12 ....

3 Fill in the gaps with an appropriate form of the verb in brackets.

1 For a long time people ......thought..... (*think*) the giant panda was a type of raccoon.

2 At the beginning of the experiment, the chemicals .... (*place*) in the beaker.

3 In medieval times the earth .... (*believe*) to be flat.

4 Up until now students .... (*allow*) to wear what they want, but the new head-teacher has decided to introduce a uniform.

5 I can't drive you to the airport because my car .... (*service*) tomorrow.

6 Next year the new theatre .... (*open*) by some of Britain's biggest acting stars.

7 It .... (*expect*) that the President will resign due to the recent revelations.

8 Chocolate .... (*make*) from the bean of the cacao tree.

9 This report .... (*claim*) that there is corruption throughout the company.

10 Several students .... (*know*) to have cheated in their exams.

11 People need .... (*encourage*) to use public transport if we want to reduce our carbon emissions.

12 I went on holiday because I really needed .... (*take*) a break.

4 Underline the correct words.

> **Air pollution in cities is growing at an alarming rate. What measures could be taken to address this problem?**

Air pollution can **1** define / be defined as the addition of something harmful to the air at a faster rate than it can **2** absorb / be absorbed. Everyone should be concerned about air pollution. It **3** affects / is affected us all, and as it **4** continues / is continued to worsen, so the environmental impact increases.

One of the major causes of air pollution in cities is car use. Cars **5** use / are used for even the shortest of journeys, and all efforts by governments to encourage people **6** to use / to be used public transport seem to be failing. Industry is another major cause of pollution in our cities, but fortunately, new industrial sites **7** are building / are being built away from large urban centres.

It **8** says / is said that there are too many contributing factors for us to **9** to decide / to be decided exactly which one is the main problem, but I believe that one of the most serious problems that needs **10** to tackle / tackling is the use of the car. In some cities laws **11** have passed / have been passed concerning car use. Athens, for example, only **12** allows / is allowed a certain number of cars into the city centre each day. In my opinion, this is a good idea. With this kind of law, people have no choice and **13** force / are forced to use buses and trains. This ensures governments **14** know / is known that public transport **15** will use / will be used, and can therefore justify the investment and expense of ensuring the system works properly.

Another thing governments could do is to force people to **16** have their cars checked / check their cars for carbon emissions and fine people with cars that produce high levels of harmful gases.

D Test practice

Academic Writing Task 1

You should spend 20 minutes on this task.

The diagram shows how fruit is canned.
Summarise the information by selecting and reporting the main features, and make comparisons where relevant.

You should write at least 150 words.

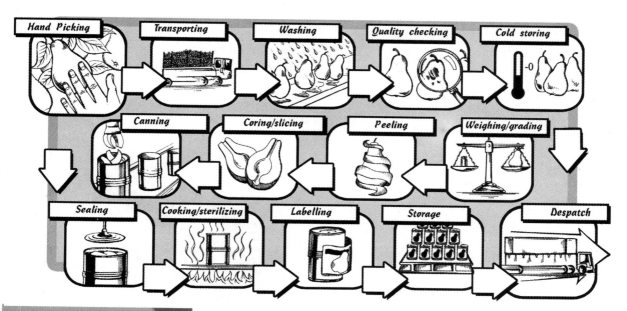

Grammar focus task

Look at these sentences describing the flowchart. Rewrite them using a passive verb. Then put the sentences in the correct order according to the flowchart.

1 They allow the cans to cool.
   Passive: ....

2 They sterilize the cans using a special heating process.
   Passive: ....

3 They take the fruit to the cannery in large trucks.
   Passive: ....

4 They check the fruit before storage and they reject any poor quality fruit.
   Passive: ....

Now write your own answer.

23 Linking ideas
conjunctions, adverbials and prepositions;
linking expressions

A Context listening

1 You are going to hear a student presenting a report on eating fish. Before you listen, match the words (1–9) to the definitions (a–i).

1	staple (*adj*)	a	advantages and disadvantages
2	controversy	b	be greater than
3	benefits and risks	c	main / basic
4	consumption	d	a heavy silver metal
5	mercury	e	harmful to the body
6	poisonous	f	contact with
7	dose	g	disagreement
8	exposure to	h	amount
9	outweigh	i	eating

2 🎧23 Listen and say whether these statements are true or false.

1 Eating fish might be bad for the heart.
2 Eating fish is good for the growth of the brain.
3 Some fish may contain a poison.
4 The Fisheries Scholarship funded this student's project.
5 The Fisheries Scholarship influenced the results of the study.
6 Comprehensive information is available about the pros and cons of eating fish.
7 The research noticed strong negative effects on the brain from the mercury contained in fish.
8 The student concludes that it is better for one's health to avoid eating fish.

3 Fill in the gaps in the extract from the talk with the words from the box.
23◄◄ Listen to the second half of the recording again and check your answers.

| although | despite | finally | firstly | however | in spite of |
| secondly | to sum up |

We discovered that, **1** .... the literature available on the risks and benefits of fish consumption, there are still important gaps in this information. **2** .... these gaps, **3** ...., decisions about how to advise people on fish consumption should be made based on what we know now.

4 ...., in terms of heart disease, it has been shown that consuming even small quantities of fish can lower your risk of heart disease by 17%. **5** ...., consuming fish is known to have a beneficial effect on brain development. **6** ...., **7** .... exposure to mercury through eating fish can have a negative effect on IQ levels, the effects that have been observed are relatively small.

8 ...., it would seem that the health benefits of eating fish outweigh the risks.

4 Which of the words in the box is used:

1 to show contrast? ....

2 to give one idea in a list of ideas? ....

3 to introduce the conclusion? ....

23

B Grammar

1 Ways of linking ideas（连接观念的形式）

我们用连词（如*but*，*because*）来连接一个句子中的两个从句：

clause 1 | clause 2

Fish has long been a staple food in many cultures, **but** *there has been some controversy recently about the benefits and risks of fish consumption.*

clause 1 | clause 2

Fish is known as a 'brain food' **because** *it is beneficial to the development of the brain.*

我们可以用副词表达式（如*consequently*，*however*）连接两个单独的句子的观念。它们通常在句子或从句的开头：

Fish is known as a 'brain food' because of the benefits it has for brain development. **However**, *recent studies have shown that fish can also contain mercury.*

有些副词表达式可以放在句中不同的位置：

People **therefore** *are unsure of whether to eat fish.*
People are **therefore** *unsure of whether to eat fish.*
People are unsure **therefore** *of whether to eat fish.*

我们可以在名词短语或-*ing*形式前使用介词（如*in spite of*，*because of*）：

The match was cancelled **because of the snow**. (**not** ~~because of it snowed~~)
In spite of *losing the first game, the team went on to win the tournament.*

2 Linking expressions（连接表达式）

Adding information

conjunctions:	*and*, *as well as*
adverbials:	*also*, *anyway*, *besides*, *furthermore*, *in addition*, *likewise*, *moreover*, *similarly*

我们用这些表达式给出附加信息：

Fish supplies us with substances that might protect against heart disease. **Moreover**, *in many cultures fish is known as a 'brain food'.*

Sequencing

adverbials: *first*, *next*, *after that*, *then*; *firstly*, *secondly*, *finally*

Firstly, *secondly*和*finally*用于排列论证中的要点：
Firstly, *in terms of heart disease, it has been shown that consuming even small quantities of fish can lower your risk of heart disease by 17%.* **Secondly**, *consuming fish is known to have a beneficial effect on brain development.* **Finally**, ...

First, *next*, *after*和*then*描述了进程中的活动顺序：
First *the fruit is picked by hand.* **Then** *it is transported to the factory.*

Cause, reason, result

> **conjunctions:** *because, so*
> **adverbials:** *therefore, consequently, so, thus, as a result*
> **prepositions:** *because of, due to, on account of, owing to*

Because 引出某事的原因，*so* 引出结果：

reason

*I eat fish three times a week **because** <u>it protects against heart disease</u>.*

result

*Fish protects against heart disease **so** <u>I eat it three times a week</u>.*

Therefore, consequently, so, thus 以及 *as a result* 引出某事的结果或行为：
***As a result**, people are unsure whether to increase or decrease the amount of fish they eat.*
可以用 *because of, due to, on account to* 和 *owing to* 来引出某事的原因在
*The match was cancelled **because of** the snow. (**not** ~~because of it was snowing~~)*
*The buses were all running late **owing to** the bad weather.*

⚠️ 可以用 *due to, on account to* 和 *owing to* + *the fact that* 带从句：
*The match was cancelled **due to the fact that** it was snowing.*

Contrasting

> **conjunctions:** *but, although, though*
> **adverbials:** *alternatively, however, in contrast, nevertheless, on the contrary, on the other hand, yet*
> **prepositions:** *in spite of, despite*

两个相反的观念之间我们用 *but*：
*Fish has long been a staple food in many cultures, **but** there has been some controversy recently about the benefits and risks of fish consumption.*

Although 可以出现 两相反观念的开头或中间。两个从句之间用逗号：
***Although** the work was supported by grants from the Fisheries Scholarship Fund, this did not affect the research findings.*
*The work was supported by grants from the Fisheries Scholarship Fund, **although** this did not affect the research findings.*

in spite of 和 *despite* +名词 / -*ing* 可以用在 相反观念的开头或中间：
***In spite of the considerable amount** of literature on the risks and benefits of fish consumption, there are still important gaps in this information. (**not** ~~in spite of there is a considerable amount~~)*
*I eat fish regularly for health reasons **despite not** lik**ing** it much. (**not** ~~despite I don't like it~~)*

⚠️ 可以用 *despite* 和 *in spite of* + *the fact that* 带从句：
*I eat fish regularly for health reasons **despite the fact that** I don't like it much.*

201

Giving examples

> **adverbials:** *that is to say, in other words, that is (i.e.), for example*

我们用这些表达式来连接两个用不同方式给出同样信息的从句或给出例子：
*There has been some controversy recently about the benefits and risks of fish consumption. **For example**, we know that fish supplies us with polyunsaturated fatty acids, substances that might protect against heart disease.*

Grammar extra: Written and spoken English

有些连接表达式在书面（正式）语或口语中更为常用。

书面语：*thus, therefore, finally, furthermore, hence, moreover, nevertheless, in addition, firstly, secondly, finally*
*Regular comsumption of fish can lower your risk of heart disease by 17%. **Furthermore**, it can have a beneficial effect on brain development.*

口语：*so, then, anyway*
*Eating fish is good for you **so** I try to eat it regularly.*

C Grammar exercises

1 Choose the best endings for these sentences.

1 I hurt my knee quite badly so

(a) I had to go to hospital.   b I didn't have the right running shoes.

2 One way to improve your health is to eat more fruit and vegetables. Alternatively,

a you could increase your risk of heart disease.   b you could exercise more.

3 Humans like to form social groups. Likewise,

a many other mammals live independently of each other.

b many other mammals live together in small communities.

4 I didn't work hard at school. Consequently,

a I did well at university.   b I failed most of my exams.

5 I believe travelling can help us to understand other cultures. Furthermore,

a it can help you to become more independent.

b it can be a lonely experience at times.

6 In spite of the fact that learning to speak a foreign language requires a lot of time and effort,

a many people give up after a short time.   b many people manage it successfully.

7 In my experience, vegetarians tend to be quite healthy. In contrast,

a many meat-eaters do not have a healthy diet.   b they look after their bodies well.

8 Fifty per cent of all newspaper readers in this country only read the sports section of the paper. In other words,

a many people are not interested in news.

b sports are reported very well in the newspaper.

9 Sydney is the biggest city in Australia, yet

a it isn't the capital.   b it is the oldest city.

10 You wouldn't be allowed to drive in my country because

a there is no point in getting a car.   b you need to be over 21.

11 Studies suggest that although sales of cookery books have increased significantly in the past five years,

a we spend less time than ever in the kitchen.   b we enjoy experimenting.

12 There are delays on all trains due to the fact that

a passengers should allow extra time.   b there is a shortage of drivers.

2 Underline the correct linking expressions.

> *It is generally accepted that smoking causes the deaths of large numbers of people. In order to address this problem governments should ban smoking in public places.*
>
> *To what extent do you agree or disagree with this statement?*

Many people think that the best way to reduce deaths from smoking is to ban smoking in public places. **1** However, / In addition, it is not as simple as that. There are several reasons why I do not consider this approach to be suitable.

2 Alternatively, / Firstly, banning activities often increases their popularity by making them seem more exciting. **3** Furthermore, / In contrast, most smoking takes place in the privacy of people's homes, and would **4** therefore / nevertheless not be affected by the ban. **5** Thirdly, / Similarly, a ban on smoking would make extra demands on the police.

6 Although / Despite the ideas behind banning smoking in public places are good, an alternative approach needs to be taken, in my opinion. Schools should lead the way in discussing the harmful effects of smoking not only on the smokers themselves but on others around them. **7** In addition, / Consequently, parents need to support these efforts by encouraging their children to understand the negative aspects of smoking.

If we adopted these measures, I believe fewer people would take up smoking **8** as a result / moreover. To some extent these things are already happening. **9** And / Nevertheless, further efforts are needed.

3 Fill in the gaps with the linking expressions in the box.

as a result	because	but	firstly	for example	however	~~moreover~~	similarly

1 Regular exercise increases the blood flow to your heart and keeps your heart healthy. ....*Moreover*...., it provides you with a general sense of well-being.

2 In times of recession people stop spending, which can have serious consequences for the economy. .... , poor sales can lead to closures of some businesses.

3 In this talk I will outline several possible reasons for melting polar ice caps. .... , it could be because of climate change. Another reason could be ...

4 These days many famous musicians are getting involved in political causes. .... , famous actors are often seen on television promoting some charity or other.

5 Pets can have a calming effect on their owners. .... , having a pet can increase stress due to the demands made on the owner to look after the pet properly.

6 Some people believe that we have too many public holidays, ... I believe they are a good idea .... it is important to find time to celebrate traditions.

7 In my city there are too many cars on the road and there are always traffic jams. .... , it is difficult for people to judge how long their journeys will take.

4 Write one or two sentences with a similar meaning to the sentences below, using the words in brackets and any other words you need.

1 Despite the rise in profits this year, our company is still losing money. (*although*)
   Although there has been a rise in profits this year, our company is still losing money.

2 The head of my department called an emergency meeting so I had to cancel all of my afternoon appointments. (*because*)

....

3 It is now much cheaper to rent a DVD at home so fewer people are going to the cinema these days. (*due to*)

....

4 The cost of basic foods has risen because petrol prices increased last month. (*As a result*)

....

5 Although there are over 30 girls on this course, the boys still outnumber the girls by two to one. (*but*)

....

6 Although there are some advantages to the pace of modern life, it also has its disadvantages. (*However*)

....

7 The numbers of red deer in the wild increased slightly in the 1980s, although the increase was not sufficient to take them off the endangered species list. (*in spite of*)

....

Academic Reading

You should spend about 20 minutes on **Questions 1–12** which are based on the Reading Passage below.

Experience versus *speed*

Certain mental functions slow down with age, but the brain compensates in ways that can keep seniors as sharp as youngsters.

Jake, aged 16, has a terrific relationship with his grandmother Rita, who is 70. They live close by, and they even take a Spanish class together twice a week at a local college. After class they sometimes stop at a café for a snack. On one occasion Rita tells Jake, 'I think it's great how fast you pick up new grammar. It takes me a lot longer.' Jake replies, 'Yeah, but you don't seem to make as many silly mistakes on the quizzes as I do. How do you do that?'

In that moment, Rita and Jake stumbled across an interesting set of differences between older and younger minds. Popular psychology says that as people age their brains 'slow down'. The implication, of course, is that elderly men and women are not as mentally agile as middle-aged adults or even teenagers. However, although certain brain functions such as perception and reaction time do indeed take longer, that slowing down does not necessarily undermine mental sharpness. Indeed, evidence shows that older people are just as mentally fit as younger people because their brains compensate for some kinds of declines in creative ways that young minds do not exploit.

Just as people's bodies age at different rates, so do their minds. As adults advance in age, the perception of sights, sounds and smells takes a bit longer, and laying down new information into memory becomes more difficult. The ability to retrieve memories also quickly slides and it is sometimes harder to concentrate and maintain attention.

On the other hand, the ageing brain can create significant benefits by tapping into its extensive hoard of accumulated knowledge and experience. The biggest trick that older brains employ is to use both hemispheres simultaneously to handle tasks for which younger brains rely predominantly on one side. Electronic images taken by cognitive scientists at the University of Michigan, for example, have demonstrated that even when doing basic recognition or memorization exercises, seniors exploit the left and right side of the brain more extensively than men and women who are decades younger. Drawing on both sides of the brain gives them a tactical edge, even if the speed of each hemisphere's process is slower.

In another experiment, Michael Falkenstein of the University of Dortmund in Germany found that when elders were presented with new computer exercises they paused longer before reacting and took longer to complete the tasks, yet they made 50% fewer errors, probably because of their more deliberate pace.

One analogy for these results might be the question of who can type a paragraph 'better': a 16-year-old who glides along at 60 words per minute but has to double back to correct a number of mistakes or a 70-year-old who strikes keys at only 40 words per minute but spends less time fixing errors? In the end, if 'better' is defined as completing a clean paragraph, both people may end up taking the same amount of time.

Computerized tests support the notion that accuracy can offset speed. In one so-called distraction exercise, subjects were told to look at a screen, wait for an arrow that pointed in a certain direction to appear, and then use a mouse to click on the arrow as soon as it appeared on the screen. Just before the correct symbol appeared, however, the computer displayed numerous other arrows aimed in various other directions. Although younger subjects cut through the confusion faster when the correct arrow suddenly popped up, they more frequently clicked on incorrect arrows in their haste.

Older test takers are equally capable of other tasks that do not depend on speed, such as language comprehension and processing. In these cases, however, the elders utilize the brain's available resources in a different way. Neurologists at Northwest University came to this conclusion after analyzing 50 people ranging from age 23 to 78. The subjects had to lie down in a magnetic resonance imaging (MRI) machine and concentrate on two different lists of printed words posted side by side in front of them. By looking at the lists, they were to find pairs of words that were similar in either meaning or spelling.

The eldest participants did just as well on the tests as the youngest did, and yet the MRI scans indicated that in the elders' brains, the areas which are responsible for language recognition and interpretation were much less active. The researchers did find that the older people had more activity in brain regions responsible for attentiveness. Darren Gleitman, who headed the study, concluded that older brains solved the problems just as effectively but by different means.

Questions 1–3

Choose the correct answer A, B, C or D.

1 The conversation between Jake and Rita is used to give an example of

    A the way we learn languages.
    B the changes that occur in our brains over time.
    C the fact that it is easier to learn a language at a young age.
    D the importance of young and old people doing things together.

2 In paragraph six, what point is the analogy used to illustrate?

    A Working faster is better than working slower.
    B Accuracy is less important than speed.
    C Accuracy can improve over time.
    D Working faster does not always save time.

3 In the computerized distraction exercises, the subjects had to

    A react to a particular symbol on the screen.
    B type a text as quickly as possible.
    C move an arrow in different directions around the screen.
    D click on every arrow that appeared on the screen.

Questions 4–7

Complete each sentence with the correct ending A–F.

Write the correct letter A–F next to Questions 4–7 below.

4 According to popular psychology
5 Researchers at the University of Michigan showed that ·
6 Michael Falkenstein discovered that
7 Scientists at Northwest University concluded that

    A the older we get the harder it is to concentrate for any length of time.
    B seniors take longer to complete tasks but with greater accuracy.
    C old people use both parts of their brain more than young people.
    D older people use their brains differently but achieve the same result.
    E the speed of our brain decreases with age.
    F older people do not cope well with new technology.

Questions 8–12

Complete the summary below.

*Choose **NO MORE THAN ONE WORD** from the passage for each answer.*

Write your answers in spaces 8–12 below.

People's bodies and **8** .... grow older at varying stages. As we age our senses take longer to process information and our aptitude for recalling **9** .... also decreases.

However, older people's brains do have several advantages. Firstly, they can call upon both the **10** .... and **11** .... which is already stored in their brain. Secondly, although the **12** .... of each side of their brain is reduced, they are able to use both sides at once.

Grammar focus task

These extracts are from the text. Without looking back at the text, match the beginnings (1–7) and endings (a–g).

1 ... evidence shows that older people are just as mentally fit as younger people because

2 ... although certain brain functions such as perception and reaction time do indeed take longer,

3 Although younger subjects cut through the confusion faster when the correct arrow suddenly popped up,

4 Just before the correct symbol appeared, however,

5 The ability to retrieve memories also quickly slides and

6 Drawing on both sides of the brain gives them a tactical edge, even if

7 ... when elders were presented with new computer exercises they paused longer before reacting and took longer to complete the tasks, yet

a the speed of each hemisphere's process is slower.

b they more frequently clicked on incorrect arrows in their haste.

c the computer displayed numerous other arrows aimed in various other directions.

d they made 50% fewer errors.

e their brains compensate for some kinds of declines in creative ways that young minds do not exploit as well.

f it is sometimes harder to concentrate and maintain attention.

g that slowing down does not necessarily undermine mental sharpness.

24

Showing your position in a text
pronouns; adverbs; verbs; adjectives

A Context listening

1 You are going to hear two students, Nick and Tina, discussing a topic with their tutor. Look at the pictures below. What do you think the topic is?

2 🎧 24 Listen and decide whether these statements are true or false.

1 Tina believes that her time at school was good for her.
2 Nick had a bad experience at school.
3 Nick believes that the boy who was bullied probably feels bad about his school days.
4 Nick likes the idea of staying at home all day.
5 Tina's friend was able to meet new friends easily.
6 Tina believes that you receive a better standard of education in school.

3 24◀◀ Listen again and fill in the gaps.

1 Well, I'm a bit like you, Tina. I went to a normal school and, ... , I had a great experience there. Mind you, ... that being educated at home would be good for some children. There was a boy in my class who was bullied by some older boys, and .... he must look back at his school days and feel really bad.

2 Yes, I think that's a good point. But, ... , schools do seem to be more overcrowded and less well-funded these days and .... the advantages of home education in terms of the quality of education. That's .... the way my friend felt. Mind you, ... she finds it hard to interact in large groups of people. And, ... , she doesn't have a great relationship with her parents these days. .... she had enough of them as a child!

4 Look at your answers in Exercise 3 and find examples of:

1 two verbs that express the speaker's attitude or opinion ....
2 three adverbs that show how the speaker feels about the idea ....
3 two adverbs that show possibility ....

B Grammar

在讲话或写作中，可以选择语言来表明我们的感情，态度，判断和信念。雅思写作部分的 *Task 2* 一般是要考生讨论一个主题。考生必须决定在该主题上的定位是什么并通过语言来证明它。

1 Pronouns（代词）

在正式写作中，第一人称代词（如 *I, you, we*）并不十分普遍，但可以用它们：

◆ 用 *I* 或 *we* 给出我们讨论中的话题所持有的观点：
   I would argue that all children should attend school.

◆ 通常用 *we* 或 *us* 表明我们是群体中的一部分并和读者有一致的认同。 比较：
   *Is it better for **us** to educate **our** children at home rather than send them to school?*
   *Is it better for **parents** to educate **their** children at home rather than send them to school?*
   第一句中 *us* 的使用将注重客观评论的文章变得更加富有主观性。

2 Adverbs（副词）

为了表明对某事的态度、感受或评价，我们可以用：

◆ 单个副词（如 *actually, frankly, fortunately, unfortunately, personally, luckily, interestingly, naturally, surprisingly*）：
   Frankly, I'd be totally bored staying at home all day.
   *But, **unfortunately**, schools do seem to be more overcrowded and less well-funded these days.*

   在讲话中，经常会用 *actually* 来纠正某人的观点或表明我们不同意已经说过的某些事：
   Actually, she believes that she received a better education as a result.

◆ 副词短语来表达讲话者总的看法（如 *broadly speaking, by and large, in general, overall, on the whole, to a great extent*）：
   *But, **in general**, I don't think it is a good idea.*

◆ 表述观点的副词短语（如 *in my/our view, in my opinion*）：
   In my opinion that's a disadvantage.

为弱化辩论的语气，我们可以使用表可能性的副词（如 *certainly, definitely, maybe, perhaps, possibly, presumably, probably*）：
*Well, that's **certainly** the way my friend felt.*
Perhaps she had enough of them as a child!
*So, **maybe** that's a result of her education experience.*

为表明信息来自他处／他人，我们可以用副词短语来转述他人的观点（如 *apparently, according to (somebody), evidently*）：
According to my friend they did fun things like going out for walks.
Apparently there is a network of parents who teach at home. (someone else told me this)

Position of adverbs

评价副词经常出现在句首或句尾（如 *according to, fortunately, interestingly, luckily, surprisingly, unfortunately*）：
Interestingly, she doesn't have a great relationship with her parents these days.
*She doesn't have a great relationship with her parents these days, **interestingly**.*

很多副词也可以出现在主动词之前或*be*后面：

*It is **probably** best.*

*He would **possibly** feel quite differently.*

⚠ *Definitely*一般不用于句首：

*I am **definitely** coming to the party.* (**not** ~~Definitely I am coming to the party.~~)

3 Verbs （动词）

为表达我们的观点或感受，可以使用 *think, suppose, believe, feel, guess, see* 等动词：

*I **think** that's a good point.*

*I can **see** that being educated at home would be good for some children.* (= I can understand)

当主语是 *I* 时，有时在前面加上 *personally*：

***Personally**, I feel the teachers did a really good job.*

为表明我们是在表述我们的观念而不是事实或听起来更加谨慎，可以用表达可能性的情态动词（如 *may, might, could, must, can*）及像 *seem* 或 *appear* 这类的动词：

*I think he **must** look back at his school days and feel really bad.*

*Schools **seem** to be more overcrowded and less well-funded these days.*

4 Adjectives （形容词）

我们可以使用形容词：

◆ 来表达感受 (*e.g. glad, delighted, overwhelmed*)：

*Anyway, I'm **glad** that my parents didn't educate me at home.*

◆ 用*it* + *be* + 形容词 + *that*来表达可能性和观点（如 *clear, possible, probable, likely*）：

*Yes, but **it is likely that** those people will be very similar.*

C Grammar exercises

1 Underline the correct word or phrase in the sentences below.

1 I'm very worried about the plans to build a new shopping centre here. _According to_ / _Apparently_ my friend they want to knock down some of the houses.

2 _Apparently,_ / _Personally,_ I believe that we will live longer in the future.

3 Joshua is working this weekend so _presumably_ / _actually_ he will have some time off at a later date.

4 We cannot say for sure but _definitely_ / _perhaps_ an advertising campaign would encourage people to recycle their waste more.

5 _Overall,_ / _Luckily,_ we can see that the experiments done by the early scientists have had a great effect on our lives today.

6 We should _probably_ / _personally_ all reflect on the way we live our lives and try to be more environmentally aware.

7 _Certainly,_ / _Surprisingly,_ John agreed to come when I invited him – I hadn't expected that!

8 _In my opinion_ / _Unfortunately_ the number of students leaving university without completing their degrees is rising.

2 Put the words in brackets into the sentences below in a suitable place. There may be more than one possible answer.

1 I ∧ believe she is the right person for the job, but I feel she may need some further
   certainly
   training. (_certainly_)

2 The start of the course has been delayed because the tutor is ill. (_apparently_)

3 I want to go to university when I leave school. (_definitely_)

4 I was late for the exam because my bus didn't come, but the exam hadn't started on time so I only missed a few minutes. (_luckily_)

5 The university has decided to close the music department. (_unfortunately_)

6 It is time to reorganise our company structure. (_perhaps_)

7 My tutor was impressed with the effort I had put into my assignment, but suggested a few changes. (_On the whole_)

8 It is true that people are living longer today than in the past. (_probably_)

3 Replace the underlined part of each sentence with an adverb from the box.

actually	~~apparently~~	evidently	frankly
on the whole	possibly	surprisingly	unfortunately

1 <u>I've heard that</u> he is a teacher. _Apparently_.

2 <u>To be honest</u> I don't really like this kind of literature. ....

3 <u>I found it unexpected that</u> the survey revealed that university students today spend longer on their work than in the past. ....

4 <u>I'm not happy about it but</u> I can't come to your party because I'm working. ....

5 <u>To sum it up, it seems that</u> people prefer to spend festivals with their families or friends rather than alone. ....

6 <u>From what I have read in the journal, it seems that</u> scientists believe the new drug will work. ....

7 <u>I am not absolutely certain about this but</u> if we reduce the amount we consume, we will become happier. ....

8 <u>As a matter of fact</u> I think this is the best piece of work you've done so far. ....

4 Put the words or expressions in brackets into a suitable place in the model answer and make any other necessary changes.

Many people have changed from a mainly meat-based diet to a vegetarian one in recent years. What are the possible reasons for this and to what extent do you consider it a sensible option?

There are many reasons why people follow a vegetarian diet. Firstly, it is because ∧ it is wrong to kill
they believe that

animals. This ∧ ~~is~~ due to religious beliefs or it is their own personal philosophy. (they believe that; may be; could be)
may be

Another motivation for stopping eating meat is health. The high fibre content of a vegetarian diet reduces the likelihood of suffering from some bowel problems and heart disease. In addition, fewer vegetarians than meat-eaters are overweight. A further advantage is that a vegetarian diet is cheaper than eating meat. (it is possible that; according to research; seems to; can be)

Nevertheless, there are some disadvantages. Vegetarians lack a lot of the vitamins and minerals that are present in meat, such as iron or vitamin B12, or calcium if you do not include dairy products in your diet. There is also the social problem of not being able to eat food available at parties and restaurants. However, in terms of health a vegetarian is more likely to be healthy than a non-vegetarian and the advantages outweigh the disadvantages. (it is clear that; can; overall; personally I feel that)

D Test practice

Academic Writing Task 2

You should spend about 40 minutes on this task.

Write about the following topic:

> *School children are becoming far too dependent on computers. This is having an alarming effect on reading and writing skills. Teachers need to avoid using computers in the classroom at all costs and go back to teaching basic study skills.*
>
> *Do you agree or disagree?*

Give reasons for your answer and include any relevant examples from your own knowledge or experience.

Write at least 250 words.

Grammar focus task

Look at the sentences from a model answer to the question above. Fill in the gaps using the words in the box.

| actually | definitely | frankly | I believe | in my opinion |

1 Modern technology does a lot of our thinking for us and as a result .... we are losing our ability to work things out for ourselves.

2 Rather than holding students back, I believe modern technology has .... improved standards of education considerably.

3 .... handwriting and spelling skills have .... deteriorated in recent years.

4 ...., I find some notes or texts which are handwritten impossible to read.

Now write your own answer.

Nominalisation in written English
forming nouns from other parts of speech
(verbs, adjectives and linking words)

A Context listening

1 You are going to hear Julie describing what happened when she was stung by a bee. Which symptoms do you think she had?

> itching   pain   redness   shaking   sneezing   swelling

2 🎧25 Listen and check if you were right.

3 25◀ Listen again and answer these questions.

1 What was unusual about what happened when Julie was stung by a bee? ....

2 Where did she get stung? ....

3 How did it feel? ....

4 What happened to her foot? ....

5 What other effects were there? ....

4 Read this written scientific account of the effects of bee stings.

> Following a bee sting the normal reaction is burning pain, redness, irritation and itching. After a person has been stung by a bee once, they may become allergic to the bee's venom. There is a 60% risk of a serious reaction upon re-sting. In this situation there may be swelling in the area around the bite, it may become red and sore, the victim may have breathing difficulties, a dry cough, abdominal pain and vomiting. In extremely serious cases, the throat may swell, blocking the airway and the heart may stop.

Look at the <u>underlined</u> words in the extracts from what Julie said. How are these words expressed in the written text?

1 I was really surprised by how much <u>it hurt</u>. ....

2 <u>It itched</u> a bit too. ....

3 My foot began to go red and <u>swell up</u>. ....

4 Then I began to find it <u>difficult to breathe</u> and <u>kept coughing</u>. ....

5 Compare the language in the written report with the spoken language.

1 What happens to the spoken verbs in the written report? ....

2 What are the most common verbs in the written text? ....

B Grammar

当选择在句中以名词短语的形式而非以动词的形式给出主要信息时，可将此称为"名词化"。

1 Nominalisation in written English（书面英语中的名词化）

在口语中我们常用主语＋动词来描述一个事件：

subject + verb
I reacted badly.

subject + verb   + verb
Then really quickly **my foot began to go red** *and* **swell up**.

在正式的书面英语中，所使用的语言更客观，所以经常用名词形式来取代动词。书面的科学报告用如下方式描述同一反应：

noun   noun   noun   noun
Following a bee sting the normal **reaction** *is* **redness**, **irritation** *and* **itching**.

noun
In this situation there may be **swelling** *in the area around the bite.*

在口语例子中，事件是用动词 (*go red*, *swell up*) 表述的。在书面语例子中，事件已经变为用名词来表述 (*redness*, *swelling*)。注意：书面语例子中唯一的动词就是非行为动词*be*。

也可以将一些形容词变为其名词形式。比较：
The cathedral is **tall** *and can be seen from all over the town.*
The cathedral's **height** *makes it visible all over town.*

口语与书面语的一般区别是：

口语	书面语
◆ 行动或事件用动词表达 *swell up*	◆ 行动或事件可以用名词或名词短语表达 *swelling*
◆ 事件发生在人身上或由人施行 *I reacted badly, my foot began to go red*	◆ 事件的客观表述 *the normal reaction is ...*
◆ 人称代词用作主语 *I, she*	◆ 名词用作主语 *a person, the throat*
◆ 动词经常是行动或事件动词 *reacted, trod, itched*	◆ 动词经常不是行动或事件动词 *be, have*
◆ 句子中有许多词汇	

2 Reasons for using nominalisation（使用名词化的理由）

Making texts impersonal and authoritative

通过将动词转化为名词形式，可以使文章看上去更客观，更具权威性。一般不常使用人称代词（如*I, you, he*）。

比较：

Following a bee sting __the normal reaction__ is __burning pain__, __redness__, __irritation__ and __itching__. In this situation there may be __swelling__ in the area around the bite.

*Then really quickly **my foot began to go red** and **swell up**. **It just got bigger** and bigger. **It itched** a bit too. **I was really surprised by how much it hurt**.*

名词化用法下面都已划了横线。口头报告更加个人化并使用了主动动词。

Adding information

名词化在学术写作*Task 1*中特别有用，因为我们可以给名词添加信息：

◆ 计数：*the **two** charts*

◆ 描述：*the two **coloured** charts*

◆ 分类：*the two coloured **bar** charts*

对于动词，却不能做同样的事。只有通过将动词转换为名词，才能在文中以如此简练的方式增加信息词。

Avoiding repetition

当我们想回过头来指前面提到过的观念时（参见Unit 21），可以用名词化来避免重复。

*The number of unemployed **increased** by 5% last month. The reason for **this increase** is still unclear.*

名词化也可以用来解释前面所说的话。在雅思听力和阅读测试中，不同的词被用于文章和问题中。

比较：

Listening text:

Then I began to find it difficult to breathe and kept coughing, although I didn't have a cold.

Question:

Which TWO of the following symptoms did Julie experience?

    A breathing problems

    B shaking

    C a cough

    D a high temperature

    E chills

选项*A*和*C*是听力文章中所用动词的名词化。

C Grammar exercises

1 Write possible noun forms for the following verbs.

1 to research: *research, researcher*

2 to study: ....

3 to find: ....

4 to respond: ....

5 to measure: ....

6 to earn: ....

7 to advertise: ....

8 to examine: ....

9 to suggest: ....

10 to create: ....

2 Complete the sentences with the noun form of the adjectives in brackets.

1 The graphs show a significant *difference* (*different*) between the ages at which men and women marry.

2 The .... (*strong*) of the government's argument for changing the law is that many car accidents happen whilst drivers are speaking on their mobile phones.

3 The .... (*deep*) of the lake means that no one has ever seen the bottom.

4 Some parts of the world are not only important in terms of their biodiversity, but they also have a special .... (*beautiful*) that must be conserved.

5 This is a good essay in parts, but you need to express yourself with more .... (*clear*) at times.

6 The discovery of a new species of monkey in Africa is of great .... (*interesting*) to both naturalists and the general public alike.

7 The .... (*difficult*) facing the scientists now is how to prove their theory.

8 The results of this research need to be treated with .... (*cautious*).

9 The .... (*significant*) of the findings surprised even the researchers.

10 Many older people are afraid to go out at night due to the increase in .... (*violent*) in our larger cities.

11 The current .... (*controversial*) over pensions is likely to continue for some time.

12 We apologise for any .... (*confusing*) caused by the last-minute change to the schedule.

3 Underline the best answers.

The two pie charts show the average spending by households in a country at two different points in its economic development.

Summarise the information by selecting and reporting the main features, and make comparisons where relevant.

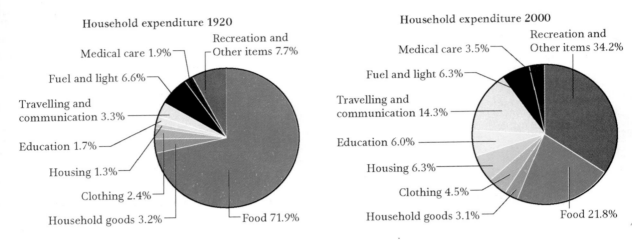

Household expenditure 1920

Recreation and Other items 7.7%
Medical care 1.9%
Fuel and light 6.6%
Travelling and communication 3.3%
Education 1.7%
Housing 1.3%
Clothing 2.4%
Household goods 3.2%
Food 71.9%

Household expenditure 2000

Recreation and Other items 34.2%
Medical care 3.5%
Fuel and light 6.3%
Travelling and communication 14.3%
Education 6.0%
Housing 6.3%
Clothing 4.5%
Household goods 3.1%
Food 21.8%

The two pie charts give information about **1** *what households spent their money on / household expenditure on goods and services* in 1920 and 2000. It is immediately obvious that **2** *there are some quite significant differences / some things are significantly different* between the two charts.

In 2000 **3** *the largest proportion of expenditure was / most money was spent* on recreation and other items whereas in 1920 it was on food, with recreation and other items accounting for just 7.7%. There is a great difference in terms of **4** *the amount of money people spent on food / food expenditure* between the two years. In 1920 nearly 72% of **5** *the total household budget / the total of what households spent* went towards food, compared to only 22% in 2000.

6 *There has been a notable increase in / People have notably increased* the amount of money spent on travelling and communications between the two dates. In addition, the charts show **7** *a significant rise in the proportion of money spent on clothing / that people spent more on clothes* in 2000 compared to 1920.

There are some similarities, however. For example, in both 1920 and 2000 **8** *people spent a similar proportion on fuel and lighting. / the proportion of fuel and lighting expenditure was roughly the same.*

4 Fill in the gaps in the second sentences with nouns so that they have a similar meaning to the first sentences.

1 a <u>She wrote books</u> that children enjoyed.

  b Children enjoyed .....*her writing*..... .

2 a Young girls <u>are spending increasing amounts</u> on make-up because they have been <u>influenced</u> by advertising.

  b .... on make-up amongst young girls is on the .... due to the .... of advertising.

3 a <u>I failed</u> to get good enough grades to get into university because <u>I was ill</u> on the day of the exam.

  b The reason for my .... to get good enough grades to get into university was my .... on the day of the exam.

4 a If you <u>eat</u> healthily you can <u>reduce</u> the chances of getting ill.

  b A healthy .... can lead to a .... in the chances of getting ill.

5 a If you <u>use</u> the Internet you <u>risk</u> getting viruses and <u>losing</u> important information.

  b .... of the Internet increases the .... of getting viruses which may cause the .... of important information.

6 a When people <u>are content</u> because their lives are <u>successful</u> they tend to be easier to <u>communicate</u> with.

  b .... due to personal .... tends to lead to improved .... with other people.

7 a In the thirteenth century engineers <u>developed</u> new ways to <u>construct</u> buildings which made it possible to build the soaring arches of Salisbury Cathedral.

  b .... in .... in the thirteenth century made it possible to build the soaring arches of Salisbury Cathedral.

8 a The IELTS reading module is <u>difficult</u> because it has long articles with lots of new vocabulary in them.

  b The .... of the IELTS reading module is due to its long articles containing a lot of new vocabulary.

Academic Writing Task 1

You should spend 20 minutes on this task.

The graph below shows the population figures of different types of wild birds in the United Kingdom between 1970 and 2004.

Summarise the information by selecting and reporting the main features, and make comparisons where relevant.

Write at least 150 words.

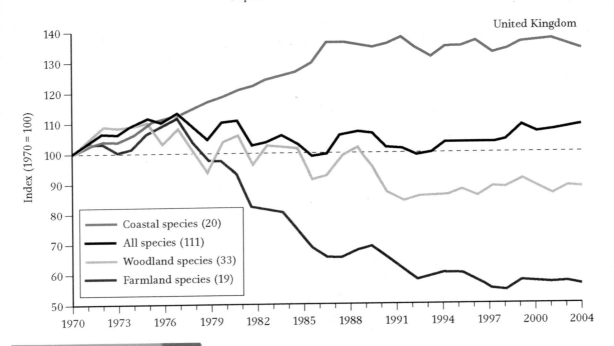

Population of wild birds: 1970–2004

Look at the extracts from a model answer and <u>underline</u> all examples of nominalisation.

1 Since 1994 there has been an improvement in numbers of all species, although the graph shows a slight decrease in 2000.

2 There was also a fall in the number of woodland birds of around 30% between 1974 and 1998.

3 It is only the coastal birds that have seen a steady increase in population over this period.

Key

Entry test

If you have the wrong answer, see the units indicated for more information.

1 B (➢ Unit 1)
2 C (➢ Unit 1)
3 B (➢ Unit 2)
4 B (➢ Unit 2)
5 C (➢ Unit 2)
6 B (➢ Unit 3)
7 A (➢ Unit 3)
8 B (➢ Unit 4)
9 C (➢ Unit 4)
10 A (➢ Unit 5)
11 A (➢ Unit 5)
12 C (➢ Unit 6)
13 B (➢ Unit 6)
14 C (➢ Unit 7)
15 B (➢ Unit 7)
16 A (➢ Unit 8)
17 C (➢ Unit 8)
18 A (➢ Unit 8)
19 B (➢ Unit 9)
20 C (➢ Unit 10)
21 A (➢ Unit 10)
22 C (➢ Unit 10)
23 B (➢ Unit 11)
24 C (➢ Unit 11)
25 A (➢ Unit 12)
26 B (➢ Unit 12)
27 A (➢ Unit 13)
28 B (➢ Unit 13)
29 A (➢ Unit 14)
30 A (➢ Unit 14)
31 C (➢ Unit 15)
32 B (➢ Unit 15)
33 A (➢ Unit 16)
34 A (➢ Unit 17)
35 C (➢ Unit 17)
36 A (➢ Unit 18)
37 C (➢ Unit 18)
38 B (➢ Unit 19)
39 A (➢ Unit 19)
40 B (➢ Unit 20)
41 B (➢ Unit 20)
42 C (➢ Unit 21)
43 C (➢ Unit 21)
44 A (➢ Unit 22)
45 B (➢ Unit 22)
46 A (➢ Unit 23)
47 C (➢ Unit 23)
48 B (➢ Unit 24)
49 C (➢ Unit 24)
50 A (➢ Unit 25)

Unit 1

A: Context listening

2 1 playing and watching football; playing the guitar in a band

3 1 T 2 F He is studying really hard for his exams this month. 3 F His parents own a restaurant. 4 F He practises the piano most mornings. 5 T 6 F His cousin is living in Thailand. 7 F He supports his local team.

4 1 sentences 3 and 7 2 sentences 4 and 5 3 sentence 1 4 sentences 2 and 6

C: Grammar exercises

1 2 b 3 a 4 b 5 a 6 b 7 a 8 b (➢ B1 and B2)

2 2 sees 3 isn't studying; don't think 4 's he doing; 's trying 5 breathe in; give out 6 want 7 drive 8 are travelling 9 runs 10 are falling (➢ B1–B3)

3 2 have (state verb) 3 is going up (*year by year* tells us this is a gradual change over time) 4 is catching up 5 know 6 is causing 7 think 8 agree (➢ B2 and B3)

4 2 ~~are increasing~~ is increasing 3 ~~decreases~~ is decreasing 4 ~~is warming~~ warms 5 ~~is rising~~ rises 6 ~~change~~ changes (be careful of verb/subject agreement) (➢ B1 and B2)

D: Test practice

Listening

Questions 1–3: multiple choice

Test tip: Read all the questions carefully before you listen. Underline or highlight any key information or words that you need to listen for (e.g. *How long is the heated swimming pool?*) Use the questions to help you find your way through the listening text. If you miss an answer, just move on to the next one.

1 A (*a heated indoor pool, which is just 15 metres long*) 2 A (*We even offer complimentary classes for beginners*) 3 C (*we can only have a maximum of seven people in the sauna at any one time, so you do need to put your name on the list for that*)

Questions 4–10: notes completion

Test tip: Read through the notes carefully before you listen and try to predict what type of information you need to hear (e.g. for question 4 you will need to write down two days of the week, or for question 5 you will need to write a time). Pay careful attention to the word limit and check your spelling at the end.

4 Tuesday; Friday (*There are classes on Monday, Tuesday and Friday in the morning*) 5 6.00/six (pm); 7.30/seven thirty (pm) (*There are classes ... every Saturday and Sunday in the evening. Those classes are a bit longer, starting at 6.00 and finishing at 7.30.*) 6 one day/1 day/once (*each day is a different level, so you only come once a week*) 7 level(s)/class(es) (*Most people start at the*

lower level, and then you can talk to the instructor about changing if you think it's too easy.) **8** Doherty (*My name is John Doherty, that's DOHERTY*) **9** 11.00/eleven (am) (*I have appointments from 9.00 to 10.30, so could you make it 11.00?*) **10** 0117 965 478 (*my number's 0117 965 478*)

Grammar focus task

1 want **2** are always looking **3** Do members have to
4 don't actually allow **5** suits **6** think

Unit 2

A: Context listening

1 A CDs   B a laptop computer   C a roast chicken   D a purse
E a handbag   F a TV

2 **1** CDs; a roast chicken; a purse   **2** B (*So you see, you do need to be careful to lock your door at all times of the day*)

3 **1** called   **2** happened; was watching   **3** used to keep
4 would leave   **5** walked   **6** didn't hear; was listening
7 went; opened; took

4 **1** sentences 2 and 6   **2** sentences 1 and 5   **3** sentence 7
4 sentences 3 and 4   **5** past simple; past continuous; *would*; *used to*

C: Grammar exercises

1 **2** was   **3** took   **4** was   **5** received   **6** meant   **7** invented
8 laid   **9** allowed   **10** replaced   **11** increased   **12** did not own   **13** walked   **14** rode (➤B1 and Appendix 1)

2 **2** made   **3** were studying   **4** was describing   **5** picked up
6 noticed   **7** was crying   **8** apologised   **9** said   **10** didn't know   **11** made   **12** happened   **13** was showing
14 was examining   **15** was smiling   **16** got   **17** said
18 laughed   **19** wasn't looking   **20** inspired   **21** started
(➤B1 and B2)
Used to is possible in **1** and **2**: *used to have* and *used to make*

3 **2** would/used to follow   **3** moved   **4** visited
5 would/used to give   **6** Did you use to have (*would* is not used with state verbs or in questions)   **7** really used to like/used to really like (*would* is not used with state verbs)
8 used to/would go   **9** used to/would spend   **10** took
11 did you use to have to (*would* is not used in questions)
12 used to have to (*would* is not used with state verbs)
13 didn't use to look forward to (*would* is not generally used with negatives) (➤B1 and B3)

4 **3** used to go   **4** ✓   **5** noticed   **6** ✓   **7** realised
8 was snowing   **9** skidded   **10** ✓   **11** phoned   **12** ✓
(background scene)   **13** stopped (event)   **14** ✓   **15** came
16 ✓ (➤B1–B3)

D: Test practice

Reading

Questions 1–9: locating information

Test tip: Scan the passage for relevant information, and then check that it matches the question exactly (e.g. for question 2 the experiment is mentioned several times but only paragraph D describes how it was done). Remember that the words in the passage may paraphrase the words in the questions.

1 E (*prey spiders did not respond to them in any way*)   **2** D (*The researchers allowed various prey spiders to spin webs in the*

laboratory and then introduced Portia spiders.*)   **3** F (*lions hunting at night, for example*)   **4** D (*To simulate the shaking effect of a breeze the zoologists used either a model aircraft propeller or attached a tiny magnet to the centre of the web*)   **5** B (*They will attack something about twice their own size*)   **6** A (*for jumping spiders that sneak onto other spiders' webs to prey on their owners, it can be the difference between having lunch and becoming it*)   **7** B (*Portia spiders live mostly in tropical forests, where the climate is hot and humid.*)   **8** B (*The fifteen known species of Portia jumping spiders*)
9 F (*Portia spiders are clearly intelligent and they often learn from their prey as they are trying to capture it. They do this by ...*)

Questions 10–13: multiple choice

Test tip: Read all the questions and options and underline or highlight any important information or key words that you need to find in the passage. Use the questions to locate the relevant part of the reading passage. If you cannot find an answer, just move on to the next one and come back to this one later.

10 A (*Portia spiders moved more when the webs were shaking (vibrating) than when they were still (motionless)* so B is incorrect; C is incorrect: *they were more likely to capture their prey during tests in which the webs were periodically shaken than in those where the webs were undisturbed;* D is incorrect: *If the spiders were placed onto unoccupied webs, they would make no attempt to change their movements*)   **11** A (*They'd make a big pluck with one of their hind legs* = make strong vibrations with one leg; B and C are incorrect: *the spiders would ... then creep forwards up to five millimetres before the vibrations died down;* D is incorrect: *the violent twanging produces a pattern of vibrations that match those caused by a twig falling onto the web*)   **12** C (*this is the first example of an animal making its own smokescreen that we know of;* A is incorrect: lions also do this; B is incorrect: Portia spiders mimic trapped insects not other prey-eating animals; D is incorrect: we are not told that spiders are the only animal that uses 'trial and error')
13 B (*Sometimes they will even take an indirect route to reach a prey spider ... When it does this, the Portia spider is actually solving problems and thinking ahead about its actions.*)

Grammar focus task

1 a   **2** c   **3** b

Unit 3

A: Context listening

1 A logical order would be: **1** F   **2** C   **3** A   **4** D   **5** E   **6** B

2 **1** C   **2** A   **3** D   **4** E   **5** B

3 **1** 've collected   **2** read   **3** 've been feeling   **4** 've just got up

4 a sentence 4 (present perfect simple)   b sentence 1 (present perfect simple)   c sentence 3 (present perfect continuous)
d sentence 2 (past simple)

C: Grammar exercises

1 **3** have already seen   **4** have just received   **5** were   **6** ✓
7 represented   **8** have played   **9** ✓   **10** have not travelled
11 went   **12** ✓ (➤B1)

2 **2** has increased (*since*)   **3** rose (*in 2005*)
4 has risen (*each year*)   **5** was (*from 1995 to 2005*)
6 have overtaken (*since 2005*)   **7** has grown (*each year*); occurred (*between 1995 and 2000*) (➤B1)

3　2 've been working　3 have now finished　4 've made
　　5 said (at last week's lecture)　6 haven't found　7 've done
　　8 used　9 went　10 learnt　11 've been wondering
　　12 've given (➢B1 and B2)

4　2 've been living (for the past three years)　3 've been studying
　　(focus on activity)　4 Have you done　5 've been (state verb)
　　6 've travelled　7 've done　8 've started　9 've been having
　　('ve been taking is also possible – focus on activity and
　　duration)　10 've just passed (recent activity)　11 've taken
　　(it's the first time)　12 've never felt ('ve never been is also
　　possible)　13 've been doing ('ve been taking is also possible –
　　focus on activity)　14 've always wanted　15 've always been
　　16 've already worked (➢B1 and B2, Grammar extra)

　　Answers will vary. Suggestions: 17 I've been studying English
　　since I was six years old.　18 I haven't studied any other
　　languages. / I have studied ... / I studied French at school but
　　I've forgotten almost everything now.　19 I've been to ...
　　20 I've been reading a lot and taking lots of practice tests.
　　21 My life has changed a great deal. I've finished university ...
　　(➢B1 and B2)

D: Test practice

General Training Writing Task 1

Test tip: Read the question carefully. Make sure you include all
the information required in your letter and make sure you stick
to the time limit so that you leave enough time to answer Task 2.
Do not write any addresses.

See model answer in unit.

Grammar focus task

1 I have lived in this town all my life　2 I have been working as
a receptionist at a local hotel　3 I have read many guidebooks

Unit 4

A: Context listening

1　1 d　2 a　3 f　4 c　5 h　6 b　7 g　8 j　9 e　10 i

2　1 January 27, 1756 / 27 January 1756 / January 27th, 1756 /
　　27th January 1756　2 one/1　3 (a) composer　4 six/6
　　5 (the) violin

3　1 was born; had already died　2 was; had also been
　　3 mastered; had copied　4 was; had written
　　5 hurried; spread　6 were; had ever been

4　1 past simple　2 past perfect

C: Grammar exercises

1　2 had entered　3 had made　4 had not discovered
　　5 had also turned up　6 had multiplied (➢B1)

2　2 had doubled　3 remained　4 began　5 had tripled
　　6 was　7 increased　8 had reached　9 had peaked
　　10 had managed (➢B1)

3　2 'd always been　3 'd heard　4 arrived　5 'd been feeling
　　6 had come　7 'd walked　8 'd learnt　9 had prepared
　　10 'd been expecting ('d expected)　11 took off
　　12 didn't feel　13 approached　14 had done　15 stepped
　　16 hadn't burnt　17 'd been hoping ('d hoped)
　　18 managed　19 'd done (➢B1 and B2, Grammar extra)

4　2 had started　3 bought　4 'd never taken　5 stayed; visited;
　　'd been; 'd liked (liked); 'd decided　6 'd been developing　7 'd
　　already discussed; 'd made; 'd phoned; felt; hadn't waited　8 'd
　　been running (➢B1 and B2)

D: Test practice

Reading

Questions 1–6: choosing paragraph headings

Test tip: Try to get the general idea of what each paragraph is
about. Make sure that the heading you choose reflects the overall
message in the paragraph and not just one fact.

1 vii (Paragraph A tells us about an advertisement for pens that
brought 5,000 people into a shop.)　2 ix (Paragraph B tells us
about earlier pens and their problems; there were 350 patents for
pens in fifty years. A patent is a formal application to
manufacture something so that no one else can copy it.)　3 vi
(Paragraph C tells us that one of the Biro brothers was annoyed
at problems he had with fountain pens, so he decided to invent a
new one.)　4 iv (Paragraph D tells us about the problem with
the first design and how this was solved with a second design
which worked better. We also learn that the brothers moved to
Argentina.)　5 viii (Paragraph E tells us that the United States
Department of War requested the pens be made in the U.S., so an
American company bought the rights from the Biro brothers.)
6 iii (Paragraph F tells us that an American man on holiday in
Argentina saw the pens and copied them back in the U.S.)

The following headings are incorrect: i (Although fountain pens
are mentioned in the text none of the paragraphs tells us that
they are no longer used = are history.) ii (The Biro brothers were
never very famous.) v (Paragraph E tells us that the United
States Department of War actually helped the progress of the
Biro pen.)

Questions 7–9: multiple choice

Test tip: Read all the questions and options and underline or
highlight any important information or key words that you need
to find in the passage. Use the questions to locate the relevant
part of the reading passage. If you cannot find an answer, just
move on to the next one and come back to this one later.

7 D (Depending on the climate or air temperature, sometimes the
pens would do both i.e. leak and clog. A is incorrect: the pens were
never manufactured; B is incorrect: there is no mention of the
manufacturing technology; C is incorrect: the first pen was
designed for use on leather – we are not told that it could not
write on paper.)　8 A (The first Biro pen, like the designs that had
gone before it, relied on gravity for the ink to flow to the ball bearing
at the tip. B is incorrect: the second pen was based on capillary
action, not the first; C is incorrect: the pen did not work with
heavy ink; D is incorrect: the pen only worked when held
upright.)　9 C (The Biro brothers had failed to secure a U.S. patent
on their invention. A is incorrect: it was Loud's patent that had
expired, not the Biro brothers' patent; B is incorrect: we know
that a patent gave the sole rights to manufacture; D is incorrect:
there is no mention of Reynolds having any contact with the Biro
brothers, and they sold the permission to Eversharp.)

Questions 10–12: short-answer questions

Test tip: Scan the text for the information you need. It is
important to write only the key words and take note of the word
limit (here you are told to write no more than two words and/or a
number).

10 leather　11 (in) Argentina (not it was in Argentina)
12 (in) 1945 (not it was in 1945)

Grammar focus task

1 had taken out; had sold   2 had patented; soon became
3 had observed   4 bought; returned; discovered; had long since
expired   5 challenged; lost; had failed

Unit 5

A: Context listening

1 hockey; Scotland and Greece
2 1 Scotland   2 four/4   3 3/three   4 mountain lodge
   5 Greece 6 three/3   7 four/4   8 (a) (small) hotel   9 islands
3 1 A   2 B   3 A   4 C   5 A
4 1 present continuous   2 *will*   3 *going to*   4 sentences 1 and 5
   5 sentences 2–4

C: Grammar exercises

1 2 will be   3 are predicted to work   4 are going to feel
   5 will certainly have   6 is likely to become
   7 are going to happen   8 will undoubtedly continue
   9 will probably result   10 will find   11 are likely to lead to
   12 will develop (➢ B2 and B3, Grammar extra)
2 2 we'll take   3 we're going to visit   4 they're holding
   5 they aren't staying   6 we'll probably do   7 we're going to do
   8 we're also going to try   9 You'll love   10 you'll probably
   end up   11 we'll see (➢ B1–B3)
3 2 'm taking   3 'll tell   4 'll pick   5 'm seeing
   6 will probably finish   7 'll need   8 'm meeting
   9 'll probably want   10 won't go on   11 will be
   12 'll see (➢ B1 and B2)
4 Answers will vary. Suggestions: 1 I'm going to visit my
   grandmother. (*I will visit my grandmother at the weekend*
   sounds like a promise rather than a planned visit.)
   2 I'm travelling to America next week.
   3 I think we will stop using fax machines. (➢ B1–B3)

D: Test practice
Reading

Questions 1–5: sentence completion

Test tip: Sentence completion with a box of possible answers is
similar to matching questions. Scan the passage for the key words
in the questions and underline or highlight them. Then carefully
read the information close to those words and try to match it to the
ideas in the options (A–F). Remember there are more options than
you need to use. Some of the extra options may not be mentioned
at all, or may be the opposite of the information in the passage.

1 F (*For some careers like medicine and law, it's essential you have
specific qualifications.*)   2 D (*Mature entrants don't always need
formal qualifications*)   3 E (*If you are interested in self-development
and meeting people, you should find out who else will be on the
course.*)   4 B (*You might prefer an open or distance learning course
if … you're at home looking after pre-school children.*)   5 C (*… and
want to be a journalist, you could write for the student newspaper or
work on the radio*)

Questions 6–9: classification

Test tip: Underline or highlight the key words in the reading passage
(e.g. *academic, vocational*). Carefully read the information nearby and
try to match the information in the passage to the facts in the
questions (6–9). Remember the words in the questions will not always
match the words in the passage exactly. Here you need to decide
whether these questions apply to only one type of course or to both.

6 C (*Further education colleges offer academic courses and work-
related courses*)   7 B (*For a career in plumbing, a vocational course
is essential.*)   8 A (*You might prefer an academic course if you like
researching, analysing and presenting arguments.*)   9 B (*A
vocational course is better if you like doing things with your hands
and working manually.*)

Grammar focus task

1 will help   2 'll need   3 'll ensure   4 am I going to do
5 will help
The future forms used are: *will, going to*
Will is used to give suggestions and advice ➢ B2
Going to is used to talk about future intentions ➢ B3

Unit 6

A: Context listening

2 Phil advises Janet to practise in front of the mirror.
3 1 will be working   2 will have given   3 will be feeling
   4 will have rehearsed   5 leaves
4 1 sentences 2 and 4   2 sentences 1 and 3   3 sentence 5

C: Grammar exercises

1 2 won't (will not) be reading   3 will be playing computer games
   4 will be doing sport; studying   5 will be resting
   6 will be seeing friends (➢ B3)
2 2 will have peaked – a   3 will have risen – d
   4 will have grown – f   5 will have gone up – b
   6 will have increased – e (➢ B4)
3 2 ✓   3 ~~they won't ask~~ they don't ask
   4 ~~is your meeting about to start~~ does your meeting start
   5 ~~after I'll get~~ after I get   6 ✓   7 ✓
   8 ~~We're about to fly~~ We fly
   9 ~~I'll receive~~ I receive (➢ B1)
4 2 'll be travelling   3 'll hopefully have saved up
   4 get (*when* + present simple)   5 'll probably have been
   travelling (*for a few months* = duration)   6 'll have visited (*by
   then*)   7 was going to do   8 'll be starting/'m about to start
   9 won't have finished   10 find out (*as soon as*) (➢ B1–B5,
   Grammar extra)

D: Test practice
Academic Writing Task 2

Test tip: Make sure that you read all parts of the question
carefully and address each point made. Organize your thoughts
and ideas well. Do not try to memorize essays. Make sure you
have at least 40 minutes to spend on this task and try to leave
time to check you spelling at the end.

Model answer

Nowadays, most people worry about over-population and living in
crowded cities. However, it is predicted that we will have the
opposite problem by the year 2030 when one third of the
population will be aged 65 or over and birth rates are predicted
to decline. What effect will this have on our society?

By 2030 the percentage of the population aged 65 or older will
have risen significantly, to more than 30%. This means that fewer
people will be working, and therefore fewer people will be paying
income tax. In the future it may be necessary for governments to
increase the official retirement age to 70 or even older. When

today's 30-year-olds are in their sixties it is unlikely that they will enjoy the relaxed lifestyle that today's older generation can expect when they give up work. Governments will therefore need to make sure that this older generation is healthy and fit enough to continue working.

However, I believe the biggest impact will be on the younger generation. In 2030 the younger generation will need to work much harder to support the large number of older people. If this trend continues then it is possible that our entire culture will change. For example, most marketing companies today try to target the younger generation with their products and advertisements. If the majority of the population is older then this will change and companies will begin to target the older generation instead.

So, what can be done now to prevent these problems? Firstly, I believe that governments of developed countries should find ways to encourage people to have larger families and increase the birth rate. Secondly, I believe that they should encourage migration from developing countries so that the problems of over-crowding can be solved.

Grammar focus task

1 will have risen   2 will be working   3 will be paying   4 are

Unit 7

A: Context listening

2 1 A, C, G   2 B

3 1 room   2 garden   3 transport   4 60   5 week
   6 electricity

4 Group 1 nouns are countable; group 2 nouns are uncountable.
   Other countable nouns: bed, bedside table, bills, desk, garden, lamp, location, mirror, wardrobe, rent, room, types, view, week
   Other uncountable nouns: furniture, transport, electricity

C: Grammar exercises

1 2 advice   3 information   4 cakes   5 sizes   6 situations
   7 electricity (➤ B1, B2 and Grammar extra)

2 2 has come   3 were   4 shows (*data* is uncountable)
   5 is included   6 were   7 is   8 was (➤ B1 and Grammar extra)

3 2 many   3 amount   4 few   5 little (*sleep* is uncountable)/
   few (*hours* are countable)   6 much/many   7 little
   8 number   9 many   10 many   11 much (➤ B3)

4 2 something (positive statement)   3 ✓   4 Few (*places* is countable)   5 some/many (positive statement)   6 a few (a small quantity)   7 plenty of / a lot of / lots of (*much* is not usually used in positive sentences)   8 ✓   9 any (= it does not matter which time)   10 ✓ (*places* is countable)
   11 No (➤ B2 and B3)

D: Test practice

Reading

Questions 1–6: matching

Test tip: Underline or highlight each of the company names listed (1–6) in the passage. Then read the relevant information for each company carefully and match it to one of the ideas in the box. Remember there will be more ideas in the box than you need and that the words in the box will not match the words in the passage exactly.

1 D (*Corpe Nove ... has made a prototype shirt that shortens its sleeves when room temperature rises*)   2 G (*Nexia Biotechnologies ... scientists have caused a stir by manufacturing spider silk from the milk of genetically engineered goats*)   3 C (*Nano-Tex ... can make fabrics more durable, comfortable, wrinkle-free and stain-resistant*)   4 A (*Schoeller Textil ... uses nanotechnology to create fabrics that can store or release heat*)   5 B (*Created in 2003 by Quest International ... and Woolmark ... SPT is a new technique of embedding chemicals into fabric...Designers could incorporate signature scents into their collections ... Hay fever sufferers might find relief by pulling on a T-shirt* = hay fever sufferers would find relief if their medication was put into the material)   6 F (*Developed by Cargill Dow, it is the first man-made fibre derived from a 100% annually renewable resource* = environmentally-friendly)

Options E and H are not used; E refers to a material that no one has made yet (see paragraph 6) and H refers to materials made by companies not on this list (see paragraphs 7–9).

Questions 7–14: summary completion

Test tip: Read through the summary carefully and try to predict what type of information you need to find in the passage (e.g. for question 7 you will need to find the name of a company). Pay careful attention to the word limit you are given and make sure you copy the words correctly.

7 Ingeo (*Ingeo's impact on fashion will derive instead from its emphasis on using natural sustainable resources.*)   8 soya bean (*Soya bean fibre ... is a better absorber and ventilator than silk, and retains heat better than wool.*)   9 weaving (*Clunky earlier attempts involved attaching electronic components after the normal weaving process.*)   10 electronic components   11 battery (*powered by a small battery, Luminex ...*)   12 costumes (*Costumes made of the fabric wowed audiences at Verdi's* Aida *in Washington, DC, last year.*)   13 fragile (*this ultimate of ambitions has remained elusive in daily fashion, largely because electronic textiles capable of such wizardry are still too fragile to wear*)   14 accessories / handbags (*Accessories with this chameleon-like capacity – for instance, a handbag that alters its colour*)

Grammar focus task

2 C   3 U   4 C   5 U   6 C   7 C   8 C *Choice* can also be uncountable: *I don't have much choice.*

Unit 8

A: Context listening

1 environment: climate, global warming, ozone depletion
   satellites: fully-equipped, observation, launch, monitoring, outer space, instrument, operational costs, precise

2 1 in 2002   2 ten/10   3 ERS 1   4 ERS 2
   5 fifteen/15 years   6 two/2 cups

3 1 a   2 The   3 the; –   4 this   5 None

4 1 Sentence 1 = the first time it is mentioned; sentence 2 = the same satellite we have just mentioned.   2 We use *the* with superlatives; we mean scientists in general, not a specific group.
   3 2.3 billion euros   4 There are more than two countries.

C: Grammar exercises

1 3 The sun   4 the piano   5 the United Arab Emirates   6 ✓
   7 by the bus   8 a doctor   9 the (my) car   10 the river Nile
   11 ✓   12 the antiques (➤ B1)

227

2　2 ✗ (no article with countries)　3 the (referring back to Borneo which has just been mentioned)　4 a　5 the (there is only one sultan of Borneo)　6 the (there is only one eighteenth century)　7 ✗ (no article necessary when the name of the university comes first)　8 The (the findings of this study)/their (the scientists' findings)　9 the (the specific differences between this DNA)　10 the (the elephant populations already mentioned)　11 the (the scientists mentioned earlier = biologists)　12 the (the island of Borneo)　13 a (not mentioned before and only one of many which have occurred)　14 an (used to classify this group of elephants) (➢B1)

3　2 people's (people in general)　3 interviews (not referred to before and plural)　4 questionnaires (not referred to before and plural)　5 our (data for our survey)　6 Both (only two methods)　7 these (referring to something just mentioned)　8 neither (only two are mentioned)　9 Our findings (not findings in general but the ones we got from our survey)　10 This (idea just referred to: *people like to take holidays in the summer*)　11 the people　12 the survey (the one previously mentioned)　13 Beach holidays (in general not specific ones)　14 Spain (no article with countries)　15 France　16 Most (more than two were surveyed)　17 Each (*person* is singular; it would need to say *all of the people*)　18 every (*all* here means 'the whole year')　19 The price of the holiday (*holiday* = thing, not person or animal) (➢B1–B4)

4　2 Both　3 neither　4 Every (Each)　5 this (that)　6 that (this)　7 my　8 their　9 That　10 none　11 those /these (➢B2–B4)

D: Test practice

Listening

Questions 1–5: multiple choice (one and multiple answers)

Test tip: Read all the questions carefully before you listen. Underline or highlight any key information or words that you need to listen for (e.g. for question 1 you need to listen for information about Europe). Make sure you read the instructions carefully (e.g. for questions 3 and 4 you need to write two letters). Use the questions to help you find your way through the listening text. If you miss an answer, just move on to the next one.

1 C (*health-club membership has doubled there as well*)　2 A (*even if people today ate no more than the previous generation, they would still be getting fatter*)　3 & 4 B, C (*So what exactly has brought about this change in fitness levels? ... We can blame the car and other such machines ... On top of this, the changes in how and where we work have reduced the amount of daily calories people actually need.*)　5 B (*an exercise machine that did not even exist a decade ago – the elliptical cross trainer ... delivers an elliptical or swinging motion, with both the hands and feet tracing semi-circular patterns – the feet on two moving platforms rather than bicycle pedals, and the hands gripping handles that move but are not meant to support any weight, which is important as there is no seat*)

Questions 6–10: classification

Test tip: Listen carefully for the key words (e.g. *treadmill, elliptical trainer, running/road*) and match what you hear to the ideas in the questions. Remember the words in the questions will not match the words in the recording exactly.

6 C (*Running on a treadmill results in forces that are roughly two and a half times the subject's body weight*)　7 A (*But using an elliptical machine gives forces that are roughly equal to the subject's weight*)　8 A (*This is much kinder on the body and makes the impact comparable to that of walking*)　9 B (*when reaching speeds above 14 kilometres per hour or so, running on firm ground uses up substantially more calories, and therefore leads to a greater reduction in weight, than running on a treadmill – or using an elliptical machine.*)　10 B (*running on firm ground creates a greater force on the body's joints than using machines*)

Grammar focus task

1 the parents of the current generation of people
2 relying on cars and other machines and eating fast food
3 the fact that people have poor health so are looking for answers
4 45 million Americans　5 elliptical cross trainer
6 in respect of the impact on the body　7 running to gym

Unit 9

A: Context listening

2　1 A　2 B　3 A　4 B　5 C　6 A　7 C

3　1 you; mine　2 she; herself　3 me　4 I; we; they　5 myself　6 you; yourself　7 themselves　8 yours

4　I, you, she, we, they;　me, you;　myself, yourself, herself, themselves;　mine, yours

C: Grammar exercises

1　2 themselves (*these bats*)　3 their　4 they　5 their　6 their　7 its (*the bat*)　8 its　9 it　10 itself　11 their (*all bats*)　12 they　13 their　14 themselves (➢B1 and B2)

2　Dear Liz

I'm sorry I haven't emailed you for a while. I'm really busy with my studies at the moment. My course is going well and I'm enjoying ~~my course~~ it a lot. The trouble is that ~~my course~~ it takes up all my time. How is ~~your course~~ yours going?

I hope you will be able to visit me soon. I'd like you to meet my friends. My best friend here is Paul. ~~Paul~~ He lives in the flat next to ~~my flat~~ mine, and I usually eat most of my meals with ~~Paul~~ him. At the moment I'm doing most of the cooking though, because ~~Paul~~ he had an accident last week. One of the reasons for the accident is connected to some changes at the university recently. ~~The university authorities~~ They have decided that students shouldn't be allowed to bring cars up to the campus, so more and more of ~~the students~~ us are cycling. Because of this new rule, Paul was riding his bicycle to the university. While he was cycling along a car driver drove into the back of his bike. ~~The car driver~~ He didn't stop to check if Paul was okay. Luckily ~~Paul~~ he was not badly hurt and managed to pick up his bike and get to the doctor's surgery. The doctor said his finger was probably broken and strapped ~~his finger~~ it up, so he can't hold anything in his right hand at the moment and ~~Paul~~ he can't really cook for ~~Paul~~ himself. Anyway, he'd like to meet you, so we must arrange a time for you to come here.

Get in touch soon. Love Sandy (➢B1 and B2)

3　2 they　3 they　4 It　5 it　6 it (= to understand this is difficult)　7 its　8 themselves　9 they　10 There (➢B1–B3)

4   2 it is   3 it (= for people to recycle their waste)
4 their (*households* = plural)   5 it (= the government making a new law)   6 you (= everyone in general)   7 It is not practical to do this.   8 themselves (people in general)   9 it (to avoid repeating *something*)   10 the ones   11 they (to avoid repeating *the government*)   12 There   13 it easier for people to recycle   14 they (≻ B1–B3)

D: Test practice

Academic Writing Task 2

Test tip: Make sure that you read all parts of the question carefully and address each point made. Organize your thoughts and ideas well. Do not try to memorize essays. Make sure you have at least 40 minutes to spend on this task and try to leave time at the end to check your spelling.

Model answer

There is always going to be a discussion about the amount of money that is spent on space exploration. Scientific studies of the moon and the planets may provide information that is useful for us on earth. However, some people believe this cannot justify the huge amount of money spent on space research when there is a greater need for it here.

In the past, different countries used space exploration to compete with each other. For example, the US and the USSR raced each other to see who could put a man on the moon first. It would have been much easier and cheaper if they had pooled resources and information, and made a joint expedition into space. Fortunately, nowadays this is happening more and more, and thus less money overall is being wasted.

Nevertheless, some critics believe that all money given to space exploration is wasted. They argue that if the millions of dollars spent on space research were put into health and education programmes around the world, many lives would be significantly improved. It is certainly likely that if this money were invested in crop development in different parts of the world, we could save many more lives in countries where people do not have enough food. It is very difficult to argue against these criticisms.

In my opinion, we need a balance between how much money is spent on space exploration and how much money is invested into solving problems here on earth. With continued co-operation between nations over space travel more will be achieved for less money. This should leave more money to be spent on problems at home.

Grammar focus task

1 C   2 A   3 B   4 E   5 D

Unit 10

A: Context listening

2   The man visited Morocco, Turkey and India.
3   1 Morocco   2 historical buildings   3 Turkey   4 boat
5 local crafts   6 Turkish carpet   7 India   8 Museum
9 Indian silk   10 (more) remote   11 colourful   12 spiders
4   historical; beautiful; good; local; Turkish; Gujarati; great; Indian; silk; remote; incredible; colourful; poisonous

C: Grammar exercises

1   3 tall old trees   4 interesting wild animals   5 blue and yellow stripes   6 dark wooden floor   7 ✓   8 a beautiful ancient ruined castle   9 ✓   10 narrow and winding (*and* is needed because the adjectives come after the noun)
11 busy and noisy   12 happy childhood memories (≻ B1)
2   impressively; slightly; steadily; sharply; steep (≻ B2)
2a impressive b impressively
3a dramatically b dramatic
4a steadily b steady   5a steeply; sharply b steep; sharp
(≻ B1 and B2)
3   2 surprising – b   3 frightened – g   4 satisfying – e
5 interested – h   6 relaxing – d   7 exciting – a   8 tired – f
(≻ B1)
4   2 work hard   3 often say   4 take action immediately
5 really important   6 act responsibly   7 can install easily
8 work well   9 safely inside   10 absolutely essential (≻ B2)

D: Test practice

Reading

Questions 1–8: multiple matching

Test tip: Read the questions (1–8) carefully to identify the kind of information you need to find; simply scanning the text for a key word is not enough. Remember the words in the questions will not always match the words in the passage exactly.

1 A (*and an outdoor theatre hosts dance and drama performances on weekends*)   2 B (*displays rare specimens of animals, ores, and species of insects ... shellfish, insects, butterflies and birds*)
3 E (*This is the sole museum in Korea dedicated to sports* = the only one)   4 C (*Audio guides, touch screens, and video rooms all help to bring the ancient world alive here*)   5 D (*this museum is located on the former site of Kyonghee-gung palace*)   6 A (*Recently, a time capsule containing 600 items representing the lifestyle of modern-day people of Seoul was buried to celebrate the city's 600th anniversary. In 2394, it will be opened!*)   7 C (*housing art and archaeological relics from Korean prehistory*)   8 D (*the museum offers art courses every Friday*)

Question 9–14: identification of writer's views (Yes / No / Not Given)

Test tip: *Yes* means the ideas or opinions in the statement match the ideas or opinions in the passage. *No* means that the ideas or opinions in the statement are incorrect and do not match the ideas or opinions in the passage. *Not Given* means that these ideas are not mentioned in the passage.

9 No (*... 49 companies that sell or make rucksacks; few* has a negative meaning)   10 Yes (*consider what you want your rucksack for*)   11 Not given (We are only told that the writer has a backpack and that it is big enough: *My current backpack is a Craghopper AD30 (30 litres) which is just big enough.* There is no information about how comfortable it is.)   12 No (*Today you can get quite technically advanced backpacks boasting excellent features: ... clever ventilation systems to keep your back cool*)   13 Yes (*choose a backpack that fits the length of your back. Being six feet I need a long, thin rucksack rather than a short, wider one.*)   14 Yes (*Last, and probably least, we have the look of the sack to consider*)

Grammar focus task

a frequency   b manner   c time   d intensity   e place

Unit 11

A: Context listening

3   1 T   2 F Runners aged 50 and over are actually speeding up
more rapidly that younger people.   3 F Women aged 60–68
running the New York marathon run on average four minutes
faster each year.   4 F They are just as likely to achieve their
peak fitness as younger athletes.   5 T

4   faster and fitter; less rapidly than; two minutes faster; less
likely than; weaker; less active than   1 sentence 1 (*fitter,
faster*) sentence 4 (*likely, younger*) sentence 5 (*weaker, active,
younger*)   2 sentence 2 (*rapidly*) sentence 3 (*faster*)
3 *Faster* is both an adjective and an adverb.

C: Grammar exercises

1   2 the smallest   3 better (best)   4 more effective
5 the most exciting   6 braver   7 happier   8 most expensive
9 heavier (➢ B1)

2   3 friendlier / more friendly   4 hotter   5 colder (and colder)
6 not as good as   7 spicier   8 more delicious   9 the best
10 not as expensive   11 earlier   12 more quickly
13 The longer   14 the faster (➢ B1 and B2)

3   2 fewer   3 most   4 twice   5 more   6 less
7 lowest/smallest   8 highest/biggest/largest/greatest
9 significantly/considerably (much/far)   10 as
11 slightly/even (➢ B1, B3 and B4)

4   2 more silver me̶d̶a̶l̶s̶ as than gold   3 ✓   4 the second h̶i̶g̶h̶
highest   5 l̶e̶s̶s̶ fewer silver medals than gold medals
6 m̶o̶r̶e̶ g̶o̶o̶d̶ better than   7 as well as   8 m̶o̶r̶e̶ (much) lower
9 significantly more successful   10 two more gold medals
t̶h̶a̶t̶ than   11 ✓   12 the w̶o̶r̶s̶e̶ worst (➢ B1–B4)

D: Test practice

Academic Writing Task 1

Test tip: Make sure you read all of the information provided very
carefully. Look at the statistical information you are given and
choose the most important features. Look for data which is the
same or similar and features which show important differences or
changes.

Model answer

The chart provides a summary of the average number of hours
married men and women work every day both inside and outside
of the home. In both age groups shown, the total number of
hours worked by married women is greater than the total number
of hours worked by men. Whilst women aged 45 to 64 may work
fewer hours inside the home, they work the greatest number of
hours per day due to the extra hours of paid work that they do.

Men aged 25 to 44 spend only slightly more time working outside
of the home than men aged 45 to 64, but this figure is
significantly higher than the number of hours of paid work that
women of the same age do.

Women in the 25 to 44 age group work almost as many hours
inside the home as outside, and there is only a slight difference in
the 45 to 64 age group. However, men work on average three
times longer outside of the home than inside.

Grammar focus task

1 greater than   2 fewer; the greatest   3 slightly more;
significantly higher than   4 as many   5 three times longer

Unit 12

A: Context listening

2   The study showed that there were more fish in areas with
rubbish. The team decided to put rubbish back into some
areas of the harbour.

3   1 h   2 c   3 g   4 f   5 a   6 e   7 b   8 d

4   noun + preposition: sea tulips with bright red bodies; the
rubble of the past; other possible sites with submerged
rubbish
noun + past participle: the areas cleared of rubbish
noun + -ing: other debris lying on the sea floor
noun + to-infinitive: a decision to expand our study

C: Grammar exercises

1   2 of   3 in   4 of   5 for   6 of   7 to   8 on   9 in
10 with (➢ B1)

2   1 working; moving   2 buying; produced; grown
3 concerning; made; manufactured; resulting (➢ B2 and B3)

3   2 The number of people buying their own home is increasing.
3 The proposal made by the education department was
rejected by the government.   4 We have computer software
to predict (for predicting) earthquakes.   5 A new dictionary
containing more words than ever before is about to be
published.   6 My favourite novel is a story based on the
author's own experience. (➢ B1–B3)

4   I recently had a wonderful holiday in Crete with my friends.
When we arrived we saw a bus waiting to take us to our hotel.
The hotel was nice with good views of the sea. The location
was also very good with lots to do nearby. There are lots of
Minoan sites to visit. It's a lovely island with beautiful
beaches. We spent our time sightseeing, lying on the beach
and walking. Actually, it was the walking that I liked best. We
did one amazing walk through the Samarian Gorge. It took all
day, but was well worth it. We saw a snake curled up on a
rock. And lots of lizards and birds. We got really hot and were
very tired when we arrived at the beach at the end of the long
walk. It was great to see the sea sparkling in the sun. We ran
into the water to cool down. It was the best holiday ever.
(➢ B1–B3)

D: Test practice

Reading

Questions 1–5: multiple choice

Test tip: Read all the questions and options and underline or
highlight any important information or key words that you need
to find in the passage. Use the questions to locate the relevant
part of the reading passage. If you cannot find an answer, just
move on to the next one and come back to this one later.

1 D (*the more paper qualifications you hold and the higher your
grades, the less able you are to cope with problems of everyday life
and the lower your score in practical intelligence*)   2 C (*Deficit
refers back to the final idea mentioned in paragraph 3: some high*

scorers failed to achieve in real life what was predicted by their tests)
3 D *(Instead of asking what intelligence was and investigating whether it predicted success in life, Professor Sternberg asked what distinguished people who were thriving from those that were not.)*
4 C *(high achievers are often unable to articulate or define what they know)* **5** A *(Training new or less capable employees to become more practically intelligent will involve learning from the genuinely practically intelligent rather than from training manuals or courses)*

Questions 6–12: classification

Test tip: Underline or highlight the key words in the reading passage (e.g. *IQ, EQ, practical intelligence*). Carefully read the information nearby and try to match the information in the passage to the facts in the questions (6–12). Remember the words in the questions will not always match the words in the passage exactly.

6 C *(most older adults contend that their ability to solve practical problems increases over the years)* **7** B *(EQ includes the abilities to ... understand and empathize with others)* **8** C *(practical intelligence is scored by answers to real-life dilemmas)* **9** A *(IQ as a concept is more than 100 years old; the text also tells us that the EQ and practical intelligence tests were devised after the IQ test)* **10** C *(the best way to reach practical intelligence is to ask successful people to relate examples of crucial incidents at work where they solved problems demonstrating skills they had learnt while doing their jobs)* **11** B *(EQ includes the abilities to ... regulate moods and keep distress from swamping the ability to think)* **12** C *(in practical intelligence tests – as in real life – there are several different solutions to the problem)*

Grammar focus task

1 record numbers of high school students; top grades in their final exams; expert on intelligence; the existence of a totally new variety **2** the only explanation offered; a study just published **3** the basic skills to succeed

Unit 13

A: Context listening

2 The newspaper headline refers to a patient with amnesia that the doctors are discussing.
3 **1** F He couldn't remember his personal details.
2 F He could have come from Yorkshire. **3** T **4** T **5** F Joe thinks he could have been married. **6** F He's been able to find his parents. **7** F She thinks that he must have hit his head. **8** F She thinks he could make a total recovery.
4 Ability: could; couldn't; be able to
Certainty and impossibility: will; must; can't
Possibility: could; might

C: Grammar exercises

1 **2** was able to / could (*could* is more natural) **3** managed to (*could* is not used to talk about a specific occasion) **4** didn't manage to / couldn't **5** can/ will be able to (*can* is being used to give permission) **6** can (it sometimes happens) **7** managed to **8** will be able to / will manage to **9** was able to (≻B1–B2)
2 **2** a **3** a **4** b **5** b **6** a **7** b **8** b (we do not use *could not* for possibility) (≻B2–B3)

3 **2** Their jobs at the temple may/might/could have provided **3** they may/might/could have grown **4** she may/might/could have been **5** she must have worried **6** she could not (cannot) have imagined (≻B3)

4 Almost every family has a television these days, and many children watch a whole range of programmes every day. Some people believe that television ~~is~~ can be harmful to children, saying that it ~~influences~~ may/can influence behaviour in a negative way.

There are a lot of programmes on television that are not educational and that contain violence and bad language. However, watching violence on television ~~encourages~~ can/may encourage violent behaviour in children. This ~~is~~ may be true in cases of children who have already exhibited violent tendencies, but it ~~isn't~~ can't be true of all children, otherwise we would have an epidemic of child crime. It is also argued that bad language on television ~~encourages~~ can/may encourage the same in children.

However, overall I believe that restricting the viewing of children to mainly educational programmes shown at a time of day when there is no violence or bad language ~~will overcome~~ may overcome any risks of television being a bad influence. (≻B1–B4)

D: Test practice

Listening

Questions 1–10: summary completion

Test tip: Read through the information in the summary carefully before you listen and try to predict what type of information you need to hear. Pay careful attention to the word limit and check your spelling at the end.

1 clothing *(initially, it was only ever used on clothing)* **2** modern *(the use of soap for personal hygiene was unheard of until fairly recently and this is considered to be a relatively modern notion)* **3** practical skills *(what these people lacked in technology they certainly made up for in practical skills)* **4** wealthy *(soap would most likely have only been available in the wealthy communities)* **5** Iron Age *(there is no real evidence that the British colonies of the Iron Age had access to such a product)* **6** written texts *(we have had to rely almost entirely on written texts for our discoveries)* **7** wool *(The first known written mention of soap was on Sumerian clay tablets dating from about 2500 BC. The tablets spoke of the use of soap in the washing of wool.)* **8** vegetables *(Egyptians ... made soap by combining alkaline salts and oil which they extracted from vegetables)* **9** metal blade *(they reached a steamy room where dirt was sweated out and scraped away with a metal blade)* **10** soap factory *(During the excavation of Pompeii, a city that was buried under the eruption of Vesuvius in 79 AD, an entire soap factory was revealed)*

Grammar focus task

1 may be able to find (possibility) **2** must have provided (possibility) **3** could have discovered (ability) **4** might have observed (possibility) **5** have been able to make (ability)

A: Context listening

1 They discuss transport, langue lessons, work permits and accommodation.

3 1 'll need to allow 2 should try to use 3 'll have to learn 4 should always carry 5 'll need 6 have to get 7 mustn't dress 8 needn't buy 9 ought to take

4 strong obligation or necessity: mustn't, have to, need
advice or suggestions: should, ought to
no obligation or necessity: needn't, don't need to

C: Grammar exercises

1 2 must not 3 have to (a fixed appointment = external obligation) 4 didn't need to go (I did not go) 5 must (formal notice) 6 mustn't (*don't have to* = it is not necessary) 7 had to (past tense) 8 have to / must (*must* is more natural if this is a written instruction) 9 'll have to 10 needn't have worried (I did worry) (➤B1 & B2)

2 1 won't have to / needn't / don't need to 2 has to / must / needs to 3 Do you have to; didn't have to; had to 4 didn't have to / didn't need to; will have to 5 mustn't; have to; do you really have to 6 have to; have to; should / must (➤B1–B3)

3 3 must ~~to~~ encourage 4 ✓ 5 ~~also should~~ should also reduce 6 ✓ 7 ✓ 8 ought to try 9 ~~must~~ had to walk (past tense) 10 should ~~trying~~ try 11 will ~~must~~ have to make / must make 12 ~~mustn't~~ don't have to make / needn't make / don't need to make (➤B1–B4)

4 2 have to consider (ought to consider) 3 have to have 4 ought to work 5 don't have to travel 6 ought to learn 7 mustn't shout 8 must always walk 9 ought to find out 10 do you have to arrange 11 have to have 12 ought to organise (have to organise) (➤B1–B4)

D: Test practice
Reading
Questions 1–6: multiple matching

Test tip: Read the questions (1–6) carefully to identify the kind of information you need to find; simply scanning the text for a key word is not enough (e.g. bicycles are mentioned several times in the passage but question 3 asks you to find information about keeping a bicycle secure). Remember the words in the questions will not always match the words in the passage exactly.

1 D (*In the case of a pupil being absent from school, please telephone on the first day in all instances*) 2 F (*If a pupil appears to be doing too little work, parents should contact the form teacher at once.*) 3 J (*Any bicycles brought onto school grounds should be clearly labelled with the owner's name and must be left locked in the bicycle sheds provided.*) 4 C (*The school stongly disapproves of pupils taking paid employment.*) 5 G (*Homework can be excused only after the receipt and approval by the teacher concerned of a letter from a parent setting out the reasons.*) 6 H (*During the holidays the school and its grounds are out-of-bounds for all pupils, unless accompanied by a teacher.*)

Questions 7–13: identification of information in the text (True / False / Not Given)

Test tip: *True* means the ideas or opinions in the statement match the ideas or opinions in the passage. *False* means that the ideas or opinions in the statement are incorrect and do not match the ideas or opinions in the passage. *Not Given* means that these ideas are not mentioned in the passage.

7 False (*the material you cover is the same as in the courses offered on campus*) 8 Not given (There is no information about how study materials will be delivered. Although there is a *shipping and handling fee*, we do not know if this relates to posting course materials, and some materials may be delivered online.) 9 False (*All Independent Study students must purchase a Study Guide*) 10 False (*This fee entitles a student to free replacement copies of end-of-course documentation for life.*) 11 False (*A course can be finished in a minimum of two weeks per module*) 12 True (*... and must be finished in a maximum of four weeks*) 13 True (*Modules cannot always be completed in the minimum amount of time.*)

Grammar focus task

1 must (obligation) 2 must (obligation) 3 need to (necessity) 4 should (advice) 5 need to (necessity)

A: Context listening

2 He mentions voluntary redundancy and good business sense.

3 1 'll be offering 2 hope 3 Are these cuts 4 hasn't been doing 5 has 6 are you saying 7 are not 8 decided to change

4 1 announced 2 hoped 3 asked 4 denied 5 said 6 claimed 7 assured 8 promised

5 Reporting verbs are used to indicate the way in which things were said in Exercise 4. There are changes in tense, word order and pronouns.

C: Grammar exercises

1 2 (that) I was doing it the following 3 (me) if I felt 4 that her classes had been 5 me (that) I'd made 6 (that) I was feeling 7 me not to 8 (that) I'd worked 9 (that) I thought I'd be 10 was doing (➤B1, B3 and B4)

2 2 urge 3 reminded 4 complained 5 suggested 6 insisted 7 refused 8 apologised 9 advised 10 warned (➤B2)

3 2 encouraged students ~~to~~ take out 3 ~~did I want~~ if/whether I wanted 4 ~~that they should~~ to vote 5 ~~making~~ to make 6 promised ~~to~~ mark 7 ~~going~~ to go 8 ~~were my hobbies~~ my hobbies were 9 complained ~~about~~ the quality 10 announced ~~about~~ the changes 11 ~~to pay~~ on paying 12 ~~would I~~ I would (➤B2 & B4)

4 2 encouraged me to apply for the job. 3 refused to help me. 4 agreed to go to the meeting. 5 denied causing (having caused) the accident. / that he had caused the accident. 6 apologised for losing my application form. 7 asked why there aren't (weren't) many poisonous snakes in Britain. 8 asked if (whether) I was going to the lecture the next day. / if I'm going to the lecture tomorrow. 9 she suggested (that) I have (had) a day off. 10 persuaded Dan to go (come) to the theatre with her. (➤B1–B4)

D: Test practice

Listening

Questions 1–3: sentence completion

Test tip: Try to identify the type of information you need before you listen (e.g. for question 2 you need to listen for a date, or for question 3 you need to listen for a place). Pay careful attention to the word limit and check your spelling at the end.

1 (columns of) (hot) air (*They actually work by using the sun to make columns of hot air that rise upwards through the centre of the tower.*) **2** seventeenth/17th century (*The first time solar energy was produced was in the seventeenth century*)
3 Spain (*he chose Spain to build the first tower*)

Questions 4–8: flowchart completion

Test tip: Completing a flowchart is similar to completing notes. Read through the flowchart carefully before you listen and try to predict what type of information you need to hear (e.g. for questions 4 and 5 you need to listen for a type of material). Pay careful attention to the word limit and check your spelling at the end.

4 concrete (*They're constructed out of high-strength concrete*)
5 plastic (*a sunlight collector which is basically a large sheet of plastic*)
6 greenhouse (*it acts like a greenhouse*) **7** rises (*this hot air rises up the chimney or the tower and drives the turbines at the top*)
8 two hundred / 200 (*it can generate 200 megawatts of power*)

Questions 9–10: multiple choice (multiple answers)

Test tip: Read all the questions carefully before you listen. Underline or highlight any key information or words that you need to listen for. Some of the options may not be mentioned at all; others will be incorrect. Pay attention to how many choices you need to make (here you need to choose two letters).

9 and 10 B, E in any order (*One problem they do have is that a lot of the energy in the sunlight is lost in the form of heat from the collector ... keeping them stable is another drawback*)

Grammar focus task

Suggested answers: **1** asked **2** explained **3** denied
4 admitted **5** insisted

Unit 16

A: Context listening

1 She wants to work in a zoo or a safari park.
2 **1** She is doing a diploma course in animal management.
  2 She enjoys feeding the animals most. **3** She has overcome a fear of snakes.
3 **1** to do **2** to study **3** working **4** taking **5** cleaning
  6 treat **7** handle **8** feeling **9** to do **10** bark; to be
  11 to work
4 **1** decide, choose, remember, tell, would like **2** start, prefer, not mind, remember **3** let, make, hear,
  Remember can be followed by either the *to*-infinitive or *-ing*.

C: Grammar exercises

1 **2** to add **3** to have **4** to do **5** to finish **6** working / to work **7** writing / to write **8** to complete **9** to get
  10 to show **11** putting **12** to be **13** to email
  14 to remember (➤ B1 and B3)
2 **2** looking **3** to become **4** cleaning **5** falling
  6 not to worry **7** to take **8** to renew **9** rising
  10 to bring (➤ B3)

3 **3** ✓ **4** tried very hard to please **5** have made me feel
  6 made me want **7** ✓ **8** will stop making **9** ✓
  10 don't mind working **11** ✓ **12** doesn't force them to teach **13** ✓ **14** let their students decide (➤ B1–B4)
4 **2** did not feel like waiting **3** finished (had finished) talking
  4 tried to find **5** failed to do **6** saw me standing
  7 needed (had needed) to send **8** carried on looking
  9 have bothered to write **10** started eating / to eat
  11 considered leaving **12** expected him to get
  13 hope to receive **14** advise you to give (➤ B1–B4)

D: Test practice

Reading

Questions 1–6: identification of information in the text (True / False / Not Given)

Test tip: *True* means the ideas or opinions in the statement match the ideas or opinions in the passage. *False* means that the ideas or opinions in the statement are incorrect and do not match the ideas or opinions in the passage. *Not Given* means that these ideas are not mentioned in the passage.

1 True (*understanding how consumers make decisions and the crucial role of packaging in this process, has been a neglected area of research so far*) **2** True (*'heuristic processing' ... is based on very simple rules: ... choose what a trusted source suggests*) **3** False (*'heuristic processing' ... requires comparatively little effort ... 'systematic processing' involves much deeper levels of thought ... This form of thinking, which is both analytical and conscious, involves much more mental effort.*) **4** Not given (the text does not give us any information about who developed this concept) **5** True (*'systematic processing' involves ... taking account of the product information, including its price, its perceived quality and so on*)
6 False (*Under heuristic processing, for example, consumers may simply need to be able to distinguish the pack from those of competitors.*)

Questions 7–8: multiple choice

Test tip: Read all the questions and options and underline or highlight any important information or key words that you need to find in the passage. Use the questions to locate the relevant part of the reading passage. If you cannot find an answer, just move on to the next one and come back to this one later.

7 D (*testing the effectiveness of your packaging can be ineffective if the methods you are employing concern one form of thinking ... but your consumers are purchasing in the other mode*) **8** A (*getting consumers to change brands may involve developing packaging that includes information that does stimulate systematic processing*)

Questions 9–13: summary completion

Test tip: Notice that the summary has a title; this helps you to locate the part of the text being summarized. Read through the information in the summary carefully and try to predict what type of information you need to find in the passage. Pay careful attention to the word limit and make sure you copy the words correctly.

9 advantages / characteristics (*A crucial role of packaging in this situation is to communicate the* <u>characteristics</u> *of the product, highlighting its* <u>advantages</u> *over possible competitors.*) **10** situation (*people only engage in effort-demanding systematic processing when the* <u>situation</u> *justifies it*) **11** information (*people have an upper limit to the amount of* <u>information</u> *they can absorb. If we present too much, therefore, they will become confused. This, in turn, is likely to lead them* *to disengage and choose something else.*) **12** ingredients (*will not be able to deal with things they do not already understand, the <u>ingredients</u> of food products, for example*) **13** simple (*Our research has differentiated between people with a high need for thinking – who routinely engage in analytical thinking – and those low in the need for cognition, who prefer to use very <u>simple</u> forms of thinking.*)

Grammar focus task

1 developing **2** looking at; thinking about **3** to be able to **4** to be able to **5** to be **6** thinking **7** making **8** to change; developing; to challenge

Unit 17

A: Context listening

2 They talk about a car, travelling and investing the money.

3 1 c 2 h 3 f 4 a 5 g 6 b 7 d 8 e

4 provided that; unless; as long as
None of the sentences refer to events in the past.

C: Grammar exercises

1 2 e 3 b 4 d 5 f 6 h 7 a 8 g (➤B1 and B2)

2 1 became; were (was); 'd hate 2 didn't have; wouldn't know; don't find (can't find); 'll find; will save; do 3 will surprise; are used to 4 kept; 'd take; don't have; 'll have to (➤B2 and B3)

3 2 don't have 3 ✓ 4 will probably 5 start 6 have 7 isn't 8 ✓ 9 wouldn't be able 10 ✓ 11 met 12 might not happen (may not happen) 13 need 14 help (➤B1–B3)

4 2 As long as 3 unless 4 unless 5 in case 6 as long as 7 Provided that 8 When 9 if 10 unless (➤B4)

D: Test practice

Reading

Questions 1–3: multiple choice

Test tip: Read all the questions and options and underline or highlight any important information or key words that you need to find in the passage. Use the questions to locate the relevant part of the reading passage. If you cannot find an answer, just move on to the next one and come back to this one later.

1 C (*its sweet white buds hang from the trunk and along a few fat branches*) **2** B (*using temporary plantings of banana to shade the cacao while it's young*) **3** A (*In the United States, for example, imported cacao is the linchpin of an $8.6 billion domestic chocolate industry that in turn supports the nation's dairy and nut industries.*)

Questions 4–9: locating information

Test tip: Scan the passage for relevant information, and then check that it matches the question exactly (e.g. for question 4 you need to find a list of countries or places, not just one). Remember that the words in the passage may paraphrase the words in the questions.

4 E (*from South America and the Caribbean to West Africa, east Asia, and New Guinea and Vanuatu in the Pacific*) **5** H (*One such disease, witches broom, devastated the cacao plantations in the Bahia region of Brazil*) **6** C (*which they frothed up with water and spices to make bracing concoctions*) **7** D (*In the last 200 years the bean has been thoroughly democratized – transformed from an elite drink into ubiquitous candy bars, cocoa powders and confections. Today chocolate is becoming popular with new markets opening up in Eastern Europe and Asia.*) **8** F (*groves like this may produce*

annual yields of 50 to 60 pods per tree for 25 to 30 years) **9** C (*In 1753, the Swedish botanist Carolus Linnaeus gave the cacao tree genus the name* Theobroma)

Questions 10–13: notes completion

Test tip: Read through the notes carefully and try to predict what type of information you need to find in the passage (e.g. for question 12 you need to identify a farming method). Pay careful attention to the word limit and make sure you copy the words correctly.

10 disease (*try to address this problem by establishing <u>disease</u> resistant plants*) **11** (local) middlemen (*Most are at the mercy of <u>local middlemen</u> who buy the beans then sell them for a much higher price to the chocolate manufacturers. If the situation is to improve for farmers, these people need to be removed from the process.*) **12** sustainable (*ensure that <u>sustainable</u> farming practices are used*) **13** profits (*Typically, farmers who grow cacao get a pittance for their beans compared with the <u>profits</u> reaped by the rest of the chocolate business ... They also need to empower the farmers by guaranteeing them a higher price for their beans so that they will be encouraged to grow beans and can maintain their way of life.*)

Grammar focus task

1 scoop **2** let **3** dry **4** roast **5** happens **6** become **7** grind **8** press **9** will obtain

Unit 18

A: Context listening

1 Simon regrets buying a new car because it has cost him a lot of money.

2 1 F 2 T 3 T 4 F 5 F

3 1 'd bought; wouldn't have needed 2 wouldn't be; hadn't almost doubled 3 'd waited; 'd have managed 4 'd listened; would have happened 5 'd taken; 'd own

4 1 past perfect; past time 2 sentences 1, 3 and 4; *would have* + past participle 3 sentences 2 and 5; *would* + infinitive without *to*

C: Grammar exercises

1 2 would (might) have got 3 would (might) have received 4 'd made 5 would (might) have been 6 'd planned 7 'd prepared 8 would (might) have restricted 9 'd started 10 wouldn't have been 11 hadn't left 12 would (might) have been able 13 'd come 14 would (could) have helped (➤B1)

2 2 had been any germs 3 wouldn't have abandoned his research 4 hadn't seen Fleming's research papers 5 hadn't worked with RAF 6 wouldn't have decided 7 wouldn't have failed 8 hadn't opposed (➤B1)

3 2 ~~would you done~~ would you have done 3 ~~am starting~~ would be starting 4 ~~would have kept~~ had kept 5 ~~didn't have~~ hadn't had 6 ~~was very excited~~ 'd be very excited 7 ~~might make~~ might have made 8 ~~will be~~ would be 9 ~~didn't make~~ wouldn't have made 10 ~~didn't go~~ hadn't gone (➤B1 and B2)

4 2 wish you'd asked 3 wish I hadn't chosen (shouldn't have chosen); should have chosen 4 wish I'd studied 5 wish he'd stop 6 should have let 7 wish I had 8 wish it would stop 9 wish I hadn't done (shouldn't have done) 10 shouldn't have told (➤B3 and B4)

D: Test practice

Reading

Questions 1–8: classification

Test tip: Underline or highlight the key words in the reading passage (e.g. *giant panda*, *spectacled bear*). Carefully read the information nearby and try to match the information in the passage to the facts in the questions (1–8). Remember the words in the questions will not always match the words in the passage exactly. Here you need to decide whether these facts apply to only one animal or to both.

1 A (*the giant panda has evolved a sixth digit*) **2** B (*The spectacled bear is a more frequent climber ... They also construct tree nests to act as a bed.*) **3** C (*Both are survivors of an ancient lineage dating back 18 million years*) **4** B (*Spectacled bears are highly adaptable and are found in a wide range of habitats including rainforest, dry forest and coastal scrub desert.*) **5** A (*They* (giant pandas) *also both have a distinctive cry which they use to communicate with others in their group.* Here the giant panda is being compared to the red panda.) **6** C (*They* (giant pandas) *feed mainly on the ground but are capable of climbing trees as well. The spectacled bear is a more frequent climber*) **7** C (*the giant panda supplements its diet with meat which it scavenges. Spectacled bears eat carrion, too, and some have been known to kill small calves*) **8** A (*the red panda, a member of the raccoon family ... The giant panda shares many physical characteristics with the red panda*)

Questions 9–13: sentence completion

Test tip: First identify the type of information you need to find (e.g. for question 1 you need to find out why a giant panda eats constantly). It may help to turn the sentences into questions (e.g. what do spectacled bears build to help them reach their food?) Make sure you stick to the word limit.

9 carnivore (*This is rather strange given that its physiology is typical of a* carnivore) **10** digest (*A panda manages to* digest *only about 17% of the bamboo it eats*) **11** hibernate (*Unable to store fat effectively, it continues eating in the bitterly cold winter, at a time when many other bears* hibernate.) **12** (tree) nests / platforms / a (tree) nest / a platform (*They also construct* tree nests *to act as a bed as well as a* platform *to feed from fruit-laden branches.*) **13** eye patches ('*In pandas, a stare is a threat,*' *Schaller says.* '*The* eye patches *enlarge the panda's small, dark eyes tenfold, making the stare more powerful.*')

Grammar focus task

1 had had; would/might have been able to **2** had not dissected; might/would not have thought **3** did not resemble; might/would not have been **4** had not contradicted; might/could/would have been

---

Unit 19

A: Context listening

2 She is worried about: finding maths difficult, being unprepared to teach, controlling the class and pupils being rude to her.

3 **1** interested in **2** share **3** with **4** impressed by **5** learning about **6** warned **7** about **8** good at **9** experience of **10** worried about **11** shout at

4 **1** warn; learn **2** worried **3** good **4** shout **5** interested **6** experience **7** share **8** impressed

---

C: Grammar exercises

1 **2** A **3** C **4** C **5** B **6** B **7** A **8** B (➤B1 & B2)

2 **2** ~~amongst~~ between **3** ~~about~~ for **4** ✓ **5** ~~to~~ at **6** ~~to~~ for **7** ~~about~~ of **8** ~~in~~ by **9** ~~at~~ with **10** ✓ **11** ~~in~~ on **12** ~~in~~ at (➤B1, B3 & B4)

3 **2** bad for **3** effect on **4** depend on (rely on) **5** obsessed with **6** true for **7** worried about **8** choose between/from **9** rely on (depend on) (➤B1–B3)

4 **2** for **3** by **4** for **5** about **6** for/of **7** for **8** at **9** of **10** with **11** by **12** of **13** for **14** of (➤B1–B4)

D: Test practice

Listening

Questions 1–2: multiple choice

Test tip: Read all the questions carefully before you listen. Underline or highlight any key information or words that you need to listen for (e.g. *How far away is the nearest big town to Greenville?*) Use the questions to help you find your way through the listening text. If you miss an answer, just move on to the next one.

1 C (*but emergency services have to drive 500 kilometres to reach us from the closest large town*) **2** B (*thanks to the arrival of Doctor Jones earlier this year, we no longer have to drive so far if anyone gets sick*)

Questions 3–10: notes completion

Test tip: Read through the notes carefully before you listen and try to predict what type of information you need to hear (e.g. for question 6 you will need to listen for a measurement, or for question 10 you will need to listen for a month or date). Pay careful attention to the word limit and check your spelling at the end.

3 contact / call / telephone (*Well, immediately after the storm has passed, the first thing you need to do is* call *the national weather station.*) **4** report card (*After that you simply have to complete what they call a* report card) **5** (local) (news)paper (*keep an eye out for any reports in the* local newspaper *of storms or storm damage. You need to cut these out and send them in as well.*) **6** two centimetres / 2cm (*report any that is* two centimetres *in diameter or bigger*) **7** large/big trees (*They also need to know about damage caused by high winds, especially if it uproots* large trees. *... restrict it to those big enough to cause a problem, especially on our roads.*) **8** training (*... we'll be conducting* training *next month. This will only take up a day so don't worry too much about it.*) **9** police (*If you do have the time and would like to come along then you'll need to talk to the* police *who are coordinating the event*) **10** October (*you'll need to put your name down by the end of* October *at the very latest*)

Grammar focus task

1 about **2** about **3** at **4** about **5** about **6** about **7** to

---

Unit 20

A: Context listening

2 The problems mentioned are: the ladder left out, the letters in the letterbox, the open window, overhanging branches.

3 **1** where there are **2** that could become **3** that can check **4** which have **5** who can collect

4 **1** *Where* refers to a place. **2** *That* and *who* are used to refer to people. **3** *That* and *which* are used to refer to things.

C: Grammar exercises

1 2 who/that; e   3 which/that; i   4 where; a   5 when/that; f
6 who/that; c   7 who/that; g   8 why; j   9 whose; h
10 whose; b   The relative pronoun can be left out in
sentences 6 and 8 (➤B1 & B2)

2 2 Some students take a year out before university, which allows
them to work or travel.   3 The Guggenheim Museum, which is
in Bilbao, only displays contemporary art. / The Guggenheim
Museum, which only displays contemporary art, is in Bilbao.
4 My English teacher, whose lectures are very interesting, is
leaving.   5 The lecture, which was about current economic
policy, was not very easy to understand. / The lecture, which
was not very easy to understand, was about current economic
policy.   6 My parents arrived in New York in 1951, where they
stayed for the rest of their lives.   7 I gave my assignment to
the faculty secretary, who was not very friendly. (➤B3)

3 2 which I saw ~~them~~ advertised   3 exhausting, ~~that~~ which is
not   4 the lecture which you gave ~~it~~ on Wednesday
5 It's the one which ~~in~~ you have written your lecture notes in.
6 today's newspaper, which has   7 those bread rolls ~~what~~
(which/that) we had   8 a person ~~who~~ whose life is full
(➤B1–B4)

4 2 which/that; i   3 which/that; e   4 which; h
5 which/that; c   6 where; b   7 which/that; f   8 which; a
9 which/that; d   (➤B1–B4)

D: Test practice
Reading

Questions 1–4: sentence completion

Test tip: First identify the type of information you need to find
(e.g. for question 1 you need to find a disease or health problem).
It may help to turn the sentences into questions (e.g. what is the
name of the process that helps keep plants in good condition?)
Make sure you stick to the word limit.

1 heart disease (*Recognised as the type of fatty acid most able to
protect against heart disease*)   **2** drought (*a project that aims to
develop more drought-tolerant sunflowers*)   **3** transpiration
(*Transpiration is the mechanism by which plants lose water through
their leaves. This system is thought to facilitate the passage of minerals
through the plant and is vital for healthy plants.*)   **4** wind (speed),
humidity (*the research team discovered that its initial approach did not
cater for changes in wind speed … The team therefore needed a
technique to measure temperature continuously that would allow it to
examine the effects of other variables such as humidity*)

Questions 5–12: locating information

Test tip: Scan the passage for relevant information, and then
check that it matches the question exactly (e.g. for question 7 you
need to find a mention of two processes used by plants, or for
question 11 you need to look for a number). Remember that the
words in the passage may paraphrase the words in the questions.

5 H (*The sunflower canopy had to be complete, with no visible soil, so
that the thermometers would only measure the temperature of the plants
and not the surrounding environment.*)   **6** F (*The robot runs on an
oblong track around the experimental plot and the thermometers
operate on each side of the track.*)   **7** C (*Plants undergo photosynthesis
to produce energy in the form of sugar. This involves allowing carbon
dioxide to enter the leaves through pores called stomata. Transpiration
is the mechanism by which plants lose water through their leaves.*)

8 I (*The team and their robot have already made a major breakthrough
in the Australian wheat industry with Drysdale Wheat.*)   **9** G (*If the
skies darken due to rain, heavy cloud cover or sunset, the robot makes its
way back to the garage to wait.*)   **10** B (*a robot developed by the
Australian National University's Research School of Biological Sciences*)
11 H (*Eight varieties of sunflower were examined.*)   **12** D (*by
measuring the temperature of the leaves, scientists can determine how
much water is being lost through transpiration.*)

Grammar focus task

1 defining relative clause; *that* refers to *a project* and acts as the
subject of *aims*   **2** non-defining relative clause; *which* refers to
wind speed and acts as the subject of *could*   **3** non-defining relative
clause; *where* refers to *a garage* and acts as the object of *waits*
4 defining relative clause; *who* refers to *an agronomist* and acts as
the subject of *could*   **5** non-defining relative clause; *which* refers
to *Drysdale Wheat* and acts as the subject of *signalled*

Unit 21

A: Context listening

3 1 I live   2 do you do   3 I always do; I go; they always put;
it costs   4 I always do; I work; there are   5 I did try; I didn't
like; can I ask; You can't

4 In the conversation the subjects are mostly personal
pronouns: *I, you*
In the written report the subjects are mostly noun phrases:
*These supermarkets; The people who were interviewed; the
respondents.*

C: Grammar exercises

1 2 the government needs is a lot more loyal supporters
3 we want is action   4 I don't enjoy is watching TV
5 is the bride who is the most important person at a wedding
6 is the causes of poverty (that) governments should be
dealing with, not the results of it   7 was when I was ill in
hospital as a child that I first decided to study medicine
8 is your family that suffer the most   (➤B4)

2 2 f *These* refers to *changes*.   3 g *It* refers to *a camera*.   4 c
5 e   6 a *This* refers to the *primary role* of the camera.
7 b   (➤B3)

3 2 This rise   3 Many countries   4 a solar roof   5 A one
kilowatt solar panel   6 Solar panels , solar water heaters and
wind generators   7 they   8 These renewable energy systems
9 the government   (➤B1, B3 and B5)

4 2 ~~children need to~~ experience   3 ~~these foods~~ tend not
4 It is often the lack of experience of eating different kinds of
foods that   5 ~~experiencing a wider variety of foods~~ can
therefore lead   6 ~~To provide support and help to parents is
important.~~ It is important to provide support and help to
parents.   7 ~~No child would feel ashamed or embarrassed by
the contents of their lunch boxes with this system.~~ This
system would ensure that no child felt ashamed or
embarrassed by the contents of their lunch boxes.
8 Eating ~~a healthy diet~~ healthily   (➤B1–B4)

D: Test practice
Academic Writing Task 2

Test tip: Make sure that you read all parts of the question
carefully and address each point made. Organize your thoughts

and ideas well. Do not try to memorize essays. Make sure you have at least 40 minutes to spend on this task and try to leave time at the end to check your spelling.

Model answer

Nowadays most children regularly play games on a computer or on their television. These games have become more violent over the past few years. In fact, many parents worry about this and the effect these games are having on their children. Some are concerned that playing violent games might encourage them to become aggressive in real life. What we need to establish is whether or not this is actually true.

First, it may help to look back at the games that children used to play many years ago before the invention of computers. In those days children would probably have played popular board games such as Monopoly or chess, or they may have played card games or some type of outdoor sport. These sports or games would probably only have encouraged children to become more competitive rather than violent.

However, throughout history children have always played fighting games with toy or pretend weapons. Even now many parents will buy a toy gun or sword for their child. Why do we never read reports in the media about the impact plastic weapons could have on children? Perhaps this is because the link between play fighting and actual fighting is not very strong.

In conclusion, the way children play games has changed with the times but the ideas behind those games have actually changed very little. Just as playing at soldiers did not increase violence in the past, I believe that playing computer games will not lead to an increase in violence in the future. I think that if we looked more closely at life in our major cities then we would find there are many other possible causes for the increase in crime and violence.

Grammar focus task

The new information is underlined.

Nowadays most children regularly play games on a computer or on their television. These games have become more violent over the past few years. In fact many parents worry about this and the effect these games are having on their children. Some are concerned that playing violent games might encourage them to become aggressive in real life. What we need to establish is whether or not this is actually true.

Unit 22

A: Context listening

1 1 f 2 d 3 a 4 b 5 g 6 h 7 e 8 c

2 1 They need to go to the library and fill in a form and have their photo taken. 2 It is a group which represents students' views to the university. 3 It is responsible for extra facilities around the campus that are not related to study e.g. restaurants, entertainment and sports facilities.

3 1 Do they process; are processed 2 does the university run; is run 3 do you choose; is chosen

4 They become the subject of the passive verb.

C: Grammar exercises

1 2 are peeled 3 are soaked 4 are put 5 are sliced 6 are rinsed 7 are fried 8 are removed 9 are then left 10 are added 11 be distributed 12 sold (➢B1 and B2)

2 2 ~~has changed~~ has been changed 3 ~~might have been happened~~ might have happened 4 ~~have given~~ have been given 5 ~~have been benefited~~ have benefited 6 ~~have been suggested~~ have suggested 7 ~~are continued~~ continue 8 ~~are being become~~ are becoming 9 ~~feels~~ is felt 10 ~~have been come~~ have come 11 ~~has affected~~ has been affected 12 ~~will use~~ will be used (➢B1–B3)

3 2 are (were) placed 3 was believed 4 have been allowed 5 is being serviced 6 will be opened 7 is expected 8 is made 9 claims 10 are known 11 encouraging (to be encouraged) 12 to take (➢B1–B4)

4 2 be absorbed 3 affects 4 continues 5 are used 6 to use 7 are being built 8 is said 9 to decide 10 tackling 11 have been passed 12 allows 13 are forced 14 know 15 will be used 16 have their cars checked (➢B1–B5)

D: Test practice

Academic Writing Task 1

Test tip: Study the diagram carefully to identify all of the key stages and make sure that you don't miss any important information out of your description. You may need to change the words on the diagram (e.g. to change verbs to nouns) to make them fit grammatically into your sentences.

Model answer

The diagram shows how fresh fruit is canned. First the fruit is picked from trees by hand. It is then transported to the cannery by large trucks. At the cannery the fruit is washed and quality checked, and any poor quality fruit is rejected. The good quality fruit is put into cold storage. When it is ready for canning the fruit is weighed and graded. The grading ensures that fruit of a similar size is kept together. After this the fruit is peeled and the cores are removed. It is then sliced into the required sizes and put into cans. Juice or syrup is also added to the cans. Once the cans have been filled they are sealed and cooked over heat to ensure that the cans are sterilized. When the cans are cool, a label is attached and they are placed into storage. The canned fruit is now ready to be despatched to supermarkets and sold.

Grammar focus task

1 The cans are allowed to cool. 2 The cans are sterilized using a special heating process. 3 The fruit is taken to the cannery in large trucks. 4 The fruit is checked before storage and any poor quality fruit is rejected.
The correct order is: 3, 4, 2, 1

Unit 23

A: Context listening

1 1 c 2 g 3 a 4 i 5 d 6 e 7 h 8 f 9 b

2 1 F 2 T 3 T 4 T 5 F 6 F 7 F 8 F

3 1 in spite of 2 Despite 3 however 4 Firstly 5 Secondly 6 Finally 7 although 8 To sum up

4 1 in spite of; however; despite; although 2 firstly; secondly; finally 3 to sum up

C: Grammar exercises

1 2 b 3 b 4 b (result) 5 a 6 b (contrasting idea) 7 a (contrasting idea) 8 a (restates the previous idea) 9 a (contrasting idea) 10 b (reason) 11 a 12 b (reason) (➢B1 and B2)

2   2 Firstly (the first idea in a list)   3 Furthermore (adds to the previous idea)   4 therefore (this idea is a result of the previous one)   5 Thirdly (introduces a third important point)   6 Although (introduces a contrasting idea: *despite* cannot be followed by a subject + verb)   7 In addition (adds further information)   8 as a result (this idea is the result of the previous one)   9 Nevertheless (gives contrasting information) (➤B1 and B2)

3   2 For example   3 Firstly   4 Similarly   5 However   6 but; because   7 As a result (➤B1 and B2)

4   2 I had to cancel all of my afternoon appointments because the head of my department called an emergency meeting.   3 Fewer people are going to the cinema these days due to the fact that it is now much cheaper to rent a DVD at home.   4 Petrol prices increased last month. As a result, the cost of basic foods has risen.   5 There are over 30 girls on this course but the boys still outnumber the girls by two to one.   6 There are some advantages to the pace of modern life. However, it also has its disadvantages.   7 In spite of the fact that the number of red deer in the wild increased slightly in the 1980s, it (the increase) was not sufficient to take them off the endangered species list. / In spite of the slight increase in the number of red deer in the wild in the 1980s, this was not sufficient to take them off the endangered species list. / Red deer were not taken off the endangered species list in spite of the fact that their numbers in the wild increased slightly in the 1980s. (➤B1 and B2)

D: Test practice

Reading

Questions 1–3: multiple choice

Test tip: Read all the questions and options and underline or highlight any important information or key words that you need to find in the passage. Use the questions to locate the relevant part of the reading passage. If you cannot find an answer, just move on to the next one and come back to this one later.

1 B (*In that moment, Rita and Jake stumbled across an interesting set of differences between older and younger minds.*)   **2** D (*In the end, if 'better' is defined as completing a clean paragraph, both people may end up taking the same amount of time.*)   **3** A (*subjects were told to look at a screen, wait for an arrow that pointed in a certain direction to appear, and then use a mouse to click on the arrow as soon as it appeared on the screen. The other arrows were used to distract the subjects.*)

Questions 4–7: sentence completion

Test tip: Sentence completion with a box of possible answers is similar to matching questions. Scan the passage for the key names or words in the questions and underline or highlight them. Then carefully read the information close to those words and try to match it to the ideas in the options (A–F). Remember there are more options than you need to use. Some of the extra options may not be mentioned at all, or may be the opposite of the information in the passage.

4 E (*Popular psychology says that as people age their brains 'slow down'.*)   **5** C (*scientists at the University of Michigan for example, have shown that ... seniors exploit the left and right side of the brain more extensively than men and women who are decades younger*)   **6** B (*Michael Falkenstein ... found that when elders were presented with new computer exercises they paused longer before reacting and took longer to complete the tasks, yet they made 50% fewer errors*)

7 D (*Neurologists at Northwest University came to this conclusion after analyzing 50 people ... Darren Gleitman, who headed the study, concluded that older brains solved the problems just as effectively but by different means.*)

Questions 8–12: summary completion

Test tip: Read through the information in the summary carefully and try to predict what type of information you need to find in the passage. Pay careful attention to the word limit and make sure you copy the words correctly.

8 minds (*Just as people's bodies age at different rates, so do their minds.*)   **9** memories (*As adults advance in age, the perception of sights, sounds and smells takes a bit longer, and ... The ability to retrieve memories also quickly slides.*)   **10 & 11** IN EITHER ORDER: knowledge, experience (*On the other hand, the ageing brain can create significant benefits by tapping into its extensive hoard of accumulated knowledge and experience.*)   **12** speed (*Drawing on both sides of the brain gives them a tactical edge, even if the speed of each hemisphere's process is slower*)

Grammar focus task

1 e   **2** g   **3** b   **4** c   **5** f   **6** a   **7** d

Unit 24

A: Context listening

1   The topic is whether children should be educated at home or at school.

2   1 T   2 F   3 T   4 F   5 T   6 F

3   1 fortunately; I can see; I think   2 unfortunately; I can see; certainly; I think; interestingly; Perhaps

4   1 see; think   2 fortunately; unfortunately; interestingly   3 certainly; perhaps

C: Grammar exercises

1   2 Personally,   3 presumably   4 perhaps   5 Overall,   6 probably   7 Surprisingly,   8 Unfortunately (➤B2)

2   2 Apparently, the start of the course has been delayed because the tutor is ill. / The start of the course has been delayed because, apparently, the tutor is ill. / The start of the course has been delayed because the tutor is ill, apparently.   3 I definitely want to go to university when I leave school.   4 I was late for the exam because my bus didn't come, but luckily the exam hadn't started on time so I only missed a few minutes. / I was late for the exam because my bus didn't come, but the exam hadn't started on time, so luckily I only missed a few minutes.   5 Unfortunately, the university has decided to close the music department. / The university has decided to close the music department, unfortunately. / The university has unfortunately decided to close the music department.   6 Perhaps it is time to reorganise our company structure.   7 On the whole, my tutor was impressed with the effort I had put into my assignment, but suggested a few changes. / My tutor was impressed with the effort I had put into my assignment on the whole, but suggested a few changes.   8 It is probably true that people are living longer today than in the past. (➤B2)

3   2 Frankly,   3 Surprisingly,   4 Unfortunately,   5 On the whole,   6 Evidently   7 Possibly,   8 Actually, (➤B2)

4 There are many reasons why people follow a vegetarian diet. Firstly, it is because <u>they believe that</u> it is wrong to kill animals. This <u>may be</u> ~~is~~ due to religious beliefs, or it <u>could be</u> ~~is~~ their own personal philosophy.

<u>It is possible</u> that another motivation for stopping eating meat is health. <u>According to research,</u> the high fibre content of a vegetarian diet <u>seems to</u> reduces the likelihood of suffering from some bowel problems and heart disease. In addition, fewer vegetarians than meat-eaters are overweight. A further advantage is that a vegetarian diet <u>can be</u> ~~is~~ cheaper than eating meat.

Nevertheless, <u>it is clear that</u> there are some disadvantages. Vegetarians <u>can</u> lack a lot of the vitamins and minerals that are present in meat, such as iron or vitamin B12, or calcium if you do not include dairy products in your diet. There is also the social problem of not being able to eat food available at parties and restaurants.

<u>Overall,</u> however in terms of health a vegetarian is more likely to be healthy than a non-vegetarian and <u>personally I feel that</u> the advantages outweigh the disadvantages. (➤ B1–B4)

D: Test practice
Academic Writing Task 2

Test tip: Make sure that you read all parts of the question carefully and address each point made. Organize your thoughts and ideas well. Do not try to memorize essays. Make sure you have at least 40 minutes to spend on this task and try to leave time at the end to check your spelling.

Model answer

Nowadays, modern technology has totally changed our approach to study. In many countries students no longer have to copy notes by hand from the blackboard; instead the teacher gives them a photocopy. Rather than messy ink and pen, students present a typed-up copy of their assignments. Their computer even checks their spelling as they go. In fact, some people believe that modern technology does a lot of our thinking for us and, as a result, we are losing our ability to think for ourselves.

In my opinion, spelling skills have definitely deteriorated in recent years. So many young people use mobile phones to send text messages where speed and conciseness are more important than spelling or grammar. Some teachers complain that these students take the same attitude towards their written assignments.

On the other hand, typed assignments are much easier to read and are much neater. Frankly, I find some notes or texts which are handwritten almost impossible to read. Doctors, for example, have often had a reputation for illegible handwriting, which could lead to disastrous medical mistakes. Perhaps it is time we focused not on handwriting but on presenting information as accurately as possible.

One advantage of computers is that access to the Internet has opened up a world of learning to us. We no longer have to wait for a book that has already been borrowed from the library before we can do our research. In fact, the Internet can clearly be used to research information in the same way as a library but more conveniently.

On the whole, rather than holding students back, I believe modern technology has actually improved standards of education considerably.

Grammar focus task

1 I believe (in my opinion)   2 actually
3 In my opinion (I believe); definitely   4 Frankly

Unit 25

A: Context listening
2 She experienced itching, pain, swelling and redness.
3 1 She had a very bad reaction and had to go to hospital.
2 On her foot.   3 It hurt. / It was very painful.   4 It went red and swelled up.   5 Her foot itched, it was difficult for her to breathe and she kept coughing.
4 1 burning pain   2 itching   3 swelling
4 breathing difficulties; a dry cough
5 1 The verbs are changed to nouns. 2 be, become (non-action verbs)

C: Grammar exercises
1 2 study; studies; student   3 findings; find   4 response; respondent   5 measurement; measure   6 earnings; earner
7 advertisement; advertiser; advertising   8 examination; examiner
9 suggestion   10 creation; creator; creativity (➤ B1)
2 2 strength   3 depth   4 beauty   5 clarity   6 interest
7 difficulty   8 caution   9 significance   10 violence
11 controversy   12 confusion (➤ B1)
3 2 there are some quite significant differences   3 the largest proportion of expenditure was   4 food expenditure   5 total household budget   6 There has been a notable increase in
7 a significant rise in the proportion of money spent on clothing
8 the proportion of fuel and lighting expenditure was roughly the same. (➤ B1 and B2)
4 2 Spending (expenditure); increase; influence   3 failure; illness
4 diet; reduction   5 Use; risk; loss   6 Contentment; success; communication   7 Developments; construction   8 difficulty
(➤ B1 and B2)

D: Test practice
Academic Writing Task 1

Test tip: Spend time studying the information first. The title given may help you with your first sentence, but try to use different words and don't just copy words from the question paper. Try to identify key areas in the data (e.g. where the data changes considerably or where there is no change over a period of time). Do not miss out any important details in your description and make sure you stick to the time limit so that you leave enough time to answer Task 2.

Model answer

The total number of all species of wild birds in the UK has been relatively stable over the last two decades, although there were significant drops in numbers between 1977 and 1979 and again in 1982 and 1986. Since 1994 there has been an improvement in numbers of all species, although the graph shows a slight decrease in 2000.

In contrast, the population of farmland birds has suffered a severe decline, particularly in 1978 when numbers fell dramatically. The rate of decline in the population appears to have slowed and it has remained relatively stable since 2000.

There was also a fall in the number of woodland birds of around 30% between 1974 and 1992. The population increased slightly in 2000 but it had dropped again by 2004.

It is only coastal species that have seen a steady increase in population over this period. Their numbers dropped slightly in 1995 and again in 2003 but the overall trend has been a positive one.

Grammar focus task

1 an improvement in numbers; a slight decrease   2 a fall in the number of woodland birds   3 a steady increase in population

Recording scripts

Recording 1a

Interviewer: Excuse me. I'm conducting a survey on how people spend their free time. Do you mind if I ask you a few questions?

Pete: Oh, er, OK. I'm just waiting for my friends – they're always late, so I should have a few minutes!

Interviewer: Right, now, can I have your name?

Pete: It's Peter, Peter Harley – H A R L E Y.

Interviewer: And do you work or are you a student, Peter?

Pete: Well, both actually. I'm studying really hard for my exams this month – I'm doing maths at university – but I also help my parents out. They own a restaurant and I work there as a waiter in the evenings, so I don't get a lot of free time during the week.

Interviewer: It sounds as if you're very busy.

Pete: Yes, I am, and my mum's always saying I don't help enough in the restaurant! But I do manage to find some free time most days.

Interviewer: Great. Now, can you have a look at this list and tell me whether you do any of these things and if so, how often?

Pete: Sure. OK, well, I love music and I'm learning to play the piano. I get up really early and practise for an hour or so just about every day. I also play the guitar in a band with some other friends. We used to practise together at least three times a week but these days we only manage to meet about once every two weeks.

Interviewer: What about the next thing on the list: computer games? I assume you're too busy to play them.

Pete: Well, I used to play them all the time but now I'm too busy studying and I don't miss them at all!

Interviewer: And do you use a computer for other things?

Pete: I use the Internet just about every day for my studies, and I also use it to keep in touch with my friends and family. My cousin is living in Thailand at the moment and he sends me regular emails to let me know how much fun he's having! He's always visiting exciting places.

Interviewer: Yes, the Internet is making it much easier for people to stay in touch with each other. Now, how about team sport?

Pete: Actually, I joined the local football team when I was at school and I still play once a month provided I can get to training. I much prefer playing football to watching it on TV, though I do occasionally watch a match if there's a big final or something.

Interviewer: What about going to watch live matches?

Pete: I'd love to be able to afford to go every week because I support my local team, but students don't generally have much money, you know! I can't remember the last time I went to a live match. Oh, sorry, I can see my friends – I have to go now.

Interviewer: Thank you for your time.

Recording 1b

Man: Westfield Sports Centre, can I help you?

Woman: Yes, I hope so. I've recently moved to the area and I want to do some sports activities.

Man: Well, we have excellent facilities, including a new gymnasium and several tennis courts. Our tennis team are always looking for new people.

Woman: Oh, I was never any good at gymnastics and I don't think I've got the time to put into learning tennis. No, I'm more interested in swimming, and I'd also like to take a few yoga classes if I can.

Man: OK, well, we have three swimming pools: an Olympic size 50 metre pool and a 25 metre pool, which are both outdoors, and a heated indoor pool, which is just 15 metres long but is very popular with our members in the winter!

Woman: I bet it is! Do members have to pay to use the pools?

Man: Well, members don't pay for the pools if they just want to swim laps on their own. We even offer complimentary classes for beginners, but we do charge a small fee if you want to take part in the advanced training sessions, and there's also a fee for our water-based keep-fit class.

Woman: Right. And would I need to book any of the facilities or can I just come whenever I want?

Man: We don't actually allow anyone to book the swimming lanes or the gym equipment, but for safety reasons we can only have a maximum of seven people in the sauna at any one time, so you do need to put your name on the list for that.

Woman:	Fine. Now, I'd also really like to take a yoga class. Do you have any?
Man:	Yes. There are classes on Monday, Tuesday and Friday in the morning from ten till eleven, and then every Saturday and Sunday in the evening. Those classes are a bit longer, starting at six and finishing at seven thirty.
Woman:	Right, I'll just make a note of that. So, does that mean that if I enrol I can come on each of those days?
Man:	No, each day is a different level, so you only come once a week.
Woman:	Oh, I see. Well, I've been doing yoga for a little while now, but I am still finding it quite difficult. Which level do you think I should choose?
Man:	Most people start at the lowest level, and then you can talk to the instructor about changing if you think it's too easy.
Woman:	OK. How much are the classes?
Man:	They're £1.50 an hour for members.
Woman:	Great. Now, I'd like to come in and look at the facilities. Would someone be able to show me around?
Man:	Yes, no problem.
Woman:	Who should I ask for?
Man:	Ask for me. My name is John Doherty – that's D O H E R T Y.
Woman:	And should I just ask for you at the reception?
Man:	Actually, my office is on a different level. Take the lift up to level one and you'll see my name on the door right in front of you.
Woman:	Great. I'd like to come tomorrow if that's OK. What time suits you?
Man:	Well, I have appointments from nine to ten thirty, so could you make it eleven?
Woman:	I'm sure that will be fine, but can I just take your direct number in case something else crops up?
Man:	That's a good idea – my number's 0117 965 478.
Woman:	Great. I think that's everything, so I'll see you tomorrow. Oh, my name's Alison Martin, by the way.
Man:	Thanks, Alison. See you tomorrow.

Recording 2

Presenter:	Today's guest is Bill Murphy, who worked for the police force for over 17 years until his retirement last week. Welcome to the show, Bill. You're going to tell us how to protect our homes, is that right?
Bill Murphy:	Thank you, yes, that's right. As you say, I used to work for the police force and I must have seen hundreds of burglaries during that time. Unfortunately, burglary seems to be on the increase; the number of burglaries in our area rose by 25% last year. What's so frustrating is that it's possible to prevent many burglaries. For example, a few weeks ago a woman called to report a robbery at her house. It happened at five in the afternoon while she was watching the news on TV in a room at the back of the house. Her son was also at home; he was doing his homework in his bedroom when the burglar came into the house.
Presenter:	So, how did the burglar break in without anybody hearing him?
Bill Murphy:	Well, this woman used to keep the front door locked at all times, but when her son got older he often went out to visit his friends after school, so she would leave the door unlocked whenever she was at home so he could come and go easily. The burglar simply walked in through the front door, which was unlocked, and no one heard a thing. So you see, you do need to be careful to lock your door at all times of the day.
Presenter:	Absolutely. And what did the burglar steal?
Bill Murphy:	On this occasion, the burglar came in through the front door, picked up the woman's handbag and while she was watching the TV, he emptied it out and stole her purse. The son didn't hear anything because he was listening to music and working on his computer upstairs. Then the burglar went into the front room, opened all the cupboards and took a valuable collection of CDs. But the surprising thing is that after that he went into the kitchen and stole the roast chicken the woman had cooked for dinner! So you see, it really is important to ...

Recording 3

Sue:	Hi Carl. Have you written your assignment yet?
Carl:	Hi Sue. No, I haven't, but I've been trying to get some ideas together.
Sue:	What sorts of things have you been doing?
Carl:	Well, I've worked really hard for the last two weeks and I've nearly finished all the books on the reading list. I've made quite a lot of notes but they're not very structured. What about you?

Sue:	I did the reading a few weeks ago, and I made notes on the most important things. I've written a rough plan this morning, and I was going to make a start on writing the assignment today but I've decided I need to read the most important parts of the books again before I do that. I'm actually finding it quite hard. It's the first time I've ever had to write such a long essay so I'm a bit nervous about it.
Carl:	Yes, it's the longest essay I've ever had to write as well. I find all the reading so difficult. I read five books last week, and they all said different things!
(Pause)	
Sue:	I find the best approach is to read only the sections that you need in order to answer the question. You don't usually have to read the whole book. I've collected plenty of information for the assignment that way.
Carl:	That's good advice. I've been trying to read the whole of each book, and the more I read, the more confused I get. I probably wasted a lot of time last week.
Sue:	Oh, I'll tell you what other things I found really helpful. When I was in the library last week, I read those leaflets called 'How to get the best out of the library' and 'How to write assignments'. They really helped. Have you read them?
Carl:	No, I haven't even seen them. I'll have to get hold of a copy; they sound very useful. I really need some direction. I find I'm so tired at the moment. I've read six articles this week but I can barely remember what they said! In fact, I've been feeling tired since I started this course!
Sue:	Hmm, I know what you mean. I felt like that as well at the start until one of my tutors told me it was far more important to get enough rest than to stay up late studying. I've gone to bed early every night since then and I manage to concentrate for longer during the day, so in the end I do actually get more done. I went to bed at ten thirty last night and I feel great.
Carl:	Well, I've just got up and I'm already tired. I must try going to bed earlier – at least till I've done this assignment.
Sue:	Yeah, it should help.

Recording 4

Good morning and welcome to today's talk on famous composers. Today we're going to look at the remarkable career of Wolfgang Amadeus Mozart. Mozart was born in Salzburg on January 27, 1756, the last of seven children. However, when Mozart was born, five of his siblings had already died in infancy or early childhood. His only surviving sibling was his sister, Nannerl, who was five years older. Mozart's father, Leopold, was a composer and his grandfather had also been a musician. Times were hard and the family had been struggling for some time.

When she was eight, Nannerl began keyboard lessons with her father. Mozart's sister was extremely gifted at the keyboard and she had been making excellent progress when her brother, then aged three, demanded to be taught as well. In just 30 minutes Mozart mastered the piece of music, which his father had copied into Nannerl's notebook. Wolfgang's achievement was followed in rapid succession by others. By the time he was six, the little boy had written a composition of his own into the notebook. And by age seven, he had taught himself how to play the violin without ever having received a lesson.

When Leopold Mozart saw how extraordinary his son was, he decided not to waste Wolfgang's precocious talents and took him on a tour across Europe with his sister. At Linz, Wolfgang gave his first public concert. Among the audience were some important statesmen who were astonished and hurried on to Vienna to spread sensational reports of what they had seen. By the time he was 17, Mozart's reputation had already begun to spread through Europe and his family were richer than they had ever been before.

Recording 5

Amanda:	Hi Tim, just ringing to see if you've got the details of the hockey team's trip for next month.
Tim:	Hi Amanda. Yes, I went to the travel agency this morning. I've got the details right here in front of me.
Amanda:	Oh, great. Well, why don't you tell me all about it and I'll pass on the information to the rest of the team.
Tim:	Good, well, first of all we're flying to Scotland. We'll have to get up really early because our flight leaves at six thirty in the morning. We're playing four matches there, which I know sounds like a lot but we'll also have three days free. So, we're going to hire a bus and then drive through the mountains and we'll probably stay in some sort of mountain lodge there.
Amanda:	Sounds wonderful. I hope the weather's good.
Tim:	Me too, but it'll probably rain every day.

Amanda:	Still, not to worry – I'm sure we'll enjoy it whatever the weather. Where to after that?
Tim:	From there we fly to Greece. We were supposed to be playing five matches there but two have been cancelled, so it's only three now. Still, that means there's a bit of free time to do some tourist things as well, as we now have four days free altogether.
Amanda:	Great. What about accommodation over there?
Tim:	Well, it's more luxurious than last year's camping trip, so I think everyone will be happy with it. This time we're staying in a small hotel near the centre of Athens for a few days, and then we're going to get a boat to a couple of the islands, although we haven't decided which ones yet.
Amanda:	I'm sure we'll have good weather there, anyway, so lots of time for sunbathing on the beach.
Tim:	Yes, I think it'll be extremely hot there.
Amanda:	You're right – we'll probably end up wishing we were back in Scotland! Well, we're certainly going to have a varied trip.
Tim:	Yes. In Scotland we're probably going to do lots of walking and in Greece we're going to be lying on the beach. I imagine we'll even get a bit of a tan.
Amanda:	I think it's going to be a great trip!
Tim:	Ha! Just don't forget to concentrate on your game! Oh, and one more thing, don't forget that the manager is having a party just after we get back to celebrate the team's great results last season, and the best player on the tour will get a special trophy.
Amanda:	Wow! Don't worry, I'll let everyone know.

Recording 6

Phil:	Hey Janet, have you finished the report yet? Sarah was asking about it.
Janet:	I'm afraid not. I'm about to go to Rome for a conference and I won't be able to finish the report before I go.
Phil:	Oh. When do you think it will be ready?
Janet:	The conference only lasts three days, so I'm not in Rome for long – just the weekend. Then I'll be working on the report all next week.
Phil:	Can you do it before we have the departmental meeting at the end of the month?
Janet:	Oh, I'll easily have finished it by next Friday. I've got it in my diary.
Phil:	That's great. I'll be seeing Sarah at lunch, so I'll tell her.
Janet:	Thanks.
Phil:	Are you giving a talk at the conference?

Janet:	Yes, the same one I gave last month on plant diversity and environmental changes. By the end of the year I will have given the same talk at six conferences! Luckily it's a different audience each time, but I'll soon be getting polite requests to do something different! The funny thing is I still get nervous every time before I give it.
Phil:	Oh come on, I don't believe that.
Janet:	No, it's true. I'll be feeling really nervous when I get to Rome. I won't be able to relax until I'm actually giving my talk. Don't you get nervous when you give talks at conferences?
Phil:	Not really, although I always make sure I prepare well. I always practise in front of a mirror. I look a bit of an idiot, but no one can see so I don't mind. I'm giving a talk in London next month and by the time I give the talk I'll have rehearsed it at least ten times. Practising like that makes me feel confident – you should try it.
Janet:	That's a good idea. But even practice doesn't seem to help me.
Phil:	Well, good luck, I'll be thinking of you in Rome. When are you leaving?
Janet:	Well, I was going to leave this morning but they cancelled my flight, so I'm on the evening flight. Actually, I'd better get a move on, as the train to the airport leaves in 20 minutes.

Recording 7

Sara:	Alan! Will you help me write this advertisement for the spare room?
Alan:	Yes, we've got so much space. It would be great to get some money to help with the rent.
Sara:	Now, we need to make it sound inviting.
Alan:	Well, the room might be on the small side but the windows are very big so the natural light is really nice. Few rooms have such good natural light.
Sara:	Yeah, it's a great room for working in during the day, and it's also got a great view of the garden.
Alan:	Exactly. What shall we say about the furniture?
Sara:	Well, it's not luxurious but it is very comfortable. The room has everything you need. Oh, except they will need to bring their own lamp; both of the lights in the ceiling are really old and not very bright.
Alan:	That's true. But it has got a nice bed.
Sara:	Yes, and it's got a great wardrobe, which has even got a few shelves for clothes as well. They will need to bring their own mirror if they want one, though.

Alan:	Yes – there isn't one in the room at the moment. Now, there's no room for a bedside table but there is a good study desk in there.
Sara:	Yes, I wouldn't mind a desk like that myself, actually. It's better than mine. It's got three drawers – mine hasn't got any at all.
Alan:	Why don't you put it in your study then?
Sara:	It's too big. There isn't much room in there.
Alan:	I suppose not, because the desk has got shelves on top as well. They're really handy for putting books on. Now, what else?
Sara:	What about the location? We could say it's close to transport. We're really lucky because we've got the bus and the train nearby.
Alan:	That's true. And what shall we say about the rent? Shall we ask for £50 a week or is that too little?
Sara:	Well, let's say it includes electricity and any other household bills and make it £60. Our expenses are bound to go up with an extra person in the house.
Alan:	Yes, you're right, I hadn't thought of that! Now, pass me the newspaper.
Sara:	I thought you'd already read the news today?
Alan:	Yes, I have, but there are lots of advertisements for accommodation and I want to look at them before we finish ours.

Recording 8a

Good morning everyone. As part of the conference on environmental awareness I'd like to talk to you this morning about an exciting development in monitoring climate change: Europe's technological showpiece, Envisat. Envisat is a fully-equipped observation satellite and it is the largest, most technologically advanced, and most powerful one that the European Space Agency (the ESA) has ever created.

The satellite was launched in 2002 and is on the trail of climate change, delivering up-to-the-minute information about our changing environment. Seeing the earth from outer space highlights how tiny and fragile this planet of ours is. Envisat helps people to understand that and encourages us to protect our blue planet as our place of birth, and as the ancestral home where our children and grandchildren will live after us.

With its ten instrument systems Envisat is equipped with the best eyes possible and offers everything that scientists could wish for. This unique flying environment station follows in the footsteps of the successful remote sensing satellites ERS1 and ERS2, which were both launched in the 1990s.

Climate protection is a challenge for our entire society. The ESA contributes to such endeavours and has provided impressive scientific results in the field of atmosphere, ozone and climate monitoring, and more. The total cost of the Envisat programme is 2.3 billion euros over 15 years. Included in this sum is the development and construction of the instrument systems as well as the cost of the satellites, the launch and the operational costs. Each European citizen has therefore invested seven euros in the environment or about the cost of two cups of coffee per year. For that, every citizen will have access to precise information about changes in the environment including global warming, ozone depletion and climate change. This information is absolutely essential and long overdue as the basis for political decisions. The gas envelope around the earth is not determined by political boundaries and none of our countries is able to ignore the implications of global warming.

Recording 8b

Hello everyone and welcome to today's talk about the current trends in health and fitness. Nowadays, it seems as though everyone in the wealthiest parts of the world is battling with their weight and as a consequence, more and more people are joining local gyms or buying home-exercise machines.

In fact, according to the International Health, Racquet and Sportsclub Association, membership in health clubs in America doubled from a little over 17 million in 1987 to more than 36 million in 2005. While the figures for Europe are harder to come by, evidence over the past decade suggests that health club membership has doubled there as well.

What few people nowadays realize is that the average person in the developed world is now burning 800 fewer calories a day than a generation ago. This means that even if people today ate no more than the previous generation, they would still be getting fatter. Unfortunately, instead of eating less than their parents did, as they should, many people consume a lot more.

So what exactly has brought about this change in fitness levels? Well, people in developed countries are not only eating more but are also doing less exercise. Increased technology has not helped. The car and other such machines designed to help reduce our work load are as much to blame as deep-fried fast food. On top of this, the changes in how and where we work have reduced the amount of daily calories people actually need. Such factors are taking their toll on our health, with health costs soaring.

And this is where exercise machines come in. Walking machines or treadmills and the like may not be the most efficient way of burning off those excess calories and boosting cardiovascular fitness but they are certainly the most common. According to the Sporting Goods Manufacturing Association International, some 45 million Americans used a treadmill in 2003. That's an amazing number of people and an awful lot of treadmills.

Having said that, an exercise machine that did not even exist a decade ago – the elliptical cross trainer – is fast replacing the traditional treadmill. As its name implies, the machine delivers an elliptical or swinging motion, with both the hands and feet tracing semi-circular patterns – the feet on two moving platforms rather than bicycle pedals, and the hands gripping handles that move but are not meant to support any weight, which is important as there is no seat. Since the machine was introduced in 1998, the number of people using elliptical machines in America has tripled to more than 11 million a year.

We have been doing some tests to find out if these machines are actually any better than the previous machines or if they are just another passing trend. Dr John Porcari, a professor of exercise and sport science, believes that ellipticals are at least better than the previous exercisers, but no better than treadmills in terms of increasing cardiovascular fitness. In one set of tests, Dr Porcari measured the oxygen consumption, heart rate and calorific expenditure of 16 volunteers, and found that there was virtually no difference between elliptical machines and treadmills. But elliptical machines have a lower impact on the user than running, claim their manufacturers. True, says Dr Porcari, who measured the 'ground reaction forces' of the test subjects on the various machines. Running on a treadmill results in forces that are roughly two and a half times the subject's body weight. But using an elliptical machine gives forces that are roughly equal to the subject's weight. This is much kinder on the body and makes the impact comparable to that of walking. In that respect, ellipticals are superior.

However, those who do not want to shell out for fancy exercise machines will be heartened by the results of a seminal study in 1969 by Lewis Pugh, a British physiologist, which has been confirmed many times since. Dr Pugh found that, when reaching speeds above 14 kilometres per hour or so, running on firm ground uses up substantially more calories, and therefore leads to a greater reduction in weight, than running on a treadmill or using an elliptical machine. Dr Pugh attributed the difference to air resistance. Manufacturers of exercise machines point out, correctly, that running on firm ground creates a greater force on the body's joints than using machines, in particular the knees and ankles. But, what they don't say is that modern running shoes go a long way to reducing the impact of such forces. So, perhaps the best exercise of all is simply to leave the car at home, and run to the gym – and then right past it. After that, just keep going and going and going ...

Recording 9

Mrs Smith: Hello, you must be Chi Wen. I'm Mrs Smith, but my homestay students all call me Lucy.

Chi Wen: Oh, hello, Lucy. I'm very pleased to meet you.

Mrs Smith: So, how long have you been in Australia, Chi Wen?

Chi Wen: Well, I only arrived last month and I'm still finding it all a bit strange, actually.

Mrs Smith: Oh, don't worry. I'm sure it won't take long to settle in. If you like, I can introduce you to a friend of mine, Yi Ling. She's a student from China who stayed with me last year. I know she's really enjoying herself here in Australia.

Chi Wen: Oh, that would be nice.

Mrs Smith: Now, I have had a lot of students staying with me over the years and I do have a few rules.

Chi Wen: Oh, of course.

Mrs Smith: First of all, my husband and I want everyone to feel at home so we treat everyone as if they were a member of our own family.

Chi Wen: That sounds lovely.

Mrs Smith: I cook and serve dinner for everyone at six. We also make everyone speak English at dinner; it's really important to practise your English as often as you can.

Chi Wen: I see, that's a very good idea. And what about other meals? Can I cook for myself?

Mrs Smith: Yes, everyone makes their own breakfast. I do the shopping, and I always make sure there is plenty of food in the fridge so you can prepare yourself a packed lunch to take to college if you like.

Chi Wen: Yes, I've noticed that in Australia you often eat sandwiches for lunch.

Mrs Smith: Well, we often eat lunch in a bit of a hurry, so sandwiches are very convenient. Now, do you have any other questions about the house rules?

Chi Wen: What about laundry? Can I use the washing machine?

Mrs Smith: Oh, yes. I expect everyone to wash and iron for themselves, although I can put a load of washing on if you need me to. I will give you clean bed sheets every week. I clean the kitchen and the living areas myself but I expect all my students to help out and clean their own rooms.

Chi Wen: I have one other question. I don't have a mobile phone here yet. Can I use yours to make a couple of local calls?

Mrs Smith: That shouldn't be a problem. Just let me know when you want to use it.

Recording 10

Good evening, everyone. As many of you know I often travel for my job as a rug buyer and this evening I've been asked to give a talk about travelling in Europe and Asia. I'll try to pass on some useful advice for those of you who are planning to travel there yourselves. At the end of my talk, I'll be happy to answer questions.

My first piece of advice is to work hard on your research before you go if you want to make your trip enjoyable and rewarding. I plan my trips very carefully for at least three months before I leave, reading about the places I am going to visit on the Internet and in books.

I had a very memorable trip recently, starting out in Morocco. The city of Marrakech is an absolutely amazing place to visit and well worth adding to your itinerary. Try to stay near the old part of the city. There are so many historical buildings and so much to see. The mosques in particular are very beautiful.

After leaving Morocco I took a long tiring boat ride to Turkey. It was well worth the trip, especially if you like local crafts. I bought a beautiful Turkish carpet in one of the villages while I was there. The man that sold it to me spoke very good English and he told me all about the different styles of carpet. I was fascinated to see the extraordinary range of patterns.

I left the small mountain villages of Turkey to travel to the huge, crowded cities of India. India is a fascinating country, and I have always enjoyed my visits there. Everywhere you go the people are very welcoming and friendly towards visitors. They always seem pleased to see you. It's easy to see why India is such a popular destination for travellers.

One of the highlights for me on this visit was the Gujarati Textile Museum. It was the first time I had been there. If you are interested in textiles, this museum is really impressive, with lots of information and some absolutely stunning examples of Indian silk embroidery, and other fabrics.

If you're interested in seeing wildlife I recommend travelling in the more remote areas of the country. I was amazed at the variety of wonderful animals which I saw on my trip and the most incredible colourful birds with vivid blue and green feathers. I also saw several poisonous spiders, although I have to say that I found the insects rather frightening!

Recording 11

The Olympics is probably the most exciting event in the sports calendar. It's one of the few opportunities we get to see some of the best athletes in the world competing against each other. And amazingly, each year they seem to be getting better and better. So, you might imagine that the Masters Games, which is for athletes aged 30 and over, would be less exciting to watch. Well, this may not be true for long because recent studies have shown that older athletes are getter faster and fitter.

Now, it's true they're not as fast as their younger counterparts, and probably younger runners will always be faster than older runners. However, runners aged 50 and over are actually speeding up more rapidly than younger people. The researchers analysed the finishing times of 415,000 runners in the New York marathon between 1983 and 1999 and discovered that finishers from the older group showed the greatest increases in speed. Interestingly, women aged 60 to 68 improved the most markedly, running on average four minutes faster each year. Men of the same age ran just over one minute faster than previously.

Not only that, a second study proved that older athletes can achieve the same degree of physical improvement as those in their twenties and thirties. In other words, they are just as likely to achieve their peak fitness as younger athletes.

25 years ago few 60-year-old men and even fewer women would have considered it possible to complete a marathon let alone set record running times. The researchers concluded that people grow weaker not simply because of age, but because they don't keep as active as they did when they were younger. It would seem that the longer athletes keep competing, the greater their chances of setting new records are.

Recording 12

Good morning, everyone. What you can see on the screen behind me is Sydney Harbour and it may surprise you to learn that this horrible rubbish lying at the bottom of the harbour was actually put there intentionally as part of a conservation project! Now, the idea of putting rubbish into the harbour instead of cleaning it out may seem absurd to you, but allow me to explain. Two years ago I was involved in a study with the University of Sydney. We were asked to try to calculate the number of fish and different species living in Sydney harbour. During this study, the divers noticed that in the areas cleared of rubbish very little life remained, whereas the old cars and other debris lying on the sea floor actually provided a rich habitat for an abundance of creatures including up to twenty species of fish, crabs and seahorses and amazing plants such as sea tulips with bright red bodies.

We realized that if you remove all of the rubbish contained in the harbour then you also take away the homes of the creatures living there. Earlier this year, with the help of the Sydney Harbour Federation Trust, we reached a decision to expand our study and start putting rubbish back into particular areas of the harbour.

So far we have used things like old car tyres and rope, but we have a plan to carry out a more detailed study to test out a variety of artificial structures and see whether the sea creatures in the harbour find these as attractive a home as the rubble of the past. We'll also catalogue the creatures living there and the data collected from the sites will be analysed to establish whether these artificial reefs have in fact helped to increase the volume of fish in the harbour.

In the meantime, if you have any suggestions of other possible sites with submerged rubbish that would be suitable for our research, please speak to me after the lecture.

Recording 13a

Deborah: Hi Joe.

Joe: Hello Deborah. Listen, have you had much experience dealing with amnesia?

Deborah: Actually, yes I have. It was a patient I had last year when I was working in a hospital in Canada.

Joe: Can you remember much about it?

Deborah: Well, a man was brought to us with some facial and head injuries and he couldn't remember who he was, where he lived or how he came to be in Canada.

Joe: Were there any clues at all?

Deborah: Well, he spoke with a strong British accent so the police realized he couldn't be Canadian. They took him to a language expert who said that he could have come from Yorkshire, in England. The police also managed to find out that he could speak French and Italian. But he couldn't remember his name, address, age, or anything. Can you imagine what it must be like to have your whole life lost like that?

Joe: Yes, it must be awful. But do you think he was genuine? He might have been trying to run away from his past or something. People can do funny things when they've experienced something terrible.

Deborah: Well, if he was, it certainly wasn't the best way to go about it, because his picture was in all the papers and on the news. He wouldn't have been able to fool everybody for so long if it wasn't true, I'm sure. At some point he was bound to have said something to give it away. No, I think he really had genuinely lost his memory and couldn't remember anything.

Joe: He could have had a wife and children waiting for him somewhere wondering what had happened. Do you know if he was married?

Deborah: Well, he can't have been, because if he'd been married, his wife would have reported him missing.

Joe: Do you know what happened to him afterwards?

Deborah: Well, apparently he's been able to find his parents and now he's back in England living with them.

Joe: That's amazing. Did you ever work out how he had lost his memory?

Deborah: Well, when he arrived at the hospital he had a head injury and no personal effects – no wallet or phone or anything. We assumed that he had probably been attacked and robbed, and he must have hit his head, resulting in the loss of memory.

Joe: It can't be easy for his parents, living with someone who doesn't remember their past. They must be having a difficult time adjusting to it all.

Deborah: Well, in my experience of these cases pieces of memory do gradually come back. He may remember some things already, and over a few years he'll probably be able to remember quite a lot. He could make a total recovery one day.

Recording 13b

Good afternoon, everyone. Today I am going to tell you about the research I have been conducting into the history of soap. While you may be able to find some information on the origins of soap, it is not a substance which has excited a great deal of study so far. What we do know is that even as long ago as 2500 BC soap was being used. Of course, initially it was only ever used on clothing rather than the body itself. In fact, although soap has existed for so many years, the use of soap for personal hygiene was unheard of until fairly recently and is considered to be a relatively modern notion. So we can only assume that other activities must have provided the basis from which this key concept arose.

To make soap you need to combine three materials in relatively exact proportions. So, how is it that these primitive people from over two thousand years ago could have discovered soap? Well, what these people lacked in technology they certainly made up for in practical skills. I carried out some experiments using basic techniques to try to find out what people without any chemical knowledge might have observed. And I was able to demonstrate that they would indeed have been able to make a soap-like substance that is not dissimilar to the one we know today.

However, it is fair to assume that, as the process requires a certain amount of time and specialization, soap would most likely have only been available in the wealthy communities. Although there are claims that the British Celts and their European counterparts used soap, there is no real evidence that the British colonies of the Iron Age had access to such a product.

Now, the history of soap is not easy to discover. As soap is an organic substance no traces of it remain in archaeological sites, so we have had to rely almost entirely on written texts for our discoveries. Fortunately there are many of these. The first known written mention of soap was on Sumerian clay tablets dating from about 2500 BC. The tablets spoke of the use of soap in the washing of wool. In another incidence, a medical document from about 1500 BC mentions that Egyptians bathed regularly. It also describes how they made soap by combining alkaline salts and oil which they extracted from vegetables.

We also know that the Romans used a mixture of earth, soda and wine to clean their clothes and pots. For the Romans bathing was not just a matter of hygiene; it was a form of relaxation, a social activity. The bather moved from room to room, getting progressively hotter, until they reached a steamy room where dirt was sweated out and scraped away with a metal blade. The Romans used scented bath oils but these were used to moisturize the skin rather than to cleanse it and there is no evidence that they used soap in this way. This is not to say that the Romans did not have soap. During the excavation of Pompeii, a city that was buried under the eruption of Mount Vesuvius in 79 AD, an entire soap factory was revealed, showing that they did in fact have access to soap but that they simply did not use it for personal hygiene.

Recording 14

Claire: Hello Jack. How much longer before you leave for Hong Kong?

Jack: Hi Claire, it's about a month now. Actually I could use a bit of advice. You used to live there, didn't you?

Claire: That's right. What sorts of things do you need to know?

Jack: Well, I've got to find somewhere to live quite quickly. The company are only paying for me to stay in a hotel for one week. Will that be enough?

Claire: Yes, you should be able to find something by then, but you'll need to allow a bit of extra time to get over the jet lag; there's a big time difference between there and the UK.

Jack: Oh, I hadn't thought of that. What's the accommodation like?

Claire: Well, the rooms tend to be smaller than here but you can get bigger places on one of the other islands. A friend of mine rented a lovely place on Lamma Island. The only problem was he had to get up really early to catch the ferry to work.

Jack: What's the transport like generally?

Claire: Fantastic! The underground system is called the MTR and there are trains every couple of minutes, so you don't have to wait for ages like we do here. You should try to use it whenever you can. The bus system is a bit more complicated because there are normal double decker buses but there are also smaller buses called 'public light buses'. They only stop when you ask them to so you'll have to learn some Cantonese if you want to take one of those. The Star Ferry is amazing. It's so cheap and you get the best view of the harbour – you really have to see it to believe it. You should always carry plenty of loose change though for the buses and the ferries.

Jack: The company has offered us Cantonese lessons when I get there. Do you think I should take them?

Claire: Oh, definitely, you must have lessons if you want to be able to pronounce things correctly. You don't need to speak Cantonese in the bigger shops but you'll need some basic phrases when you go shopping in the local market.

Jack: Is there anything else I need to know?

Claire: Well, nowadays you have to get a work permit before you go. We didn't have to worry about those when I was there.

Jack: Yes, that's already taken care of.

Claire: And you mustn't dress too casually for work. Everyone dresses really well in Hong Kong.

Jack: I'll remember that.

Claire: Oh, and you needn't buy lots of guide books before you go. You can get great ones there for a fraction of the price. Also, you ought to take lots of passport photos with you. You'll find you need lots to fill in any application forms.

Jack: Great! I'm getting pretty excited now.

Claire: I'm not surprised. Oh, one last thing ...

Jack: What's that?

Claire: You must invite me to visit you!

Recording 15a

Interviewer:	So, Mr West, what does the future hold for Angleside?
Mr West:	Well, we've just announced our future plans for the company.
Interviewer:	And how many jobs will have to go?
Mr West:	We'll be losing 100 jobs here in Swindon, and another 50 jobs will go from our Birmingham branch. However, we'll be offering voluntary redundancy and early retirement and hope to cover most of the job losses this way.
Interviewer:	And what has led to this situation? Are these cuts a result of Angleside's poor performance over the past five years?
Mr West:	No, the company hasn't been doing badly. This has nothing to do with the figures; it just makes good business sense.
Interviewer:	So are you saying that your figures are not the basis for this decision to cut jobs?
Mr West:	Absolutely. We decided to change the way we operate our business two years ago.
Interviewer:	So are you confident that the company will continue to operate into the future?
Mr West:	Yes, of course. We are completely confident about this.
Interviewer:	And how are you going to deal with the discontent of your workforce over this announcement?
Mr West:	We will do our very best to make things as easy as possible for our employees.
Interviewer:	Well, we're out of time. Thank you very much for answering my questions.
Mr West:	Thank you.

Recording 15b

At local company Angleside, up to 150 employees will lose their jobs. Christopher West, the Managing Director, announced they would be offering voluntary redundancy and early retirement and hoped to cover the job losses in this way. I asked Mr West if these cuts were a result of Angleside's poor performance over the past five years but he denied that the company had not been doing well and said that the job losses have nothing to do with the figures. West claimed that they decided to make changes two years ago. He assured me that the company would continue to operate in the future and promised to do his best for the employees.

Recording 15c

Tutor:	OK, so it's Millie's turn to give her tutorial today, isn't it?
Millie:	That's right. I'm going to talk about renewable energy sources, and specifically solar towers. I'm not sure how much you already know about solar towers, so I thought I'd start with a few questions. First of all, does anyone know how solar towers work?
Tanya:	Don't they somehow use the sun's energy to create electricity?
Millie:	Yes, in a way. They actually work by using the sun to make columns of hot air that rise upwards through the centre of the tower. Now, do you know how old this idea is?
Luke:	I would have thought it was a twentieth-century idea. That's when we've had to start thinking about how to solve energy problems, isn't it?
Tanya:	No, I read something about this last week. The first time solar energy was produced was in the seventeenth century, wasn't it?
Millie:	That's right, so it's not a modern idea at all. And Leonardo Da Vinci also made sketches of a solar tower, though he never actually built one. Their recent history starts really with a man called Jorg Schlaich.
Tanya:	Yes, I read about him. He's a professor from Germany and he needed a country with plenty of sunshine and land for his research so he chose Spain to build the first tower.
Millie:	Correct! Well, everyone seems to know something about these towers.
Luke:	Yes, but I still don't really understand how they work.
Millie:	Well, I've made a flowchart to help you. Firstly, you have to realize that they are very tall towers. They're constructed out of high-strength concrete and they can be as high as 1,000 feet; there's one being built in Australia that's one kilometre high. Now, all around the base of the tower they have a sunlight collector which is basically a large sheet of plastic. It extends out for as much as seven kilometres, and it is raised off the ground slightly so it heats up the air underneath it.
Luke:	So it acts like a greenhouse then?
Millie:	That's exactly right. In fact, they plan to try and grow plants underneath it as well.
Tanya:	So what happens to the air?

Millie:	Well, the sunlight collector heats it to 65°C – that's on average 35° greater than the outside temperature – and the laws of physics mean that this hot air rises up the chimney or the tower and drives the turbines at the top. As the turbines revolve, they generate electricity. In fact, they can generate 200 megawatts of power or enough for 200,000 houses.
Tanya:	Wow, that sounds impressive. But it can't all be good news. What are the disadvantages? I'll bet they're really expensive to operate.
Millie:	Well, no, not necessarily, because sunlight is free after all, so it's really only the initial outlay that is costly. After that they're very efficient.
Luke:	But what about at night when there is no sun?
Millie:	Well, they've managed to find a way to store the electricity produced during the day, so it's no problem at night or even on cloudy days.
Tanya:	So, there are no drawbacks then?
Millie:	I didn't say that. One problem they do have is that a lot of the energy in the sunlight is lost from the collector in the form of heat, and then, of the remaining heat, a large proportion escapes from the top of the tower. But they are still worth the investment because, as I said, sunlight is free!
Luke:	Hang on. If these towers are so tall, how do they cope in high winds? Surely they become dangerous then?
Millie:	Yes, keeping them stable is another drawback. I believe they anchor the towers to the ground with wires to stabilize them so they're not dangerous, but it is an issue.
Tutor:	You have certainly found an interesting topic today, so thanks Millie. Perhaps we can have a look at your pictures now.

Recording 16

Presenter:	Good afternoon, and welcome to Education Today. This afternoon Freya Smith tells us about her diploma course in animal management. Welcome, Freya.
Freya:	Thank you.
Presenter:	Now, tell me, Freya – was animal care something you always hoped to do?
Freya:	Oh, yes, absolutely. I've always been interested in working with animals and during my last year at school I decided to do an animal management course.
Presenter:	Right, and was it difficult to find the right course?

Freya:	No, not really. I chose to study at Fairfield College because it's got a good range of animals and everyone's really friendly.
Presenter:	So, tell us a little about the course.
Freya:	Well, we get a lot of practical experience and there's also a lot of theory, but not so much that it's boring. I want to learn to manage the animals and the business side of it. The course is only three days a week, so I've already started working part-time at a pet shop.
Presenter:	That must be interesting.
Freya:	Yes, it's quite a varied job. My favourite job is feeding the animals. Some people rush through this but I prefer taking time so I can get to know them. In fact, I like having the chance to hold them. I don't even mind cleaning them out.
Presenter:	And have you been pleased with the course so far?
Freya:	Oh yes, it's been everything I expected it to be and more, really. We've practised handling animals and they've let us treat some minor problems, like removing splinters from paws. They make us handle all kinds of animals including spiders and snakes, even if we don't want to. At first I didn't want to touch the snakes, and I remember feeling really scared, but they let us take it slowly, and taught us exactly how to hold them. As long as you remember to do it the way you've been taught, it's fine. I still don't like holding them, but I'm not scared any more. This course has taught me to respect all animals and overcome my fears.
Presenter:	What has been the most useful thing you've learned so far?
Freya:	Learning about the behaviour of dogs on the course has helped me understand my own dog better. Before, if I heard him bark, I just told him to be quiet. Now, I stop to think about why he's doing it.
Presenter:	And what do you hope to do when you've finished?
Freya:	Well, I was thinking about doing another course when I finish, but now I've decided I'm going to stop studying for a while and go out to work. I'd really like to work in either a zoo or a safari park.

Recording 17

Father:	Simon, do you have time for a little chat?
Simon:	Sure, Dad.
Father:	I just wondered if you'd thought about what you were going to do with the money your grandfather left you?
Simon:	Well, I have started to give it some thought. It's quite a lot of money so I want to make sure I don't just waste it. I had thought about leaving it in the bank for a while.
Father:	Well, unless you invest it properly, you won't earn much interest and it may lose value over time.
Simon:	Yes, but if I invest it, I won't be able to access the money quickly when I've decided what to do with it, will I?
Father:	Well, what sort of thing would you like to do?
Simon:	Well, at first I thought about taking a trip around the world, but if I went travelling, I'd lose a year of study and I wouldn't have any money left over for anything else.
Father:	Very true. If you were to spend a year travelling around the world, you'd probably need an awful lot more money than this!
Simon:	Right, so the other thing I wanted to do was buy a car.
Father:	Do you think that's a good idea? It's not just the initial cost of the car you have to consider, you know. If you own a car, you also have to pay for insurance and road tax every year and then there's the petrol ...
Simon:	Yes, Dad, but I'm planning to get a part-time job as well and it would be great if I could drive to work instead of travelling on the bus, especially if I have to work late at night.
Father:	I still think you should think about investing some of your money for the future.
Simon:	But I'm scared that if I invest it, I might lose it all when the stock market goes down.
Father:	Well, it's best not to look at it like that. You won't lose any money provided that you think of it as a long-term investment. Now, I know you want to buy a car but as long as you get a second-hand one, you should still be able to invest some of the money as well. That's what I would do if I were you.
Simon:	But Dad, there's this fantastic new car that I've seen ...

Recording 18

Anna:	Hi Simon, how are you? How is your new car going?
Simon:	Oh, don't ask me, Anna. It's a nightmare! I should never have bought it!
Anna:	Why? What's wrong? I thought you'd got one of those fancy new models?
Simon:	I did, but that's part of the problem. If I'd bought a second-hand car, I wouldn't have taken out this big bank loan I've got now.
Anna:	Oh, so I suppose you've got big repayments to make?
Simon:	Yes, and I can't sell the car until I've paid for it. But it's not only that. I had no idea running a car was going to be so expensive! I wish I'd thought about the other costs before I bought it.
Anna:	It probably wouldn't be so bad if the price of petrol hadn't almost doubled last month.
Simon:	Don't remind me – the petrol alone is costing me a fortune!
Anna:	Lucky you've got that part-time job then!
Simon:	That's just the thing. Nearly all of my wages are going on the car. If I'd waited a bit before buying the car, I'd have managed to save quite a bit by now. I might even have gone on that college trip last week; it sounded great.
Anna:	Oh, dear. Can't you ask your dad to help you out?
Simon:	No way! When my granddad left me some money, my dad didn't want me to spend it on a car. If only I'd listened to him, none of this would have happened! I wish he wasn't always right!
Anna:	Well, maybe you should value his opinions more. You do seem to argue with him a lot. If you got on better with him, you might have listened to his suggestions.
Simon:	The worst thing is, Dad wanted me to buy some shares with the money and now they've gone up by thirty per cent. I should have listened to him. If I'd taken his advice, I'd own a small fortune now instead of a big debt!
Anna:	Oh, Simon, you poor thing. I wish I could help you but I have even less money than you. At least you have a car!
Simon:	Oh, don't say that! I wish I'd never bought the car! If it weren't for the car, I'd have no money worries now.

Interviewer: Come in Sarah. I do apologize for keeping you waiting. Would you like a cup of tea or coffee?

Sarah: That's very kind of you, but I'm fine thanks.

Interviewer: Now, I just want to run through a few questions with you. Firstly, why have you applied for this course?

Sarah: Well, I've always been interested in teaching and I've just finished my first degree at Stamford University, so I'd like to gain a teaching qualification.

Interviewer: Right, and can you explain your reasons for choosing our college specifically?

Sarah: Well, that's easy. My brother lives in the city and I'm hoping for a place on this course because then I'll be able to share a flat with him.

Interviewer: Oh, I see. So there isn't anything about our course that attracts you?

Sarah: Oh, I didn't mean it like that. I was really impressed with the description of the course in your prospectus. I haven't applied to the other university in the city because their course didn't appeal to me as much.

Interviewer: That's interesting. Can you say a bit more about what interests you about this course?

Sarah: Well, I like the structure of it and the fact that all the focus in the first term is on theory. I like the idea of learning about teaching before being asked to do it. Do you see what I mean?

Interviewer: Yes, and it sounds like a good reason to apply for our course. Have you talked to anyone who has done this course?

Sarah: Yes, my friend did it last year. She warned me about all of the hard work! But that's OK, I expect to work hard.

Interviewer: Excellent! Now, do you have any concerns about the course?

Sarah: Well, I must admit there are some aspects of the course that I'm a bit scared of.

Interviewer: Oh, what are they?

Sarah: Well, you can see from my application form that I'm not very good at maths. Will that cause me any problems?

Interviewer: That's very honest of you, but there is no need to worry about that. It's not important for this course.

Sarah: Oh, that's a relief. But the thing I'm most worried about is the classroom practice.

Interviewer: Well, most people are frightened of being in front of a class for the first time, but the tutors will help you to feel more confident.

Sarah: I haven't had any real experience of teaching and I'm worried about not being able to control a class, and the pupils being rude to me. If they shout at me in class, I'm not sure what I'll do.

Interviewer: That's a common worry but you will be taught how to deal with those things by the tutors on the course. In the end, of course, you have to take responsibility for what happens in your classroom, but you will be much better able to cope after training.

Sarah: Well, that makes me feel a bit better. Thanks.

Interviewer: Right, well, I don't want to make you late for your train. Thank you for coming and we'll be in touch soon by email, if that's okay.

Recording 19b

Hello everyone and welcome to Greenville community centre. Today we're going to be talking about what we as a community can do to help each other in severe weather. Our lovely little village is, as you know, quite remote. There may be other similar sized communities only 25 kilometres away but emergency services have to drive 500 kilometres to reach us from the closest large town. That can mean a wait of up to ten hours before help arrives.

Having said that, we are very lucky in that we've always had our own fire service and, thanks to the arrival of Dr Jones earlier this year, we no longer have to drive so far if anyone gets sick. What we don't have, and are unlikely to get in the near future, is a weather station.

Now, the National Weather Bureau can provide a lot of helpful information and even warn us about severe storms, but they can only do this if they build up a database of information and to do that they need local help. That means us. What we'd like to do is set up a group of volunteer storm spotters to pass information on to the Weather Bureau.

So, what do these storm spotters have to do? Well, thankfully you don't have to be particularly skilled at anything. Quite simply, immediately after a storm has passed, the first thing you have to do is call the national weather station to let them know. After that you have to complete a report card, which is very simple and won't take more than a few minutes to do. The only other thing they ask is that we keep an eye out for any reports in the local newspaper of storms or storm damage. You need to cut these out and send them in as well. Damage that makes news here is unlikely to make it into the national papers, so these can be an important source of extra information.

So that's all as far as the duties go. Now, what sort of thing do you need to report? Well, they don't want to hear about every single storm that we have, only the ones that bring some unusual conditions. For example, we don't need to call them just because there is hail, but we should report any hailstones that are two centimetres in diameter or bigger. They also need to know about damage caused by high wind, especially if it uproots large trees. Again, don't contact them every time you see a tree fallen over. You should use your common sense and restrict it to those big enough to cause a problem, especially on our roads. They'd also like to hear about very heavy rainfall and more especially any localized flash floods.

So, what should you do if you care about our community and you want to help? Well, obviously you'll need a bit more information and preparation than I've given you today so we'll be conducting a training session next month. This will only take up a day, so don't worry too much about it. If you do have the time and would like to come along, then you'll need to talk to the police who are coordinating the event. And as our storm season is from November right to the end of January, you'll need to put your name down by the end of October at the very latest, but if you'd like to get in early, Sergeant Phillips is here this afternoon and he's happy to take names now. This really is important for our community, and we're hoping to get a lot of support. Thank you.

Recording 20

Presenter: Good morning, listeners! The holiday season is here and this is the time when many of us plan to get away from it all, but what about the home you're leaving behind? Well, please welcome Mike Bowers, who is going to talk about how to look after your home when you are travelling.

Mike: That's right, Matthew. Whether you're a person whose job involves a lot of travel or whether you travel for pleasure, you really need to consider who will look after your home when you are away.

Now, some people seem to think it's just a matter of locking all the doors and windows, which is fine as long as there are no nasty storms while you are away. If you're going to be away during a stormy or windy season, then you also need to take a good look outside your home. Perhaps you live in an area where there are a lot of tall trees, in which case you will need to cut off any dead branches that overhang your property.

Do you have a garden or, if you live in a block of flats, perhaps you have a balcony or veranda? If so, make sure you store away any objects that could become damaging missiles if picked up by strong wind, things like outdoor furniture or even plants, for example. These can be especially dangerous if you live in a flat which is in a large high-rise building.

Once you've taken care of the outdoors you have to consider what could go wrong inside. Remember this isn't just a house or a flat; this is your home, the place where you keep your most treasured possessions. What would happen to them in a flood, for instance? If you're leaving for an extended period of time, the best idea is to find someone that can check on your home while you're away. Perhaps you have a family member who lives close by, or you may have a neighbour that you can rely on.

Another possible problem is having your home burgled while you are away. Now, there are often very good reasons why one house is burgled and another is not. In the evening, a home that's very dark can really stand out. So why not install lights which have a timer and programme them to come on at times when you would normally be home? Also, make sure you find someone who can collect your mail for you. You'll be amazed how quickly a letterbox can become crammed full of uncollected letters and papers, which is a great help to a burglar looking for homes that are empty!

Recording 21

Student: Excuse me, can you spare a few minutes to answer some questions?

Woman: Umm, yes, I suppose so. What's it for?

Student: I'm doing a survey about people's shopping habits for a university assignment.

Woman: Oh, all right then.

Student: Great. First I need to ask about your household. Do you live alone?

Woman: No, I live with my family – my husband and three children.

Student: And how many times a week do you do the food shopping?

Woman: Well, I usually do my food shopping once a week at the supermarket.

Student: Do you usually shop alone or with someone else in your family?

Woman: Oh, I always do it on my own. If I go with the others, they always put too many things in the trolley and it costs me a fortune!

Student:	Right. And do you always shop at this supermarket?
Woman:	Yes. It's very close to my house so it's very convenient.
Student:	And do you tend to do the shopping on the same day of the week?
Woman:	Yes, actually I always do the food shopping on Thursdays because I work Monday to Wednesday and there are fewer people in the supermarket on Thursday than on Friday.
Student:	Great. Finally, would you ever consider using a computer to buy your shopping online?
Woman:	Well, I did try it once but I didn't like it.
Student:	Can I ask you why not?
Woman:	Well, what I like is being able to see the products and walking around the shop, and maybe buying things that aren't on my shopping list, you know. You can't do that on your computer, can you?
Student:	No, I suppose not.

Recording 22

Jack:	Well, firstly, welcome to the university. My name's Jack Dawson and I'm president of the students' union. I'm here to answer any questions you may have about university life. Would anyone like to start?
Student 1:	Er, yes, I'm not sure how to get a library card.
Jack:	Ah, yes, that's very important. You need to go to the reception at the library and they'll give you a form to complete. You'll also need to have your photo taken for the card.
Student 1:	I've already got a passport photo. Can I use that?
Jack:	Yes, in which case just give them your photo with the filled-in form and they will do the rest.
Student 1:	I'm keen to start using the library as soon as possible. Do they process applications quite quickly?
Jack:	Oh, yes. All applications are processed on the spot so they'll be able to issue you a card straight away. Now, are there any other questions?
Student 2:	Can you explain a little bit about the students' union? I'm not really sure what it does.
Jack:	Well, the students' union is a group which represents your views to the university.
Student 2:	So, does the university run the students' union?
Jack:	No, the union is run by students, seven students to be precise, who are called the executive committee.
Student 2:	And how do you choose the executive committee?
Jack:	Well, the executive committee is chosen by the students through an election process.
Student 2:	And what exactly do they do?
Jack:	Well, the students' union is responsible for many of the extra facilities around the campus that are not related to study. We run the restaurants and entertainment and the sports facilities, which are said to be among the best in the country. So if you think any of these facilities need improving around the campus, or if there are other services you think we need to provide, then please come to one of our union meetings and make a suggestion. Now, any other questions? Yes, at the back ...

Recording 23

Fish has long been a staple food in many cultures, but there has been some controversy recently about the benefits and risks of fish consumption. For example, we know that fish supplies us with polyunsaturated fatty acids, substances that have been found to protect against heart disease. Moreover, because it is beneficial to the development of the brain, in many cultures fish is known as a 'brain food'. However, recent studies have shown that fish can also contain mercury, which is poisonous in large doses and has been linked to lower intelligence. As a result, people are unsure whether to increase or decrease the amount of fish they eat.

We recently undertook a project to evaluate the health advice currently being given about fish consumption. Although this work was supported by grants from the Fisheries Scholarship Fund, this did not affect the research findings or interpretations of the results. We discovered that, in spite of the literature available on the risks and benefits of fish consumption, there are still important gaps in this information. Despite these gaps, however, decisions about how to advise people on fish consumption should be made based on what we know now.

Firstly, in terms of heart disease, it has been shown that consuming even small quantities of fish can lower your risk of heart disease by 17%. Secondly, consuming fish is known to have a beneficial effect on brain development. Finally, although exposure to mercury through eating fish can have a negative effect on IQ levels, the effects that have been observed are relatively small.

To sum up, it would seem that the health benefits of eating fish outweigh the risks.

Recording 24

Tutor:	Well, today's topic for debate is 'home schooling'. And the question we're asking is, 'Is it better for us to educate our children at home rather than send them to school?' What do you think, Tina?
Tina:	Well, I was educated at an ordinary school and I don't have any regrets. Personally, I feel the teachers did a really good job and that I have benefited from the experience.
Tutor:	What about you, Nick?
Nick:	Well, I'm a bit like you, Tina. I went to a normal school and, fortunately, I had a great experience there. Mind you, I can see that being educated at home would be good for some children. There was a boy in my class who was bullied by some older boys, and I think he must look back at his school days and feel really bad. If he'd been educated at home, he'd probably feel quite differently. But, in general I don't think it is a good idea.
Tutor:	So, do you know of anyone who was home-schooled?
Tina:	Yes, a girl on my course was taught at home by her mother.
Nick:	Surely her mum can't know enough to teach her everything! She must have missed out on a lot of subjects!
Tina:	Actually, she believes that she received a better education as a result.
Nick:	Frankly, I'd be totally bored staying at home all day.
Tina:	Well, according to my friend they did lots of fun things like going out for walks and looking at nature and going to the theatre to see literature in action. I can see the benefits of that.
Nick:	Yes, but what about the social aspect. Doesn't your friend feel she missed out on making new friends?
Tina:	No, I don't think so. Apparently there's a network of parents who teach at home, and they have clubs where their children meet and that's how they made friends.
Nick:	Yes, but it's likely that those people will be very similar. I doubt that they met many people from different backgrounds and cultures, which in many schools it is possible to do. In my opinion that's a disadvantage.
Tina:	Yes, I think that's a good point. But, unfortunately, schools do seem to be more overcrowded and less well-funded these days and I can see the advantages of home education in terms of the quality of education.

That's certainly the way my friend felt. Mind you, I do think she finds it hard to interact in large groups of people. And, interestingly, she doesn't have a great relationship with her parents these days. Perhaps she had enough of them as a child!

Nick:	Well, anyway, I'm glad that my parents didn't educate me at home. Some of my best friends today were friends I met at school.

Recording 25

Julie:	When I was a teenager I was stung by a bee. For most people, that's not much of a problem – it just hurts a lot. But I reacted really badly to it. I ended up having to go to hospital where they gave me an injection to stop the reaction. What happened was that I trod on a bee that was crawling along the floor in the kitchen – it was summer and I was barefoot. My first feeling was, 'Ow – that hurts!' Then really quickly my foot began to go red and swell up. It just got bigger and bigger. It itched a bit too. I was really surprised by how much it hurt. Then it got even scarier because I began to find it difficult to breathe and kept coughing. Luckily my mum was there and she said, 'Right you're going straight to hospital!' It was quite near our house, but she drove really fast. I was given an injection and soon recovered, but I have to be really careful now in case I get stung again.

Appendix 1: Irregular verbs

Verb	Past simple	Past participle	Verb	Past simple	Past participle
be	was/were	been	lie	lay	lain
beat	beat	beaten	light	lit	lit
become	became	become	lose	lost	lost
begin	began	begun	make	made	made
bend	bent	bent	mean	meant	meant
bet	bet	bet	meet	met	met
bite	bit	bitten	pay	paid	paid
bleed	bled	bled	put	put	put
blow	blew	blown	read	read	read
break	broke	broken	ride	rode	ridden
bring	brought	brought	ring	rang	rung
build	built	built	rise	rose	risen
burn	burnt	burnt	run	ran	run
burst	burst	burst	say	said	said
buy	bought	bought	see	saw	seen
catch	caught	caught	sell	sold	sold
choose	chose	chosen	send	sent	sent
come	came	come	set	set	set
cost	cost	cost	shake	shook	shaken
creep	crept	crept	shine	shone	shone
cut	cut	cut	shoot	shot	shot
deal	dealt	dealt	show	showed	shown
dig	dug	dug	shrink	shrank	shrunk
do	did	done	shut	shut	shut
draw	drew	drawn	sing	sang	sung
dream	dreamt	dreamt	sink	sank	sunk
drink	drank	drunk	sit	sat	sat
drive	drove	driven	sleep	slept	slept
eat	ate	eaten	slide	slid	slid
fall	fell	fallen	smell	smelt	smelt
feed	fed	fed	speak	spoke	spoken
feel	felt	felt	spell	spelt/spelled	spelt/spelled
fight	fought	fought	spend	spent	spent
find	found	found	spill	spilt	spilt
fly	flew	flown	split	split	split
forbid	forbade	forbidden	spoil	spoilt	spoilt
forget	forgot	forgotten	spread	spread	spread
forgive	forgave	forgiven	spring	sprang	sprung
freeze	froze	frozen	stand	stood	stood
get	got	got	steal	stole	stolen
give	gave	given	stick	stuck	stuck
go	went	gone	sting	stung	stung
grow	grew	grown	strike	struck	struck
hang	hung	hung	swear	swore	sworn
have	had	had	swell	swelled	swollen
hear	heard	heard	swim	swam	swum
hide	hid	hidden	swing	swung	swung
hit	hit	hit	take	took	taken
hold	held	held	teach	taught	taught
hurt	hurt	hurt	tear	tore	torn
keep	kept	kept	tell	told	told
kneel	knelt	knelt	think	thought	thought
know	knew	known	throw	threw	thrown
lay	laid	laid	understand	understood	understood
lead	led	led	wake	woke	woken
lean	leant	leant	wear	wore	worn
learn	learnt	learnt	weep	wept	wept
leave	left	left	win	won	won
let	let	let	write	wrote	written

Appendix 2: Phrasal verbs

These are some useful phrasal verbs. Many phrasal verbs have more than one meaning.
Check them in a good dictionary before using this list.

account for	cut down	head for	see through
act as	deal with	hear from	see to
agree to	depend on/upon	help out	send (off/away) for/to
aim at	dispose of	hold on	send out
allow for	do up	hold on to	set aside
amount to	do without	hold up	set out
aspire to	draw up	join in	set up
attribute to	eat out	keep from	settle down
base on	engage in	keep on doing	settle into somewhere
be into	enter into	keep up (with)	sort out
believe in	even out	lay off	speak out/up
belong to	fall apart	lead to	stand by
break down	fall back on	lead up to	stand for
bring about	figure out	let down	stand up to
bring back	fill in/out	let off	start afresh
bring in	find out	live on	start over
bring out	finish off	live up to	stay out of
bring up	fit in	look after	stick at
build up	focus on/upon	look ahead	stick out
call for	get across	look at	stick to
call off	get at	look forward to	stick together
call on	get away with	look into	sum up
care for	get back	look up	switch off
carry on	get in	make up	take after
carry out	get off	make up for	take away
catch up	get on	miss out on	take down
cater for	get out of	name after	take in
check in	get round to	name for	take off
check out	get through	pass on	take on
cheer up	give away	pay back	take out
clear up	give back	pick out	take over
close down	give in	pick up	take up
come about	give up	play down	think about
come across	go back	point out	think of
come along	go down	put aside	think over
come around	go into	put forward	throw away/out
come back	go off	put off	try out
come down	go on	put on	turn into
come from	go over	put up	turn out
come out	go through	put up with	turn to
come up	go together	refer to	use up
come up against	go up	relate to	wake up
come up with	hand in	result in	work at
consist of	hand out	rule out	work out
count on	have (got) on	run out	write up

CD Tracklist